Analyzing
Outsourcing

Other McGraw-Hill Books of Interest

Analyzing Outsourcing

Reengineering Information and Communication Systems

Daniel Minoli
DVI Communications, Inc.
and
New York University

McGraw-Hill, Inc.

New York   San Francisco   Washington, D.C.   Auckland   Bogotá
Caracas   Lisbon   London   Madrid   Mexico City   Milan
Montreal   New Delhi   San Juan   Singapore
Sydney   Tokyo   Toronto

For Gino, Angela,
Anna,
Emmanuelle, Emile, and Gabrielle

"...per il modello di vita di Giuseppe Verdi"

Library of Congress Cataloging-in-Publication Data

Minoli, Daniel, date.
  Analyzing outsourcing : reengineering information and
communication systems / Daniel Minoli.
       p.   cm.
  Includes index.
  ISBN 0-07-042593-0
  1. Business enterprises—Communication systems—Management.
2. Information technology—Management.   3. Management information
systems.   4. Contracting out.   5. Information service industry.
6. Computer service industry.   I. Title.
  HD30.3.M563   1995   94-22273
  658.4′038—dc20   CIP

    2 3 4 5 6 7 8 9 0   DOC/DOC   9 0 9 8 7 6 5 4

ISBN 0-07-042593-0

The sponsoring editor for this book was Marjorie Spencer, the editing
supervisor was Stephen M. Smith, and the production supervisor was
Suzanne W. Babeuf. It was set in Century Schoolbook by McGraw-Hill's
Professional Book Group composition unit.

Printed and bound by R. R. Donnelley & Sons Company.

Contents

Foreword

For the rest of this decade and well into the next century, enterprises will be asked to do more and more with less and less. Increased global competition has forced businesses and governments alike to become more productive, more decisive, and more responsive to new opportunities. The removal of trade barriers in North America and Europe only intensifies the need to triumph in a global economy. Such a rapidly changing business climate requires radically new ways of doing business. It requires facilitating technologies—including new computing environments—that maximize competitiveness in worldwide markets and allow companies to change the way they do business.

A critical tool in these endeavors is information technology and its power to help executives rethink, reshape, and ultimately reengineer the processes that deliver products and services. Executives who successfully compete in today's environment use technology to streamline business processes—to move the power of information and the power to make decisions closer to the point of sale or service.

As companies redefine the way they do business, emerging technologies—including, in particular, client-server computing—have become a key component in their success. Client-server computing transforms today's employees into tomorrow's knowledge workers, enabling them to access information instantly and make decisions quickly anywhere in the world. It offers lower processing costs than the mainframe environment, improved system flexibility, and open systems platforms. Client-server technology can successfully transform organizations into cost-effective and nimble competitors reaping sustainable and tangible benefits: faster information flows, more satisfied customers, empowered employees, leaner organizational structures, and higher margins.

But to succeed, corporations need streamlined and globally integrated operations. Above all, they need an absolute focus on their core business. That's when it may become important to outsource certain "noncore" requirements. Outsourcing is not a cure-all, however. It is a facilitator for changing the process. Outsourcing allows companies to become partners with experts. They gain access to the technology they need to beat the competition while continuing to focus on what they do best.

The decision on how to outsource is a critical one. It requires detailed analysis to ensure that the move is compatible with overall business objectives. It requires careful consideration to select the right outsourcing partner. The company chosen should have not only outstanding technical capabilities but also a philosophy that is aligned with the client's goals. And it requires an arrangement flexible enough to accommodate changing business climates and evolving technical environments.

One of these arrangements is what we at SHL Systemhouse call transformational outsourcing. Transformational outsourcing services encompass the operation of a client's mainframe applications, migration to a lower-cost and flexible client-server platform, and the operation of that distributed environment.

Unlike traditional outsourcing, which merely moves the operation of a client's mainframe applications to the outsourcer's mainframe, transformational outsourcing provides the flexibility to accommodate business change and new and evolving technologies. A company's mission-critical applications are moved to the outsourcer's mainframe only temporarily, while the organization's information systems are downsized to a client-server architecture. Then the mission-critical applications are moved from the mainframe to a distributed client-server system, where they are maintained by the outsourcer or, as another option, returned to the customer.

Transformational outsourcing provides the flexibility to accommodate change. It customizes and aligns information technologies with an organization's business strategies to facilitate the achievement of corporate-wide objectives. It allows organizations to focus on their core competencies. It also provides the tools to reengineer business processes and transform people, operations, and even technology itself. Best of all, transformational outsourcing delivers impressive results: considerable cost savings, heightened efficiency, and rapid decision making.

As more and more businesses take advantage of outsourcing, this book will prove invaluable. It covers all pertinent issues, from traditional outsourcing to transitional outsourcing, in an even-handed, unbiased manner. In so doing, it becomes a most reliable reference for information technology executives and managers. As they assess their particular situations to arrive at sound outsourcing decisions, they will discover that outsourcing, like client-server computing, is the new paradigm for harvesting the opportunities abundant in a global arena.

John R. Oltman
Chairman and Chief Executive Officer
SHL Systemhouse

Preface

The 1990s are the decade of corporate reengineering and "right-sizing." Organizations are inventorying the tasks they perform vis-à-vis their core business, and for many of these tasks, they are asking whether the task really needs to be done, or whether it can be eliminated or outsourced to an agency that specializes in such activities. Doing a job internally affords detailed control; however, this approach carries the responsibility of planning, designing, implementing, staffing, training, managing, monitoring, tracking technological development, and eventually making the transition away from the infrastructure required to support the job.

Data processing and data communications represent a substantial corporate expense: Typically from 2 to 12 percent of the organization's annual revenue is spent on these functions. For example, a company with a $1 billion annual revenue could spend $50 million a year (at 5 percent) on data processing and data communication. If a way could be found to save, say, 20 percent of this amount, this would represent $10 million each year. Additionally, the total corporate investment in the required infrastructure is typically equal to four times the yearly expenditure, so that a $1 billion company would have about $200 million tied up in PCs, workstations, LANs, servers, bridges, routers, gateways, modems, departmental systems, mainframes, communication processors, etc. Given these (estimated) figures, it is not surprising that many companies are planning to implement downsizing strategies within their corporate computing environments.

Outsourcing of various aspects of data processing and data communications is a popular trend. Outsourcing is a multibillion-dollar-a-year industry, and is expected to triple by 1997. Outsourcing has been found to be useful for companies aiming to cut costs, focus internal resources on mission-critical projects, or add new systems and applications. Outsourcing often results in cost savings in the 10 to 20 percent range, mostly because of the reduction in the number of people a company requires. Although some reports say that outsourcing is decreasing, others say it is still on the rise because of products that make it easy to manage multiple systems and/or networks from a single location, standards that make it easier to combine products, and the availability of broadband communication services, which facilitate the transport of data. The movement toward client-server architectures is sometimes, but not always, combined with a decision to outsource, so that reengineering can occur at two levels: replace the mainframe with smaller systems, and have an outside company take over, in whole or in part, the responsibility for the organization's computing tasks.

Outsourcing is taking place in many data processing and data communications areas, including the computing environment, application development, disaster recovery, document imaging, wide area communication, management of the communication, and local area networks and their management, to list just a few areas.

There are many variables when considering outsourcing. The process starts with a thorough assessment of an organization's needs, followed by the establishment of an operating baseline. Determination and documentation of service requirements comes next, along with service and performance goals. Current and future costs need to be determined, and if an outside company is to be used, a suitable billing method must also be agreed upon.

Planners must realize, however, that there are both pros and cons associated with outsourcing. No decision should be made without a thorough and balanced assessment of these factors.

This text aims at exploring these and other issues related to outsourcing. Specifically, emphasis is given to benefit *analysis*. The first chapter identifies the issues that define the current view of outsourcing. The second chapter documents aspects of the computing environment now evolving, with emphasis on client-server architectures. Chapter 3 provides some of the analytical tools required for decision making, and Chap. 4 describes outsourcing principles at the macro level. The chapters that follow examine various areas in which organizations have applied outsourcing: data processing (Chap. 5); telecommunications and local area networks (Chap. 6); and disaster recovery, archival functions, document imaging, system engineering, and international communication (Chap. 7). Issues pertaining to selecting the right vendor and writing the right contract are covered throughout the text.

Worldwide, one can label the decade of the 1990s as the New Economy, harbinger of the third millennium, characterized by the epithet "retrain or retreat." Outsourcing is but one example of this trend of looking for new ways of doing things more efficiently; clearly, among other consequences, it has employment implications. The professional must be ready to continually keep up, that is, continually retrain. This book serves that purpose.

This text is based completely on course material developed by the author at New York University's Information Technologies Institute. The packaging of the lecture notes into a book was not funded by any company or institution.

Acknowledgments

DVI Communications, Inc. and Ben Occhiogrosso are thanked for providing insight and perspective into real-world considerations based upon case studies (both data processing system and telecommunications networks) that DVI has performed over the last several years, drawn from its clientele and experience in financial services, health care, education, government, and professional services.

Prof. A. Whinston, University of Texas at Austin, is thanked for his permission to utilize very valuable published material on contracting issues, which is included in Chap. 4.

Tony Gaffney of SHL Systemhouse is thanked for providing Chap. 8, which contains a valuable discussion of transformational outsourcing and a number of case studies that put into practice many of the principles discussed in this text. The author also thanks the SHL Systemhouse crew who reviewed the book's text to give it a real-world flavor, in lieu of a clinical overtone. Dennis Maloney, Greg Jacobsen, Bill Trafford, Leo Lefebvre, Ralph Gardiner, Yolande McDonald, Rick Gray and Harry Schlough are warmly acknowledged.

The following individuals are also thanked for their moral support of this undertaking: Dick Vigilante, New York University; Lance Lindstrom, DataPro Research Corporation; Tony Rizzo, *Network Computing* magazine; Jo-Anne Dressendofer, IMEDIA; and Al Tumolillo, Probe Research Corporation.

Daniel Minoli

What Outsourcing Is and Why It Is Important

1.1 Introduction

Outsourcing, the turning over of information systems (IS) and/or communication functions, as a whole or in part, to a third-party contractor, is a newly reintroduced solution to the challenge, problem, and expense of creating and running a corporate information enterprise. Outsourcing is a new term for an old concept and is not limited to IS; it means contracting out work. The consideration is basically simple: If an outside party can do the work more efficiently and inexpensively than can the organization itself, then the outside party ought to do it; if the organization's employees can do the job better, then the work ought to remain in-house. As a result of the general restructuring and contraction of businesses in response to a changing economy, corporations are "farming out" functions to various service firms, ranging from legal to accounting, to food service, to security, to cleaning, to information technology (IT).[*,1]

Organizations now rely to an ever-increasing extent on information. Efficient information collection, processing, and distribution are making the difference between organizations that thrive and those that fade. IT expenditures in a company range from about 1 percent of total company revenue to as much as 12 percent, with an average of 5 percent; this is a substantial ongoing corporate expense. IT expenditures account for about 40 percent of most large companies'

---

*We employ the term IS to refer specifically to data processing functions; we use the term IT to refer to the total informatics technological infrastructure of a company, including data communication, imaging, E-mail, etc.

capital expenditures.[2] IT represented $190 billion of the U.S. economy in 1991, and telecommunications is equally large. Outsourcing became an important IS industry trend in the United States several years ago. Many organizations are now turning to outsourcing to help them cut costs, improve service, and focus on core business activities—about 20 percent of large U.S. IT users are expected to turn to some form of outsourcing to achieve their objectives in a better, faster, and/or cost-effective way.[3]

In addition to simple, traditional outsourcing, organizations are looking at reengineering their information technology operations. At the same time, many mainframe-based systems are being replaced with client-server architectures. This combination of outsourcing and reengineering has been called *transformational outsourcing*. Through transformational outsourcing, organizations are seeking to transform business processes and the technology infrastructure to reduce costs, improve service, and empower employees. Effective application of technologies provides the equivalent of an "enterprise on the desk," giving employees easy access to the information they have a need and a right to use in order to work more effectively. Outsourcing the "legacy" systems often allows the organization to concentrate on future business and IS requirements.

With IS outsourcing, organizations relinquish control and management of part or all of their data processing/data communications functions to a third party. Outsourcing enables customers to realize an estimated 10 to 15 percent savings on annual data center operations.* Additionally, the IS manager is able to predict future costs for the IS function, whether this function is centralized or client-server-based. Computing equipment (PCs, servers, terminals, minicomputers, mainframes, bridge, routers, etc.) can now be leased rather than purchased. In effect, the same can be said about people. They can be transferred to a support (but nonaffiliated) organization so as to help the company reduce headcount without the financial and emotional cost of termination. Advantages of outsourcing include (see Fig. 1.1)

- Minimizing the user's investment and reducing financial risk.

- Protecting against technological obsolescence.

- Reducing the user's responsibility for designing, deploying, and validating complex and evolving IS functions and networks.

- Reducing the user's responsibility for ongoing management of a complex and evolving network and IS infrastructure, and for

---

*Some outsourcing vendors have promised to reduce annual IS expenditures by 50 percent, although 15 to 25 percent savings are more common and realistic.[2,4,5]

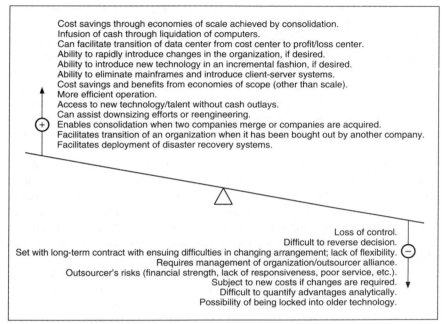

Cost savings through economies of scale achieved by consolidation.
Infusion of cash through liquidation of computers.
Can facilitate transition of data center from cost center to profit/loss center.
Ability to rapidly introduce changes in the organization, if desired.
Ability to introduce new technology in an incremental fashion, if desired.
Ability to eliminate mainframes and introduce client-server systems.
Cost savings and benefits from economies of scope (other than scale).
More efficient operation.
Access to new technology/talent without cash outlays.
Can assist downsizing efforts or reengineering.
Enables consolidation when two companies merge or companies are acquired.
Facilitates transition of an organization when it has been bought out by another company.
Facilitates deployment of disaster recovery systems.

Loss of control.
Difficult to reverse decision.
Set with long-term contract with ensuing difficulties in changing arrangement; lack of flexibility.
Requires management of organization/outsourcer alliance.
Outsourcer's risks (financial strength, lack of responsiveness, poor service, etc.).
Subject to new costs if changes are required.
Difficult to quantify advantages analytically.
Possibility of being locked into older technology.

Figure 1.1 The pros and cons of outsourcing.

understanding and applying new (and perhaps initially risky) technologies.

■ Decreasing staff numerically, ending up with a smaller number of people, who are higher-level technical specialists, planners, and contract managers; in addition to reducing the responsibility of managing a large staff, this usually also reduces the expense.

■ Achieving one-stop shopping.

Organizations are now moving toward a more "federated" structure: They want to concentrate on what they are good at, their core business, and leave the rest to somebody else.[6] Companies have long outsourced some of their functions. For example, the U.K.'s British Telecom handles its catering requirements by farming them out, at an estimated saving of 20 to 25 percent. Few organizations now undertake their own vehicle fleet maintenance, and many do not even manage their fleets. However, the issue is whether or not to outsource what are considered to be core functions. In addressing this issue, it is interesting to note that companies have different perceptions of where peripheral business ends and the core business begins. Some companies outsource parts of their operations that outsiders might think are core functions. For example, the Ford Motor Company has decided that it no longer wants to build engines and has contracted this out to Japan's Mazda—on the face of it, one would think that building engines is a core function for an automobile manufacturer.[6] Similarly, some believe that IS is part of their core business. In fact, IS is critical to their operation, as an engine is critical to a car; however, this does not imply that the organization needs to manage IS directly. For another analogy, electricity is unequivocally critical to all organizations, yet perhaps the majority of companies are not involved with its production.

As computing architectures move from the established centralized systems to newer client-server systems, which are making major inroads in the 1990s, many organizations are seeing an opportunity to upgrade their systems, reengineer the business processes,* and at the same time outsource the IS operation. Mindsets and paradigms are changing in the data processing and data communications arenas, driven by business imperatives, as shown in Fig. 1.2.

Of course there are disadvantages to outsourcing, as shown in Fig. 1.1. In particular, strategic problems associated with loss of control and other risks should not be overlooked. Some observers argue that many senior business managers have been led to believe that IS is a clerical function that can be farmed out easily; many are sold on outsourcing as a means of expense reduction (a laudable goal) without understanding its potential longer-term strategic implications. IS is

---

*Such activity is popularly known as business process reengineering (BPR). In addition to outsourcing, BPR relies on client-server technology, groupware, workflow systems, imaging,[5] artificial intelligence systems, multimedia, and object-oriented mechanisms (e.g., object-oriented fourth-generation languages).

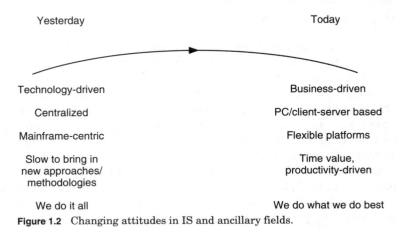

Yesterday   Today

Technology-driven   Business-driven

Centralized   PC/client-server based

Mainframe-centric   Flexible platforms

Slow to bring in   Time value,
new approaches/   productivity-driven
methodologies

We do it all   We do what we do best

Figure 1.2 Changing attitudes in IS and ancillary fields.

often the one factor that differentiates a company from its competitors; hence, before they outsource, managers must become fully aware of the strategic implications of such a decision and fully explore the risks, the side effects, and the possible downright disadvantages. While outsourcing is a contemporary trend in the computer industry, it is worth noting that it is not epidemic: Some vendors are suggesting alternatives to outsourcing, and some organizations that have tried outsourcing are pulling back.

Although much of the initial attention was focused on outsourcing facilities management, outsourcing now affects all facets of IS, including application development and communication. Table 1.1 depicts some of the areas currently undergoing outsourcing in a number of organizations. Some early outsourcers took the approach of outsourcing the *entire* corporate IS function. More recently, companies have tended to be more selective and outsource only specific applications. For example, many U.S. and Canadian companies are now moving toward *selective* outsourcing of data network functions alone to ease the load of overburdened IS departments.[8] With outsourcing, companies are going back, in a way, to the 1960s approach of timesharing, where a service bureau owned, managed, and maintained a complex computer platform and supporting infrastructure. The top reasons for outsourcing cited by IS managers, according to one study, are[8]

TABLE 1.1 IS Areas Currently Experiencing Outsourcing

Data processing functions, as a whole or in part (e.g., outsource operation of data center tape library)

Telecommunication functions, including or limited to network management

LAN and desktop computing functions (backup and management)

Help desk

Business process reengineering

Application development, including database design and management (e.g., user contract programmers)

Software distribution/management

Disaster recovery functions

Document processing and archival functions

Engineering and system integration functions

International information processing and telecommunications

- To leverage internal resources, since data network management is better handled by an outsourcer
- To save on costs, since an outsourcing contract covers equipment and services
- To acquire a complete solution and better network performance
- To improve technical expertise
- To increase competitiveness
- To learn and manage new technologies
- To improve control and security
- To stay flexible

With nearly 40 percent of U.S. corporate capital invested in information technology and with IS expenditures representing the third largest ongoing corporate expense, IS is being more closely scrutinized in an effort to cut costs and increase productivity.[4] Of 1250 U.S. corporations recently surveyed, almost all rated cost reduction as one of the main reasons for outsourcing.[9]

Advances in communication are making high-capacity digital connectivity widely available at the local level as well as at the wide area level. These advances, in conjunction with computing architectures such as client-server, enable peripherals to be remotely located, thereby facilitating outsourcing. For example, mainframes could be taken over by an outsourcer and consolidated in the outsourcer's data center, and still provide nearly transparent services to the users. Database servers can also be remotely located and maintained. Disk drives can be located remotely, enabling a company to keep a hot standby in a remote location where an outsourcer providing disaster recovery is based. Local area network (LAN) maintenance, including automatic backup, can also be outsourced. Asynchronous transfer mode (ATM) communication technology is being presented by proponents as supporting client-server computing and enabling business reengineering.[10]

An organization contemplating outsourcing must first understand the implications of such a move—its advantages and disadvantages in the organization's specific situation. The next major step is selecting the proper vendor or vendors. The third step is making sure that a solid contract is written between the two parties. Last, it is important to monitor the performance of the vendor or vendors to ascertain that the desired grade of service is consistently obtained over time.

Outsourcing can also be a profitable business for providers. The preinterest return (after depreciation) can be in the 15 to 25 percent range. The establishment of an outsourcing center provides a predictable revenue stream for 5 to 10 years, which is the typical length of a contract. Also, the provider (for example, a system integrator) can sell additional products to the client company, particularly as the technology changes and clients request new systems.

1.2   Scope of Text

This text covers contemporary issues related to outsourcing, including the aspects discussed in embryonic form above. Its purpose is to acquaint the chief information officer (CIO) contemplating such an approach, as well as the subordinates who must justify, plan, and implement such a corporate transformation (some even say metamorphosis), with the technical, economic, and administrative facets of such an important decision. Table 1.2 depicts the areas of investigation undertaken in the text. Issues pertaining to selecting the right vendor and writing the right contract are covered throughout the text. Naturally, a single book cannot equip the manager with all the required information. This text aims at describing some of the "common-experience" aspects of a decision to pursue outsourcing; other information sources—for example, the cited references—should also be consulted to obtain a more complete picture.

It is not the purpose of this text to tell the CIO and the IS manager *what to outsource* in their own company or *how to go about implementing* the many substeps required to complete an outsourcing decision. The text focuses on outsourcing *principles*. It provides input that any manager contemplating outsourcing should find beneficial, even necessary. The text does indicate areas that have been outsourced by

TABLE 1.2   A Course of Investigation

Chapter 1	Overview, purpose, and opportunities
Chapter 2	Typical computing environments now in place, including communication infrastructures
Chapter 3	Analytical decision-making tools (financial basics, decision making, economics, etc.)
Chapter 4	Outsourcing principles—a macro view
Chapter 5	Outsourcing of data processing functions
Chapter 6	Outsourcing of telecommunication and LAN functions
Chapter 7	Outsourcing of other corporate functions: disaster recovery functions, document processing and archival functions, engineering and system integration functions, and international information processing and telecommunications
Chapter 8	Transformational outsourcing/reengineering and study cases

hundreds of companies; however, the specifics for a given company have to be worked out within the particular confines of that company. Many of the implementation steps are simply a matter of common sense and good business practices. If the company needs help in carrying out some of those steps, it may be cost-effective to obtain the services of an accredited consultant.

As stressed in this text, outsourcing has to be based on analytically demonstrable facts and goals (for example, a guaranteed better grade of service at lower cost), rather than on an intangible feeling that it is generally a good thing. It is essential that the reasons be readily identifiable and quantifiable, and that they be fully evaluated before the decision to outsource is taken.[11]

This text does not take any particular point of view on outsourcing; it is neutral, arguing both sides and letting the decision maker draw the appropriate conclusion in the specific environment in question. The text examines both the advantages and the disadvantages of outsourcing. The prospective manager must determine whether the cited advantages apply to his or her environment, and the same for the disadvantages; then the manager must consider the balance and determine whether, in the specific situation, the advantages outweigh the disadvantages.

1.3   Focus on Core Business: Let Others Do Less Creative Tasks

From an accounting perspective, outsourcing is defined as "the transfer of an internal service function to an outside vendor."[12] This type of arrangement is not necessarily new and need not include all IS functions. Two outsourcing arrangements that have been used are (1) the partial transfer of computing activities and associated resources and (2) the total sale of the organization's computing assets. Each of these arrangements has advantages and disadvantages.

Partial transfer.   This approach could, for example, include outsourcing well-established IS applications, such as payroll, while developing and retaining newer and specialized decision support systems in-house. When executed properly, this type of outsourcing may result in lower costs and greater access to advanced technology. Outsourcing needs to be accomplished in such a way as not to give away the strategic part of one's business. When done correctly, the organization remains the manager of the process and decides which entity, the organization or the outsourcer, will do specific portions of the overall function. A savvy manager will outsource only his or her weaknesses while keeping strengths in-house.[12]

Purchase of assets.   Some outsourcing vendors agree to purchase the entire set of IS assets from the organization, if the organization elects to proceed in this direction. This approach to outsourcing provides an infusion of cash into the organization at the time of the transfer of the assets to the outsourcer. When, on a periodic basis, the organization pays the outsourcer, the payments are a tax-deductible expense. The physical assets need not physically move from the organization's original data center location, although the IS employees may be transferred from the original organization's payroll to that of the outsourcer, thereby shifting administrative responsibilities and hire/fire responsibilities. Ostensibly, things will appear to be the same as before the transfer: The employees will still report to the same location and have the same responsibilities.

Why is outsourcing receiving attention from many CIOs and other senior IS managers? Because outsourcing is part of the reengineering of the corporation. Outsourcing is becoming an increasingly common way to reduce the costs involved in the management of in-house services and tasks. In addition to the cost savings from reduced labor and equipment, outsourcing affords access to expertise that would have been too expensive to provide internally.

Outsourcing services are available for many functions undertaken within an organization, from telecommunications to office management to mailroom functions. Temporary help companies are also involved in the outsourcing business. They can either staff many of the available vacancies in a company with temporary workers (ideal for departments with high turnover of staff) or provide a full-time staffing coordinator to oversee the client's outsourcing needs.[13]

Data processing managers considering outsourcing of facilities management (FM) should develop an IT service management strategy in order to evaluate their options. Outsourcing pursued without such a plan could lead to an arrangement that might imperil crucial business operations. The involvement of the company's senior management at this juncture is critical.[14]

While some companies may be reluctant to turn such a crucial function as IS over to outsiders, others are finding the approach cost-effective and efficient. For example, an increasing number of manufacturing firms are finding that while manufacturing data are strategic to a company, the handling of those data is not; these companies are finding that in some cases data management is best performed by a service firm that specializes in that function.[15]

As another example, information technology training is now outsourced by many corporations in an effort to avoid the high cost of in-house training, particularly in the use of microcomputer software.

Sources estimate that the cost of information technology training in the United States in 1992 was $4.6 billion.[16] Outsourcing is becoming more popular as a source of training because of a lack of resources, financial pressures, and the proliferation of software products for which training is required.

1.3.1 The IS trends of the 1990s

The first part of the decade has brought budget pressure for IS managers, yet they are being asked by their organizations to deploy new technologies, such as client-server, and to support increased interconnection, including bringing in new broadband communication services. Also, some IS organizations have been made responsible for departmental PCs and PC networks. Surveys conducted at press time indicated that for the fifth year in a row, IS budgets are experiencing constraints.[17] From 1989 to 1993, IS budgets grew only a point or less faster than inflation, while in the past they grew at a higher rate (as high as double digits in the early to mid 1980s). In industries such as electronics, aerospace, defense, and auto making, and in government agencies, zero growth has been common in recent years.

IS managers find themselves forced to reengineer their own organizations at the same time as the corporation is undertaking more global reengineering. "IS managers are getting the message that their bosses want them to focus on cutting costs."[17] Almost three-quarters of all IS managers surveyed recently indicated that "managing" costs was their highest priority. Some areas where reductions are sought are in enhancements of legacy mainframe-based applications. In some cases these applications can consume as much as 75 percent of the total development budget. In many organizations, senior management is determined to bring that figure down, to 50 percent or even 25 percent of the total budget.[17] This has already resulted in staff cuts in the 10 to 20 percent range in a number of companies [since these IS departments are large (several thousand), the number of displaced IS employees can be high]. Companies looking at reducing these costs begin the process by comparing themselves to other companies in the same industry based on some metric, say IS budget per 1000 served customers, tons of steel produced, number of aircraft, etc. If a company finds that it exceeds the average, then it targets a reduction.

Putting a limit on IT spending is now a common corporate goal, particularly in industries where in the past technology expenditures have been high (such as financial services institutions). A 1993 survey of 500 CIOs by Deloitte & Touche found many of them planning a major client-server push in the next two years, although the mainframe still plays an important part in some industries. However, migrating applications from host-based environments to client-server architectures remains challenging.[18] This topic will be revisited in Chap. 2.

As noted, some view outsourcing as enabling the corporation to transform its IT/IS infrastructure, or even transform itself more fundamentally—namely, outsource and accomplish business reengineering at the same time. At the very least, organizations can move their legacy systems to outsourcers, but keep client-server systems inhouse, the rationale being that legacy systems may not provide the competitive advantage that client-server systems could. In addition, businesses can outsource the transition to client-server computing and use their increased leverage to get outsourcers to provide more services, such as network services.[19]

1.3.2 Some outsourcing principles

Deciding whether to outsource any part (or the whole) of an enterprise's IT infrastructure requires a careful analysis of the operational and financial implications of such a decision. Many companies have little idea of what it costs them to design, run, and manage their IT investments. Some costs are obvious, but many others are hidden (see, for example, Table 1.3).

The first step in an outsourcing analysis entails an inventory of a company's IT investment, including all fixed and variable costs. A complete inventory could take considerable time to complete, since companies may have many systems and subsystems, with associated local and interconnection networks. In many cases it is possible to obtain at least a quick initial assessment of a company's investment. Table 1.4, based on a variety of sources, including Ref. 17, shows a breakdown of IT costs in 1993, averaged over several hundred companies. Table 1.5, also based on a variety of sources, can be used to *estimate* the total IT budget in a number of industries. (This is an empirical model based on a number of studies conducted by the author; individual companies may or may not fit this first-cut assessment.)

TABLE 1.3   Examples of Hidden Costs of IT Infrastructure (Partial List, Adapted from Ref. 20)

Hardware/equipment costs
  Equipment (PCs, hubs, servers, bridges, routers, etc.)
  Site preparation
  Installation, testing, documentation
  Cables

Software
  Licenses
  Testing

TABLE 1.3   Examples of Hidden Costs of IT Infrastructure (Partial List, Adapted from Ref. 20) (*Continued*)

Installation/distribution
Documentation
Maintenance

Communication costs
Initial
Recurring

Rental costs for housing equipment
Real estate
Floor space
Air conditioning
Lighting
Sensors
Security
Planning and administration

Electric power
Principal
Backup
Planning and administration

Project feasibility study (staff time)

Project pilot

Pilot evaluation

Management review

Project implementation time/cost
Construction
Delivery costs
Testing and validating
Integration
Delays and overruns
Cost of service overlap
Specialized installation staff

Fees
Rights of way
Licenses

Taxes

System/network operation/management
Staff
Benefits
Management of staff
Facilities
Test equipment
Training
Turnover
Ad hoc maintenance
Maintenance (monthly fees)
Insurance
Cost of documentation
Capacity planning

TABLE 1.3   Examples of Hidden Costs of IT Infrastructure (Partial List, Adapted from Ref. 20) (*Continued*)

Planning and administration
Cost of network/system security (including appropriate tools)

Cost of back up system, including disaster recovery

Lost productivity

Business risk

Financial management (bookkeeping, accounting, etc.)

Cost of capital

Technological obsolescence

Cost of eventual replacement

Decommission costs

TABLE 1.4   IT Cost per Key Function

Function	Percent of IT budget
Personnel	37.75*
Hardware	23.25
Software	15.70
Overhead	6.00
Communication	5.55
Networking products	5.25
Outside services	5.10
Other	1.40
	100.00
Breakdown of Communication Budget	
Function	Percent
Network management	40
Hardware (amortized)	30
Recurring transmission costs	30

*As an estimate, this number can be partitioned as 30.75 percent for data processing, 7 percent for data communication.

Notes:

1. In the top of this table, portions of the communication costs are included in the personnel, equipment, communication, and networking entries; therefore, the top and the bottom of this table are not directly comparable. The only equivalency is that the 30 percent representing recurring charges in the bottom of this table equates with the 5.55 percent figure given in the top.

2. In recent years, communication expenditures for wide area connectivity are becoming a smaller portion of the total IT budget. This is partially achieved through Tariff 12 contracts.

3. The hardware budget (23.35 percent of the total IT budget) is further divided as follows: PCs, 7.045; workstations, 1.372; servers (application), 1.418; midrange/department systems, 4.720; mainframes, 3.092; storage, 2.232; printers and other peripherals, 2.534; other, 0.837.

TABLE 1.5 Empirical Estimator for IT Expenditures

	IS personnel (% of gross)	Hardware (% of gross)	Software (% of gross)	Overhead (% of gross)	Communication (% of gross)	Networking products (% of gross)	Outside services (% of gross)	Other (% of gross)	Total (% of gross*)
Aerospace	1.80	1.11	0.75	0.29	0.26	0.25	0.24	0.07	4.76
Airlines	4.35	2.68	1.81	0.69	0.64	0.61	0.59	0.16	11.53
Automotive	1.36	0.84	0.57	0.22	0.20	0.19	0.18	0.05	3.60
Banks	1.58	0.97	0.66	0.25	0.23	0.22	0.21	0.06	4.18
Beverages	0.38	0.23	0.16	0.06	0.06	0.05	0.05	0.01	1.01
Broadcasting	1.71	1.06	0.71	0.27	0.25	0.24	0.23	0.06	4.54
Chemicals	1.58	0.97	0.66	0.25	0.23	0.22	0.21	0.06	4.18
Financial services	1.36	0.84	0.57	0.22	0.20	0.19	0.18	0.05	3.60
Food and lodging/hotel	1.74	1.07	0.72	0.28	0.26	0.24	0.24	0.06	4.61
Food processing	0.68	0.42	0.28	0.11	0.10	0.09	0.09	0.03	1.80
Government agencies	3.40	2.09	1.41	0.54	0.50	0.47	0.46	0.13	9.01
Instruments	1.74	1.07	0.72	0.28	0.26	0.24	0.24	0.06	4.61
Manufacturing	1.85	1.14	0.77	0.29	0.27	0.26	0.25	0.07	4.90
Medical institutions	0.38	0.23	0.16	0.06	0.06	0.05	0.05	0.01	1.00
Natural resources	0.71	0.44	0.29	0.11	0.10	0.10	0.10	0.03	1.87
Nonprofit organizations	3.02	1.86	1.26	0.48	0.44	0.42	0.41	0.11	8.00
Office equipment companies	4.63	2.85	1.92	0.74	0.68	0.64	0.62	0.17	12.25
Oil service & supply	1.50	0.92	0.62	0.24	0.22	0.21	0.20	0.06	3.96
Paper and forest products	0.68	0.42	0.28	0.11	0.10	0.09	0.09	0.03	1.80
Personal care companies	1.31	0.80	0.54	0.21	0.19	0.18	0.18	0.05	3.46
Pharmaceuticals	1.66	1.02	0.69	0.26	0.24	0.23	0.22	0.06	4.40

14

Publishing	1.71	1.06	0.71	0.27	0.25	0.24	0.23	0.06	4.54
Railroads	3.46	2.13	1.44	0.55	0.51	0.48	0.47	0.13	9.15
Retailing (food)	0.38	0.23	0.16	0.06	0.06	0.05	0.05	0.01	1.01
Retailing (nonfood)	3.02	1.86	1.26	0.48	0.44	0.42	0.41	0.11	8.00
Service industries	1.41	0.87	0.59	0.22	0.21	0.20	0.19	0.05	3.75
Steel producers	1.28	0.79	0.53	0.20	0.19	0.18	0.17	0.05	3.39
Textiles/apparel	1.28	0.79	0.53	0.20	0.19	0.18	0.17	0.05	3.39
Transportation/trucking	3.40	2.09	1.41	0.54	0.50	0.47	0.46	0.13	9.01
Universities	2.99	1.84	1.24	0.48	0.44	0.42	0.40	0.11	7.93
Utilities	1.33	0.82	0.55	0.21	0.20	0.19	0.18	0.05	3.53

*Total percentage of gross revenue/budget spent on IT; average over column: 5.0 percent.
Examples of use:

- A bank with $1 billion of revenue per year would spend $41.8 million per year on IT.
- An oil company with $8 billion of revenue per year would spend $317 million per year on IT (or $0.015 × 8,000,000,000 = $120 million on personnel, or 2400 people at an average of $50,000 per person).
- The embedded base of IT equipment can be approximated as being about equal to the yearly expenditure. For example, a $1 billion bank would have about $42 million in IT infrastructure. This heuristic is based on a detailed unpublished study conducted by the author in the late 1980s that looked at the infrastructure investments of seven of the top ten data processing companies in the world, with combined data processing assets of $4 billion. (This heuristic can also be derived from the fact that hardware is about 25 percent of the total IT budget, from Table 1.4, and four-year amortization can be used; therefore the hardware is 0.25 × 4 = 1.00 of the IT budget.)

After the data collection phase, the manager can begin to explore some available outsourcing options and to some "what-if" analysis. After key areas have been identified, a more detailed economic analysis can be undertaken. At a macro level there are three clear phases to such analysis:

1. Plan
2. Implement
3. Manage

Organizations should examine their in-house resources, as well as their finances, before making an outsourcing decision.[21] The process of developing a strategy should include (1) establishing service management objectives that are linked to business goals, (2) generating proposals, (3) evaluating options, (4) identifying potential benefits and risks, and (5) making recommendations. When finalized, the strategy must define what services are to be delivered, specify which components are supported by internal and external sources, and identify the skills and controls needed to manage the internal activities and external suppliers.[14]

In an outsourcing arrangement, an outsourcer may agree to take over some existing applications and/or convert them to new (more up-to-date) applications running on a platform of choice. There may be a charge associated with the conversion. After the transfer, charges related to data center operations are based on standard metrics of system use, such as number of transactions per day, disk space used, etc.

Some organizations are now linking their compensation of outsourcing vendors to their own business performance, structuring contracts under which the organization pays the vendor a fee proportionate to how much product rolls off its assembly lines and how much the company earns. Such contracts are based on the view that the outsourcer is a business partner and should, therefore, share in its customers' success or failure. For example, Navistar International Corp. is reported to have negotiated an outsourcing agreement that directly links outsourcer compensation to productivity.[22] In some situations, the outsourcer processes transactions that directly generate revenue for the client and is paid a "commission" on each transaction. Most outsourcers are still assessing the issue of indexed compensation.

The move from mainframe computers to client-server networks is creating a challenge for negotiators of outsourcing contracts: The transfer of software licensing is emerging as an important issue as outsourcing providers seek to enter the rapidly developing client-server market. Problems have arisen when providers of outsourcing services have been prompted by vendors to sign contracts detailing their responsibilities for software originally licensed for customer use only. A ruling by the Ninth U.S. Circuit Court of Appeals reaffirmed the need for both service providers and outsourcers to maintain strict software licensing standards.[23]

There are those who see limitations and risks in outsourcing. Outsourcing has been primarily a means of cutting costs, but it has also been criticized for its tendency to result in loss of control over IS. Some believe that outsourcing tends to favor vendors over users.[21] Some view outsourcing as selling off a strategic asset (the corporate IT infrastructure) to achieve a short-term cut in operating costs. By and large, outsourcing is still viewed as a progressive approach: Once a corporation gets into such a paradigm, it is difficult to turn back and regain ownership of the IT/IS infrastructure. The earlier trend of turning over the *entire* data center to an outsourcer is slowing down, as already noted; outsourcing is now more often practiced in selected areas.

Outsourcing contracts should be entered into with caution. When negotiating outsourcing contracts, it is important for organizations to leave room for flexibility, since a contract that meets a company's current needs may not be adequate at a later time during the life of the contract.[24] Outsourcing contracts tend to be signed for periods lasting between 7 and 10 years, during which time the corporate objectives and/or the business climate may change radically. According to some studies, most organizations outsourcing their information system functions are not realizing the level of cost reductions they originally anticipated.[9]

Outsourcing network management functions can lower a company's communication costs, since companies that outsource can spend less time performing certain functions and do not have to invest money in personnel with expertise in the latest technologies, such as frame relay, switched multimegabit data service, and cell relay service, in order to support new expensive hardware and software. Outsourcers often have access to newer technologies that companies could not afford to buy themselves, and companies that outsource can save money by exploiting economies of scale. However, even in this context, outsourcing can have drawbacks, such as lack of control over the communication network and misunderstandings caused by the outsourcer's potential unfamiliarity with the company's core business.[25]

The securities industry has yet to choose the outsourcing approach. Some believe that the concept of outsourcing is contrary to the practices of securities firms, which like to maintain tight control over their computer operations.[26] Securities firms such as Lehman Brothers, Prudential Securities, and Smith Barney Shearson have reportedly considered outsourcing their information systems, but have not followed through with an implementation. One reason cited for such indecision is a lack of belief that the contracting firm could offer the same high-quality service that the securities firm offers itself. Securities companies may, however, move to partial outsourcing of those functions that do not represent core competencies.[26]

Companies contemplating outsourcing should undertake a detailed business case analysis before assuming that outsourcing will necessarily be a money-saver in their specific case. Some issues to examine are whether or not the outsourcer's economies of scale are available to the organization, and whether the outsourcer or the company can obtain the hardware for less money. When negotiating contracts, companies could use an outside consultant to evaluate different outsourcing firms' services. Companies should have a 10-year plan covering all identifiable contingencies before issuing a request for proposals, and they should retain control over the development of mission-critical applications.[24] Outsourcing can be a large, costly, and not easily reversed step. Issues to consider include whether the proposed savings can be measured against actual costs, whether outsourcing will truly address the problem or merely disguise it, and whether the contract actually will save money.[27] Chapter 3 provides some analytical techniques that can be employed in the required analysis.

Lately, corporate executives have started to view the option of outsourcing differently and are looking to a broader range of possibilities.[21] Given the limitations posed by (some) vendor contracts, companies can look into some other options. These include

- *Multisourcing.* This combines multiple deals with vendors and internal IS staff. Multisourcing, also known as partnering or selective sourcing, seeks to combine the efforts of both business and IS.

- *Temporary outsourcing partnerships.* These arrangements have a much shorter time frame than traditional outsourcing arrangements (e. g., 12 to 24 months).

- *Insourcing.* This approach is finding a place in certain corporations. Insourcing refers to the bringing back in-house of applications that had been outsourced, either by hiring consultants to reengineer the in-house MIS department or simply through competitive in-house bidding.[28] Advances in computer systems allow these corporations to perform operations that would earlier have entailed a large expense. Applications such as payroll no longer require mainframe systems, and companies are finding that they can run such applications themselves, often more expeditiously and cheaply than if they were outsourced.

According to some observers, businesses are outsourcing *less* as the trend toward smaller computers and reduced costs leads to the withdrawal of funds from centralized IS, a trend which gives companies more leverage in renegotiating contracts with vendors. Bringing work back in-house is an important leverage point.[19]

Other benefits/areas. Others see outsourcing as a way not only to reduce costs, but also to wipe out fractures and fissures that may exist in the IS organization. Cost can be reduced when employees that are part of the IS organization are transferred to an organization in which salaries and benefits are more streamlined and more in line with the market. Improvements in organizational dynamics can become necessary when the IS organization has grown by way of mergers and acquisitions, as is common in the financial services and banking industry, for example. In one case, a bank had acquired and assimilated 21 other banks. However, prior to outsourcing, IS was still run by eight IS executives reporting to eight different top executives, and there were 260 applications on eight separate platforms, slowing down the organization's ability to meet the competitive challenges. To solve the problem, consolidation of both hardware and software onto a single platform and a managerial consolidation were needed. Outsourcing enabled the organization to meet those goals on an expedited basis.[29] Temporary outsourcing, transition assistance, capability development, and complete divesting of IT functions are all options to be considered by groups looking into outsourcing.[3] One way in which companies can realize savings is by outsourcing the less creative functions of IS.[9]

Outsourcing is not limited to IS; it is being used for related business functions as well. Growth in outsourcing is anticipated in the areas of networking, integrated systems for videoconferencing, and value-added networks.[27] Outsourcing LAN administration tasks to systems integrators is gaining in popularity as networks become increasingly complex, particularly because of high levels of interconnectivity.[30] LANs are becoming more important to the corporation; in fact, an estimated 700,000 U.S. firms have installed LANs. A number of integrators are now offering network management services that may cost less than corporations pay for their own administration. Integrators are providing services such as performance tuning, security monitoring, and backup.[30] While outsourcing network management is not new, outsourced LAN administration is a new area where observers expect to see significant growth. Outsourcing's major advantage is saving money, even for companies whose LANs work well. The topic of LAN outsourcing is revisited in Chap. 6. New technologies are also part of the motivation to outsource, as many management functions can be performed remotely, eliminating the need for in-house personnel.

Network managers can approach outsourcing in a selective way. Costly or complicated parts of network operations can be off-loaded, allowing managers to focus their attention elsewhere.[31] Parts of operations can be outsourced to carriers, computer companies, or systems integrators. Interexchange carriers are emerging as effective providers because of factors such as their geographic reach and their distributed computing capabilities. Carriers can meet stringent user requirements for reliability for networks that run mission-critical applications.[31]

Local exchange carriers can also provide network outsourcing support. For example, as of press time, Pacific Bell was managing the networks of more than 50 organizations; most of these businesses outsource network services to Pacific Bell because of the high cost of managing their own networks (however, some large companies prefer to manage their own networks). Pacific Bell is using several networking tools to automate the management process, including[32] HP's Open View, Isicad Inc.'s Command data management software, and Remedy Corp.'s Action Request System trouble-ticket software. In this approach, network repairs are designated to third-party vendors; Pacific Bell then tracks the status of repairs. The company is also considering automatic inventory software that would perform data collection without an operator having to be present.

Global network outsourcing offers a number of benefits for many multinational companies. Outsourcing a company's global networking operations can reduce costs and improve management. Outsourcing offers international networking solutions to multinational companies, relieving these companies of the cost and the responsibility of managing their communications resources and allowing them to refocus instead on their core business activities.[33] However, a number of challenges exist for those businesses considering the move, including the selection of an outsourcing firm and whether to commit to full or just partial outsourcing.[34] Note that it is generally easier for data center outsourcers to upgrade their computing resources than it is for network outsourcers to keep up with changing communications technologies; this is because global networks are not as restricted geographically as corporate data centers and are not as stable.[35]

Cost is an important factor in global network outsourcing because the technologies are changing rapidly. A company outsourcing its network may find itself locked into current pricing schedules at a later date when competitors are taking advantage of cheaper services. Most observers expect a continued decline in transmission cost as additional fiber-based facilities are deployed. Companies may be considering outsourcing as a way of altering network loads, to fill in missing skills within their organization or to respond to user dissatisfaction, to improve network management uptime, as a way of transferring employees to more strategic operations, or to upgrade systems and applications. Hence, stabilizing or reducing networking costs is not the only benefit derived from outsourcing network functions.[34]

For example, Worldspan Travel Agency Information Services has contracted with AT&T for an X.25 packet data network to connect more than 8000 travel agencies to an Atlanta-based data center. The seven-year, $100 million outsourcing deal is part of Worldspan's plans to reduce costs and generate revenue for the computerized reservations system. Worldspan expects this new networking approach to improve or maintain availability and performance. Because of the outsourced network management, the operational costs were expected to be reduced by approximately 10 percent.[36]

Some networking outsourcing vendors are already planning broadband ATM networks (see Chap. 2) to support outsourcing needs.[37] The issue of telecommunication outsourcing is revisited in Chap. 6.

1.4 Outsourcing Market

In 1992, the market for data processing outsourcing was estimated at $12.2 billion ($7 billion of which was for facilities management), and proponents expect the market to grow to nearly $30 billion by 1997.[*,24] According to some surveys, 53 percent of the outsourcing market is devoted to custom development (including application development), 25 percent to system integration, and 22 percent to planning, design, and education.[39]

The outsourcing industry is growing as computing changes fuel the trend. Some well-publicized instances of outsourcing in the past few years include Enron Corp [$750 million to Electronic Data Systems (EDS)], First City Bank ($600 million to EDS), Eastman Kodak ($500 million to IBM), National Car Rental ($500 million to EDS), First Fidelity Bank ($450 million to EDS), Freeport McMoran Inc. ($200 million to EDS and then Andersen Consulting/IBM's Integrated Solutions Corp./Computerland Corp), McDonnell Douglas Corp. ($3 billion to IBM), and General Dynamics Computer Sciences Corp. (a 10-year contract worth over $3 billion). Other major recent instances of outsourcing cases include American Standard, American Ultramar, Brooks Brothers, CalFed Inc., Chase Manhattan Bank, Continental

---

*Frost and Sullivan put the 1992 outsourcing market at $18.2 billion, or 4.4 percent of the average IS budget; they expect the market to rise to $38.2 billion or 8 percent of IS budget in 1995.[9] Others use different estimates as follows: $2.7 billion (1992), with the figure rising to $8.4 billion by 1997.[38]

Bank, Copperweld, General Dynamics Corp., Hook-SuperRx Inc., Kaiser Permanente, Merrill Lynch & Co., NationsBank of Charlotte, Norrell Corp., Wabco, and Woodward Stores. An estimated 550 U.S. companies have some type of IS outsourcing.*

There are four types of outsourcing providers: computer manufacturers, telecommunications carriers, stand-alone outsourcing companies, and telecommunications equipment manufacturers.[38] Key outsourcing companies in the United States include EDS (13 percent of the 1992 market), Computer Sciences Corp. (5 percent of the 1992 market), IBM's Integrated Solutions Corp. (ISSC) (3 percent of the 1992 market),† Affiliated Computer Systems Inc. (2 percent of the 1992 market), Systematics Information Services (2 percent of the 1992 market), and others (for the balance of the market) including Perot Systems Corp. and Digital Equipment Corporation.[40] That outsourcing can be lucrative for the providers is shown by the fact that IBM's ISSC did well recently, in sharp contrast to the performance of much of the rest of the company (IBM lost $4.97 billion in 1992 because of restructuring charges and costs related to workforce reductions, but ISSC showed $1 billion of revenues and made a profit).[41]

Of companies on which data was collected by a 1993 survey, 20 percent have outsourced information systems operations, and 58 percent are considering it.[18] In the United States, just the value of *banking* outsourcing contracts signed in 1992 reached $2.5 billion. This segment of the outsourcing market is expected to be around $6 billion in 1997.[29] The market has been growing and continues to grow at a rate of about 20 percent a year. The consolidation in the banking business is driving the outsourcing trend (almost one-third of all banks now in existence will be absorbed and consolidated by 1996). The growth in the outsourcing market slowed down a few percentage points in 1993 from the earlier growth value in the low 20s. The slowdown is partly attributed to the improved financial outlook of banks, softening pressure to cut costs across the enterprise.

Canadian companies have been slower to consider IS outsourcing than their U.S. counterparts. But Canadian industry is catching up quickly. Indeed, in the first three months of 1992, the Canadian outsourcing market doubled with the award of only two major contracts. That year also saw the entry of two of Canada's corporate giants into the outsourcing provider market. The size of the Canadian outsourcing

---

*This is estimated as 20 percent of the *Fortune* 1500, 10 percent of the next 1500 companies, and 5 percent of the next 2000 companies.

†In 1992 IBM and Sears Roebuck formed a joint networking venture, Advantis, which has been characterized as the "networking arm of ISSC."[37]

TABLE 1.6   Canadian Outsourcing Market in 1992

Provider of outsourcing services	Revenues from outsourcing business (C$M)	Percent of total Canadian outsourcing market
SHL	500	42
ISM	350	29
EDS Canada	204	17
Digital Equipment Corp.	36	3
Other	100	8
Total	1190	100

market during 1991 was C$500 million. Several large corporations (SHL Systemhouse, IBM Canada, and EDS Canada) are targeting the C$3 billion market expected in 1996 and the rapid growth in outsourcing activity that was expected to begin in 1993. Table 1.6 depicts the revenues for the major providers. The picture for 1992 was significantly different from that for the 1991 market. In 1992 IBM Canada (with 1991 revenues of $4.6 billion) injected new energy and direction into Information Systems Management Corporation (ISM) by increasing its equity stake in ISM to 51 percent. ISM was the largest outsourcing provider in Canada at the time. The BCE group (with 1991 revenues of $18.8 billion) also announced its intention to acquire control of SHL Systemhouse, a Canadian multinational systems integration and computer consulting firm, making SHL Systemhouse a major national force.

In 1993, SHL Systemhouse signed a 10-year contract with Canada Post Corp. that involves the provision of complete systems management, telecommunications and data processing requirements.[42] SHL Systemhouse now handles distributed computing (mail tracking, electronic messaging, payroll administration, and financial accounting) and will support both LANs and WANs. A key facet of the contract involves the conversion of Canada Post from a mainframe system to a distributed processing system based on the client-server network architecture, a trend alluded to earlier (Chap. 8 looks at this illustrative study case in more detail).

1.5   Treatment Approach

The rest of the book will provide additional details on many of the concepts covered in summary form in this first chapter. The discussion starts with a primer on client-server computing, the target technology of many IS managers. After providing some analytical tools, each of the chapters that follow examines a different facet of outsourcing.

References

1. M. J. Major, "Who's Minding the Store?" *Midrange Systems,* 6(4):23ff, 1993.
2. L. Loh and N. Venkatraman, "Determinants of Information Technology Outsourcing: A Cross-Sectional Analysis," *Journal of Management Information Systems,* 9(1):7–24, 1992.
3. Robert Manion, "Why It Makes Sense to Break the IS Shackles (The Case for Outsourcing)," *I.T. Magazine,* 25(3):14, 1993.
4. C. Benko, "Outsourcing Evaluation: A Profitable Process," *Information Systems Management,* 10(2):45ff, 1993.
5. R. T. Due, "The Real Costs of Outsourcing," *Information Systems Management,* Winter 1992, pp. 78ff.
6. P. Morley, "The Advantages to Outsourcing," *Networking Management Europe,* January/February 1993, pp. 24ff.
7. D. Minoli, *Imaging in Corporate Environments: Technology and Communication,* McGraw-Hill, New York, 1994.
8. Charles Johnson, "Top Ten Reasons for Choosing an Outsourcer," *Computing Canada,* 19(12):43, 1993.
9. Steve Polilli, "Is Outsourcing a Bargain?" *Software Magazine,* 13(4):36, 1993.
10. McQuillen Consulting, *Early Adopters of ATM, A Report to ATM Forum,* July 1993.
11. P. Lloyd, "Outsourcing: Mutual Benefit or Mutual Risk," *Telecommunications,* February 1993, pp. 37ff.
12. J. L. Wagner, "Issues in Outsourcing," *1992 IRMA Conference Proceedings,* Idea Group Publishing, 1992, pp. 214ff.
13. Nancy Frost, "Outsourcing: The Right Move for Today's Virtual Organization," *Office,* 117(5):40, 1993.
14. John Cox, "The Essential Guide to Effective Outsourcing (Strategies for Facilities Management)," *Computer Weekly,* June 10, 1993, p. 24.
15. Larry Stevens, "Getting By with a Little Help from Your Friends," *Manufacturing Systems,* 9(3):52–55, 1991.
16. Anthony Vecchione, "Take the 'O' Train: Outsourcing PC Training (Skill Dynamics, IBM's Training Subsidiary, Acquires Catapult Inc.)," *Information Week,* 424:25, 1993.
17. J. Moad, "Tight Budgets: It's How You Cut 'Em," *Datamation,* May 1, 1993, pp. 30ff.
18. Dave Powell, "Client/Server, Re-engineering, and Outsourcing Often Fall Short of User Expectations," *Networking Management,* 11(5):6, 1993.
19. Timothy Middleton, "It's Time to Duel for Dollars; Rethinking Outsourcing," *Corporate Computing,* 2(6):27, 1993.
20. D. Minoli, *Broadband Network Design and Analysis,* Artech House, Norwood, Mass., 1993.
21. Elizabeth U. Harding, "IS Explores Multisourcing: Trend toward Selective Use of Third Parties," *Software Magazine,* 13(9):28, 1993.
22. Mark Halper, "Users Tie 'Partners' to Profits: Bottom Line Key for Outsourcing Pacts," *Computerworld,* 27(25):1, 1993.
23. T. C. Doyle, "Outsourcers: Beware of Client/Server Licensing Trap," *Computer Reseller News,* 529:2, June 7, 1993.
24. George Harrar, "Outsource Tales," *Forbes* ASAP Technology Supplement, *Forbes,* 151(12):S36, 1993.
25. Heinan Landa, "Outsourcing Network Management—Pros, Cons," *LAN Times,* 10(9):49, 1993.
26. Sheila O'Heney, "Outsourcing: Dead or Alive?" *Wall Street & Technology,* 10(6):29, 1993.
27. Dave Burkett and Bob Wiffen, "And Five Reasons Why It May Not (The Case against Outsourcing)," *I.T. Magazine,* 25(3):18, 1993.
28. Elaine Appleton, "Term Limits," *HP Professional,* 7(6):28, 1993.
29. J. Moad, "Inside an Outsourcing Deal," *Datamation,* Feb. 15, 1993, pp. 20ff.
30. Doug van Kirk, "LAN Management: The Next Wave of Outsourcing," *InfoWorld,* 15(28):52,

31. Kimberly Patch and Mary Johnston Turner, "A Fresh Outlook on Outsourcing: Users Find Farming Out of the Network Operations Pie Has Its Benefits," *NetworkWorld,* 10(8):34, 1993.
32. Sharon Fisher, "PacBell Blends Management Tools for Outsourcing Service," *Communications Week,* 450:69, April 19, 1993.
33. Gerald W. Thames, "Outsourcing Global Telecommunications," *British Telecommunications Engineering,* 11:153–157, October 1992.
34. Dave Powell, "To Outsource or Not to Outsource?" *Networking Management,* 11(2):56, 1993.
35. Dave Powell, "Outsourcing Offers Obvious Benefits, but Beware of 'Subtle Disadvantages,'" *Networking Management,* 11(3):8, 1993.
36. Paul Travis, "Worldspan Books Flight with AT&T; Travel Service Has No Reservations about Outsourcing Deal," *Information Week,* 417:46, March 22, 1993.
37. T. Wilson, "Avantis Rides Crest of Outsourcing Wave," *Communications Week,* Dec. 13, 1993, pp. 35ff.
38. "Network Outsourcing Market Could Triple by 1997," *Communications Week,* 435:32, Jan. 4, 1993.
39. W. B. Richmond, A. Seidmann, and A. B. Whinston, "Incomplete Contracting Issues in Information Systems Development Outsourcing," *Decision Support Systems,* 8(5):459–477, 1992.
40. D. Livingston, "Outsourcing: Look Beyond the Price Tag," *Datamation,* Nov. 15, 1992, pp. 93ff.
41. Bob Brown, "ISSC Subsidiary Brightens Glum Picture for Big Blue: IBM Outsourcing Group Posts Profit in Hard Times," *Network World,* 10(4):25, 1993.
42. James Buchok, "Systemhouse, Canada Post Sign 'Mega' Outsourcing Deal (10-Year Contract for SHL Systemhouse Inc.)," *Computing Canada,* 19(9):1, 1993.

2

Background: Typical Computing Environments Now in Place

Starting in the late 1980s and continuing through the 1990s, many organizations have transformed their mission-critical computing infrastructures by implementing LAN-based architectures. PCs and workstations are now almost universally connected to LANs. In turn, local or departmental LANs are connected across the corporate enterprise by multiprotocol routers; such connectivity is sought whether the organization is clustered in a building or spread out over a campus, a metropolitan area, a state, a nation, or several nations and/or continents.

Companies continue to use automation in general, and IT in particular, to improve productivity. Automation and IT have been employed by companies to "reengineer" the way corporate work is done. For example, in a traditional corporate environment, middle managers relayed filtered information from the production floor to the executive level and, in turn, dispensed directives from the executives to the workers. Now databases and telecommunication networks collect and distribute that information in a more effective and unbiased manner.[1]

A survey of 400 large companies during the period 1987–1991 indicated that their annual return on their investment in IT has averaged between 54 and 68 percent.[1] This type of return has fueled the continued introduction of this technology; however, such introduction carries its own cost, which companies are now trying to control. Therefore, IT is itself now being reengineered. Many companies are introducing client-server architectures, and sometimes take the opportunity not only to reengineer the IS environment, but also to accomplish (some degree of) outsourcing at the same time. In 1990 about 30 percent of the applications in a typical organization were client-server-based; by 1995 the percentage of client-server-based applications is forecast to be 65 percent. The client-server market is estimated at $30 billion in 1993.[2] In particular, this means that the once-safe mainframe-based data management systems are now threatened by the potential migration of data off the mainframe to a client-server environment.[3]

The focus on business accountability has led departments and workgroups to introduce workstation technology to solve problems which the traditional central IT organization was either slow or unable to deal with. This, however, resulted in islands of automation which prevented effective communication of information and access to processes and applications developed in another area. Reengineered IT organizations recognize this reality and the value of personal computers; such IT organizations see their new role as the establishment of enterprise standards to facilitate application and infrastructure interoperability. In many situations, however, the expertise to establish these standards is not available internally; the reengineering process may be more effectively done through outsourcing.

Because of the growing importance of client-server systems as part of IT reengineering, this chapter serves as a short primer in this area.* Both the advantages and the challenges of client-server computing are addressed, following our goal of wanting to provide a neutral analysis. Additionally, a short synopsis of local and remote communication technologies is provided. Not only is communication critical to client-server systems (and therefore important to discuss), but also some companies are outsourcing certain elements of their corporate networks; hence, this material serves as a primer for Chaps. 5 and 6. The discussion of outsourcing per se is resumed in Chap. 3.

The early part of this chapter tries to answer the question: What is client-server technology, and how do corporations now use it? There are doctrinaire arguments both for and against client-server design, but one size does not fit all in real life, much less in the complicated IS world; hence, some pertinent questions are[5]

- How does one sort through the claims and counterclaims on client-server computing?

- What should one look for in one's own applications and technical infrastructure?

- When should one not choose client-server?

- What becomes of the mainframe-based applications?

---

*This treatment is only an encapsulated review. For a more inclusive treatment, see Refs. 2 and 4, among others.

- Should all on-line transaction processing applications be client-server-based?

- Are small applications (e.g., XBase database applications whose roots are derived from dBASE) worth converting?

The past few years have seen large amounts of trade press extolling the potential advantages of client-server computing. More recently, as organizations have started to gain hands-on experience with client-server systems, literature and studies have emerged that make the point that when all the cost factors are appropriately accounted for (as described in Chap. 1), client-server systems may in fact be from one to two times more expensive than mainframe systems. Thus, well-defined benchmarks are sought by the user community to settle this issue. (This topic is examined in greater depth in Ref. 4.) The implications of this situation should be kept in mind while reading the rest of the text.

2.1   Client-Server Systems: Practical Definition

2.1.1   Key client-server concepts

The basics of client-server computing involve dividing the work between two computer systems. One is the system on the desktop, which is generally, but not always, referred to as the client. The other is somewhere on the network, perhaps along with other servers. Clients initiate requests for some service—for example, database lookup/update, read from/write to a remote mass storage device, dialing out on one of a pool of modems, or printing a report or document; the server accomplishes the task on behalf of the client.[5]

In the client-server arrangement, the client is the "consumer" of the services provided by the server or servers. The concept of the client-server architecture is support of a clear separation of functions: The server acts as a service provider responding to work requests from the various clients. Note that the same piece of equipment can be used as either a client or a server; what makes the difference is the software that is loaded onto the equipment. In fact, the same piece of equipment can act as a client and as a server in different instances. Table 2.1 provides a glossary of key client-server terms and concepts.

The term *client-server* is only loosely defined at the practical level. People use this term to refer to a variety of systems, from simple remote-access file systems to complex database engines. Many people hold that the terms *client-server* and *network database* are synonymous; in fact, the database server technology used in systems developed by Microsoft, Sybase, Oracle, and others fits most definitions of

TABLE 2.1   Glossary of Key Client-Server Terms and Concepts (List Not Exhaustive)

API	The Application Programming Interface, a set of call programs and functions that enables clients and servers to communicate.
Back end	The database engine. Back-end functions include storing, dispensing, and manipulating the information.
Client	A (networked) information requester that can query databases and/or seek other information from a server. At the physical device level, the client is a PC or workstation.
Common ORB architecture (CORBA)	An ORB standard endorsed by the Object Management Group (OMB).
Distributed computing environment (DCE)	A set of integrated software modules that provides an environment for creating, using, and maintaining client-server applications on a network. It includes capabilities such as security, directory, synchronization, file sharing, RPCs, and multithreading.
Distributed database	A client-server database system based on a network supporting many clients and servers.
Distributed Relational Database Architecture (DRDA)	A SAA-based enhancement that allows information to be distributed among SQL/DS and DB2 databases.
Dynamic Data Exchange (DDE)	A message-based protocol used in the context of Microsoft Windows which allows applications to automatically request and exchange information, thereby supporting interprocess communication. The protocol allows an application running in one window to query an application running in another window.
Front end	A client application working in cooperation with a back-end engine that manipulates, presents, and displays data.
Object	A named entity that combines a data structure with an associated operation. Expressed more formally, Object = {Unique identifier} $\cup$ {data} $\cup$ {operations}
Object Linking and Embedding (OLE)	A client-server capability (protocol) in the context of Microsoft Windows that enables the creation of compound documents. It is an extension of DDE's capabilities. A document (e.g., a spreadsheet, a database entry, a video clip, etc.) can be embedded within or linked to another document. When an embedded ele-

TABLE 2.1   Glossary of Key Client-Server Terms and Concepts (List Not Exhaustive) (*Continued*)

	ment is referenced, the application that created it must be loaded and activated; if, for example, an embedded object is edited, these edits pertain only to the document that contains the object and not the more general instance of the object. If the object is linked, it points to an original file external to the document; if, for example, a linked object is edited, these edits are automatically loaded onto the original document.
Object Request Broker (ORB)	Software that handles the communication tasks for messages between objects in a distributed, multiplatform environment.
Object-oriented language	Linguistic support for objects. Objects can be dynamically generated and passed as operation parameters. "Pure" languages offer no facilities other than those related to classes and objects; "hybrid" languages superimpose object-oriented concepts on an alternative programming paradigm.
Open Software Foundation (OSF)	A not-for-profit organization formed to deliver an open computing environment based on industry standards. It works with members to set technical directions and licenses software. Also see DCE.
OSF/1	OSF's multiprocessing operating system.
Relational database	A database in which information access is limited to the selection of rows that satisfy all search criteria.
Server	A computer that stores information that is required by networked clients. It can be a PC, workstation, minicomputer, or mainframe.
Windows Open Services Architecture (WOSA)	A single system-level interface for connecting front-end applications with back-end services for Windows-based applications. Using WOSA, application developers and users do not need to be concerned about conversing with numerous services which may employ parochial protocols and interfaces; these details are handled by the operating systems and not by the applications themselves. WOSA provides an extensible framework in which applications "seamlessly" access information and network resources in a distributed environment. It uses Dynamic Link Library (DLL) methods to enable software components to be linked at run time.

Table based partially on Refs. 2, 6, and 7.

client-server computing. Some view client-server as the culmination of the trend toward downsizing applications from the mainframe and the minicomputer to the desktop.[2]

The following general definition has been advanced: Client-server computing is any application in which the requester of actions or information is on one system and the supplier of action or information is on another.[8] Most client-server systems have a many-to-one design: More than one client typically makes requests of the server. Many enterprise systems fit this definition. Even a classical Systems Network Architecture (SNA) fits this definition. The program in the 3270 terminal takes data entered by a user and submits them (through a cluster controller) to a server application on a mainframe; the server processes the requests, and the resulting data are sent back to the terminal.

However, when most people talk about client-server, they have something else in mind.* Closer to the contemporary use of the term are file server systems, such as Novell's NetWare or Banyan's VINES, which respond to client requests by supplying data in various logical aggregations, typically files. Even more complex examples of client-server systems are database engines that support sophisticated data structures (examples of these systems include those developed and marketed by Sybase, Oracle, and Microsoft). These database systems respond to queries from clients, perform activities based on those queries, and return discrete responses to the clients. In some sophisticated cases, a client-server application can take a complex calculation submitted by a client and partition it into a number of smaller components. These stand-alone calculations are then submitted to a series of calculation servers in a "CPU farm" that can perform these calculations simultaneously. Once each server has responded with its subresult, the client-server application consolidates these calculation components and is able to rapidly calculate the desired final answer.

In the 1960s and 1970s, organizations looked to their central IS to satisfy evolving market and economic demands. Host-based systems provided adequate support by automating back-room tasks, such as customer information, accounting, and other batch processing jobs. Host-based systems also facilitated control functions and data integrity. The 1980s proved that host-based systems could not keep pace with the growing computing demand imposed on organizations by market and economic forces. These forces drove departments and divisions to turn to personal computers, workstations, and LANs to achieve the responsiveness they needed to run on-line mission-criti-

---

*Keeping a database on a mainframe can be considered consistent with client-server computing principles if the application that uses the database runs on a PC or workstation.

cal business applications. End users worked together to achieve a competitive advantage and fulfill their departmental mission.[3]

The PC, workstation, and LAN deployments of the late 1980s and early 1990s helped give birth to client-server computing, which efficiently integrates data, applications, and computer services. End users now respond to business demands faster using their desktop and portable computers linked to resources located throughout the network. At the same time, many IS organizations are discovering that they can lower their computing costs by off-loading processing from the mainframe to the more affordable, smaller machines that have become available.[3] While the mainframe provides an ideal level of control over data, the cost savings that organizations can experience are often perceived to be large enough to justify the migration of applications off the mainframe. As a result, IS organizations have moved toward a client-server computing architecture for both cost benefits and flexibility. Figure 2.1 depicts two examples of client-server architectures. The first example shows departmental use of client-server; the second depicts an enterprise-wide system that also includes mainframes.

2.1.2 Other related concepts

It follows from the discussion above that a client-server LAN* architecture is a computing environment in which software applications are distributed among entities on the LAN. The clients request information from one or more LAN "servers" that store software applications, data, and network operating systems. The network operating system allows the clients to share the data and applications that are stored in the server, and to share peripherals on the LAN. Figure 2.2 depicts a logical view of a client-server environment, and Fig. 2.3 depicts a physical view. Note that multiple clients can rely on a single server. Approximately 200,000† client-server systems were expected to be in service by 1993,[10] and 95 percent of companies are now investigating, developing a pilot program for, or using client-server computing, according to observers.[11]

The client is the entity requesting that work be done; the server is the entity performing a set of tasks on behalf of the client. The client system provides presentation services to the ultimate (human) user. There has been an almost universal movement toward graphical user interfaces (GUIs) as the most effective method for presenting information to people. This windowing environment allows the client system (and the user) to support several simultaneous sessions.

---

*The discussion in Sec. 2.1.2 is based on Ref. 9.
†That is about 30 percent of an estimated 700,000 companies with LANs.

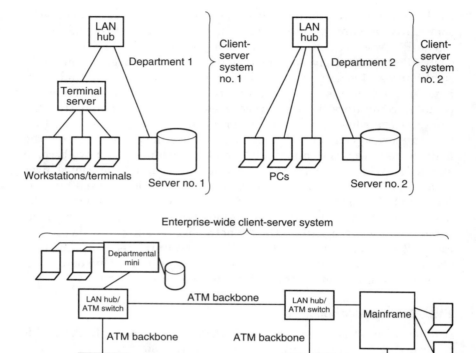

Figure 2.1 Client-server systems. Top: departmental systems; bottom: enterprisewide system.

Facilities such as Dynamic Data Exchange and Object-Linking and Embedding (see Table 2.1) provide the means to support cut-and-paste operations between such diverse applications as graphics, spreadsheets, and word processing documents.

There are three basic functions supporting computing: (1) data management, (2) processing, and (3) presentation (to user). Client-

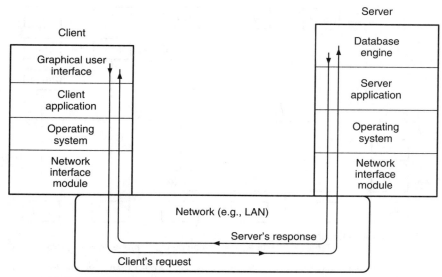

Figure 2.2 Client-server model—logical view.

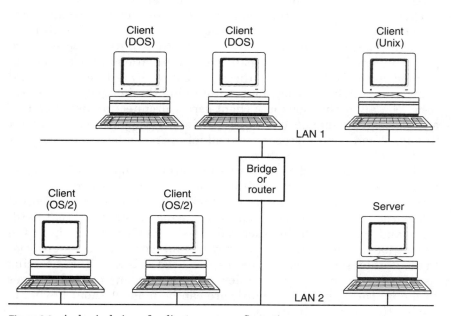

Figure 2.3 A physical view of a client-server configuration.

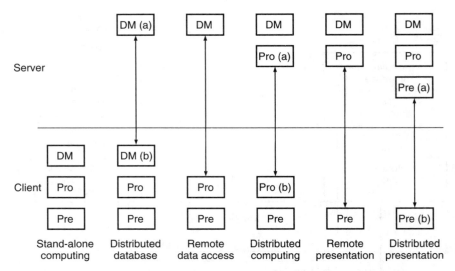

Figure 2.4 Various client-server implementations. DM = data management; Pro = processing; Pre = presentation; xxx(a/b) = function xxx partially done at point a or b.

server systems allow the distribution of these functions among appropriate devices, as shown in Fig. 2.4. Table 2.2 depicts some of the features associated with client-server implementation variations.[12,13]

The user's processor controls the user interface and issues commands across the LAN to direct the activity of the server. This is done through the use of remote procedure calls (RPCs). RPCs are software programs with distributed capabilities. Applications that are implemented on the LAN can "call" these procedures by ordering messages, translating different codes, and maintaining the integrity of the protocol. Not all applications in a client-server architecture are stored on a server; clients may also be capable of storing applications and data locally. When clients possess individual operating systems, the network is referred to as *loosely* coupled.

The goal is to have a client-server platform that operates in an open environment. In an open environment, the requester-service procedures and necessary support messages are based on well-defined standards, allowing multiple platforms (using possibly different hardware and software) to interact seamlessly. RPCs play a role in the search for openness. One of the key advantages of an open environment is that servers may grow as the need arises, without forcing users to buy from a single supplier. Additionally, any needed changes to the operating system or hardware can be made without having to modify the client applications.

Some of the benefits of using a client-server architecture include[12]

TABLE 2.2   Features Associated with Client-Server Implementation Variations

Variation	Application	Examples	Pluses	Minuses
Distributed presentation	Existing mainframe-based applications	PCs; X-terminals; X-servers	No changes to existing applications; improved human-machine interface; inexpensive desktop	Increased system computational load
Remote presentation	Independent management of user environment; new or existing applications	Workstations; PCs; DECwindow/ Motif	Server is offloaded; can be used for existing applications	Degraded performance for multi-application environments
Distributed computing	Computing components executed by most appropriate platform (array processor, mainframe, mini, etc.)	Workstations; high-end PCs; minicomputers; mainframes; adjunct processors	All resources are optimally used	Cooperative computing is required (processing must in some sense be coordinated)
Remote data access	Common data with independent applications; decision support systems	Workstations; high-end PCs; minicomputers; mainframes; SQL access; fourth-generation languages; DECquery	Reliable data; computing choices closer to user	Database machine performance affects all users
Distributed database	Resource sharing for desktop applications	Workstations; high-end PCs; minicomputers; mainframes; Oracle's Oracle Server; IBM's Database Manager; Sybase's SQL Server; Novell's NetWare SQL; Gupta's SQLBase; other fourth-generation languages	Good utilization of all devices; maximum independence	Difficult to scale up

- Increased productivity
- Control/reduction of costs by sharing resources
- Ease of management through focusing efforts onto a few servers
- Ability to adapt to new needs

In the stand-alone computing environment, all the intelligence is placed in the PC. The next step up is the static server. Here the data reside in a file server, but the file server simply stores the file in a manner functionally equivalent to storage on a local hard disk. For example, to do a sort, the entire file is downloaded to the PC, which does all the computing; the file may eventually be reloaded to the server in a sorted form. The server has no ability to manage or control the data. Two problems with this static-server architecture are[14]

- The number of simultaneous users is rather small because of performance problems related to the movement of files and indexes.

- Multiple applications usually require replication of the data into multiple databases, often with different file formats. This makes database synchronization difficult.

In a more sophisticated client-server environment, the server has the capability to perform database management. This means that the server (also known as the *back end* or *database engine*) can run a (relational) database management system using a multitasking operating system (e.g., OS/2 or Unix). See Table 2.2 under "distributed database." A relatively powerful microprocessor (e.g., 80386, 80486, or better) is required to run the multitasking operating system, the database manager, and the concurrent user sessions.

In a client-server environment, the workstation (also known as the *front end*) is responsible for presentation functions (i.e., display of data according to specified user interfaces, editing and validating data, and managing the keyboard and mouse). These functions are easy to implement, making the cost of the repetitive module (N modules for N end users) low. This provides the following advantages:[14]

- Support of many concurrent users (a few hundred)

- Reduction in cost, since front-end software is simple

- Availability of software from a variety of vendors that can perform a variety of functions and share the database

- Data integrity (single database shared by all users)

The four common methods of linking client-server applications are (1) application program interfaces (APIs), (2) database servers, (3) remote windowing, and (4) RPC software.

1. *APIs.*   A commonly used method of sharing information on a client-server network is through the use of network APIs. These are vendor-provided functions that enable application programmers to

access network resources in a standardized manner. Network APIs also allow for the connection of various applications running under the same operating system. Vendor-supplied APIs are not easily portable among different operating systems. SPX (Novell NetWare), Named Pipes (Microsoft LAN Manager), and Sockets (Berkeley UNIX) are examples of APIs. A long-term goal is to come up with vendor-independent APIs (this topic is revisited later).

2. *Database servers.*   A database server is a dedicated server in a client-server network that provides clients with distributed access to database resources. The database servers usually employ the Structured Query Language (SQL) relational database for communication between the client and the server. SQL is a de facto standard language supported by many vendors, and therefore runs on multiple platforms. (A number of vendors have introduced some syntactical differences and extensions meant to improve developer productivity; these extensions should be assessed to determine whether the benefit derived from their use outweighs the incompatibilities that may arise.)

Using SQL, database servers allow a client to download a table, as opposed to downloading the entire database. This feature reduces LAN and WAN traffic, thereby improving performance. SQL database servers extend user processing applications across various network operating systems via RPCs. SQL is a simple conversationlike language that relies on English commands such as SELECT, FROM, WHERE, etc., to perform database inquiries. For example, the user can issue the command

SELECT customer, balance FROM checking-account-list WHERE balance ≤ 1000

3. *Remote windowing.*   Remote windowing is an extension of the windowing concepts commonly used with PCs. Remote windowing allows for multivendor connectivity through the use of the Universal Terminal Standard. This concept allows multiple user processing applications to be viewed concurrently from remote locations. In order to properly distinguish Microsoft Windows from the generic concept of *windowing,* the following definition is provided: Windowing is a software feature that offers split-screen capability in which the different partitions of the display form rectangular areas. These rectangular forms, usually accompanied by GUIs, can be moved or resized on the screen. Microsoft Windows is a specific vendor application providing windowing.

4. *RPCs.*   RPCs are based on computer-aided software engineering (CASE) principles. This concept allows conventional procedure calls to be extended across a single- or multivendor network. RPCs function across several communication layers. Programmers are shielded from the networking environment, allowing them to concentrate on the func-

TABLE 2.3   Typical Client-Server Services

Database services	First-generation database services are actually file server functions with an altered interface; they execute the database engine mostly in the client. More sophisticated systems support database interactions via SQL syntax (e.g., Sybase, IBM's Database Manager, Oracle, Ingress, etc.).
Fax services	Clients can route requests for faxing, even though the fax system may be busy with another document. Requests are redirected by NOS software and managed in a fax queue. Notification of delivery is often provided. Applications themselves need not provide these capabilities.
Message services	With these services, which support buffering, scheduling, and arbitration, messages can be sent to and received from the network.
Network services	These services provide support for actual communication protocols such as TCP/IP (over Ethernet, Token Ring, FDDI, etc.), APPN, etc. They enable LAN and WAN connectivity. The application accesses the network services over the API.
Print services	Clients can route requests for printing, even though the printer may be busy with another document. Requests are redirected by NOS software and managed in a printer queue. Notification of delivery is often provided. Applications themselves need not provide these capabilities.
Remote boot services	A skeleton operating system is contained in the local workstation (e.g., on a X-terminal), and the capabilities are loaded over the network.
Windowing services	This service provides the workstation with the ability to activate, rescale, move, or hide a window. Applications themselves need not support these physical windowing capabilities (the application, using the GUI capability, places data into a virtual screen; the window service handles screen placement and manipulation).
File services	These services support access to the virtual directories and files located both on the client's hard disk and in some network server (here through redirection).

tional aspects of the applications under development. The computing industry generally describes two RPC technologies as industry standards. They are Open Network Computing (ONC) RPC (often called SunRPC), and Network Computing System (NCS) RPC. An international standard RPC based on the Remote Operations Service Element and Abstract Syntax Notation One was under development at press time.

Services.   Client workstations operate by issuing requests for services (see Table 2.3 for a typical list). The responder to such a request may be on the same processor (e.g., the request is for a locally stored file) or a remotely networked processor. The critical fact here is that the format of the request must be the same, regardless of where the responder is located. The network operating system (NOS) intercepts the request and, if necessary, translates or adds the details required by the intended responder. This NOS service is known as *redirection*. This capability intercepts the client's operating system calls and redirects them to the server operating systems. Requests such as file access, directory inquiries, printing, or application activation are trapped by the redirection software and redirected over the LAN or WAN to the correct server.

As seen in Table 2.3, application servers provide the same business functionality as was supported in the past by (more expensive) mainframes and minicomputers. These services are invoked in response to a client's request, specifically via RPCs. As already indicated, these requests are issued by the client system to the NOS. The request processing module of the client formats the request into the appropriate RPC and passes that to the application layer of the client's communication stack. What now becomes a protocol data unit (PDU) is passed further down the stack, sent over the network, and received by the server through the server's communication protocol stack. The PDU is reconstituted into the RPC, which is delivered to the server's processing logic.

RPCs standardize the way programmers write calls (invocations) to procedures (e.g., subroutines) stored somewhere in the network. If an application issues a functional request and this request is embedded in an RPC, the requested function can be located anywhere in the enterprise network (or even outside the company's enterprise network); naturally, considerations of security and access rights have to be taken into account. The RPC facility provides the invocation and execution of requests from processors running on possibly different operating systems and different hardware platforms. Many RPCs also provide data translation services; here the call causes dynamic translation of data between systems with different physical data storage formats. RPC standards are evolving and are being adopted by the industry in order to promote open environments.[2]

2.1.3 What are not considered client-server systems

The term *client-server* has a kind of understood meaning that goes beyond exact technical definition. Strictly at the system level, most applications involve some type of distributed computing, even though not all of these applications would be considered client-server systems. For example, a broker working at home can dial up a remote database server over the public switched telephone network and download some needed information to his or her PC. However, this arrangement is not considered to be a client-server application. Also, a multithreaded application is not necessarily a client-server application. A common multithreading technique is to take a parallel process—for example, printing—and run it as separate from a main task; however, these may be local functions performed on local data without client-server communication.*

There are three well-known computing environments that are *not* generally considered to be client-server systems: monolithic centralized applications, peer-to-peer applications, and messaging applications.

Monolithic applications.   A monolithic application is a single program (or a group of interrelated programs) that performs all the data interpretation and presentation as a single unit and, in a specific implementation, always runs on a single platform.[8] The application communicates with the data using normal file I/O and directly performs the data analysis and manipulation itself. (Note that a monolithic application may use a networked file service, but it is not involved with, or aware of, the client-server process.)

Peer-to-peer applications.   Strictly speaking, a peer-to-peer application can be considered a special case of client-server computing;† however, at the practical level, these applications are usually not considered client-server systems. In a peer-to-peer environment, two remote client processes can submit requests to one another over a single logical connection; each client is also a server, supporting many-to-many communication rather than the many-to-one communication typical of a true client-server system.

Messaging applications.   Most E-mail/messaging applications cannot be considered client-server systems since, typically, they do not use real-time communication between their various system components. Some on-line transaction processing (OLTP) systems use local and remote queues with continuous attempts to deliver

---

*Multithreaded applications can use client-server methods if some portions, such as print services, are located on distinct processors, servicing requests from other devices on the network.

†Some view the situation as the opposite: peer-to-peer as the general case and client/server as the special case. In this view, given the multitasking operating systems being deployed (e.g., Unix, OS/2, Windows NT, and Windows 4—Windows for Workgroups), peer-to-peer computing is expected to become the norm in the near future in LAN environments.

data, but because batched requests are generally queued before being passed to back-end service, they are not seen as client-server systems.[8]

2.1.4 Why client-server applications are being deployed

Organizations, driven by the pressures for IT cost reductions discussed in Chap. 1, properly inquire if a client-server-based solution is the correct approach to their applications development needs. Companies are now deploying client-server systems despite cultural and technical challenges that can include migrating both IS and users off mainframes and onto "foreign" platforms, coping with a myriad of standards, and ensuring that client-server data do not degrade a network's performance.[11] As discussed earlier, there are advantages to deploying client-server applications. Client-server systems typically deliver more information to the user, and they do this faster and potentially in a more readable format than legacy systems.[8] Many client-server applications can be built using off-the-shelf tools that take advantage of GUIs.

Client-server systems enable the users to be more productive through the integration of personal desktop tools and corporate systems. Mechanisms such as OLE, DDE, and CORBA (see Table 2.1) support these productivity improvements. Client-server systems leverage the business experience of the user in combination with tools that are usable by non-computer professionals.

Cost savings. Client-server applications usually result in long-term monetary savings, although these savings can be achieved only if the cost of supporting distributed applications is low.* Studies have shown that when mainframe-based legacy systems are replaced with client-server systems, their combined cost, in most cases, is less than the operating system, application software, hardware, and maintenance costs of the original system. Cost reductions are also realized by more efficient use of the computing resources. In a client-server system, the client only formulates the request for data and then processes the reduced data set returned by the server; this implies that the user requires a less powerful processor than if the client per-

---

*Experience has shown that locally supported applications require one support person per 15 to 25 users in new applications and 25 to 50 users in mature applications; remote management can support 150 to 500 users with one management person.

TABLE 2.4   Decreasing Cost of Machine Cycles

Processor	Approximate cost of PC (1993 costs)*†	Cost per MHz ($\times 10^{-5}$ $)
386SX-20‡	$1400–1700	7–8.5
386DX-33	$1500–1900	4.5–5.7
486SX-20	$1700–2100	8.5–10.5
486SX-25	$1800–2200	7.2–8.8
486DX-33	$1900–2300	5.7–6.9
486DX2-50	$2100–2500	4.2–5.0
486DX-50	$2700–2900	5.4–5.8

Processor type by clock speed (MHz)	Cost per MHz ($\times 10^{-5}$ $)	Average cost per MHz ($\times 10^{-5}$ $)
20	7–8.5	7.7–9.5
20	8.5–10.5	
25	7.2–8.8	7.2–8.8
33	4.5–5.7	5.1–6.3
33	5.7–6.9	
50	4.2–5.0	4.8–5.4
50	5.4–5.8	

*See Ref. 15.
†Range depends on size of RAM and hard drive; includes typical monitor. Additional peripherals (CD-ROM, audio/video cards, etc.) can raise the cost by another $2,000 to $3,000, or more.
‡The last term represents clock speed in MHz.

formed all the application tasks locally. In fairness, however, the cost of machine cycles has been coming down, so that these savings alone may not be as important as time goes by (see Table 2.4).

The implementation of a GUI-based presentation front end to an application (as implied in Fig. 2.4) can also result in savings because of a shorter learning time for new users and, perhaps, a shorter time to complete a given production task. This is particularly true when shortcuts are implemented, obviating the need to navigate multilayer menus. The IS organization can deliver data to end users faster in the form they want because end users choose their front-end tools and IS organizations maintain central control over the data with programmable servers and other tools.[3]

Additionally, a well-designed client-server query/response process results in less data being transmitted over the network. This eliminates (or reduces) the cost of having to incrementally upgrade the network components to provide additional bandwidth, particularly in a wide area network (WAN) context, where bandwidth costs are still nontrivial [this, however, also applies at the local level, pushing the user to higher-speed LANs—e.g., 100-

Mbit/s LANs, FDDI, and asynchronous transfer mode (ATM) LANs]. This upgrade also applies to bridges, routers, modem pools, etc. Network management tools for controlling traffic in the client-server system are essential. Also, coming changes in networking options make it critical that applications be built using standard protocols to isolate the location of the data and processing from the application. Thus, a database or application server may move from the department to headquarters as new high-capacity communication services (such as ATM) reduce the communication charges (as a result of economies of scale and integration) and provide LAN-like performance over the WAN.

Not all client-server systems now being installed, however, aim at replacing legacy systems. IS managers realize that in many cases these applications can be used to enhance the capabilities obtainable with existing systems.

Many organizations have seen client-server computing emerge in a grass-roots fashion, at the departmental level. In these organizations, success in departmental client-server computing is now driving an enterprise-wide demand for greater access to corporate data, for access to applications that were once in the hands of a few users, and for E-mail services in order to better help the department to improve productivity and remain competitive. However, client-server computing on a departmental level provides benefits only within specific departments; as a result, data are duplicated on servers or PCs by rekeying or downloading information from the mainframe (new data may also be created completely outside the mainframe environment on a network server). The desirable solution is to balance end-user responsiveness with IS control by deploying client-server computing across the entire organization. Proponents hold that client-server computing is now proving itself as an effective architecture of strategic value for linking all of an organization's computing resources, in the form of *enterprise-wide client-server computing,* as shown in Fig. 2.1 bottom.[3] In this computing environment, end users, departments, and IS can again join to create one cohesive computing environment. Front- and back-office end users anywhere in the organization can now access corporate data on their desktops. Central control of data is put back in the hands of central IS.

Challenges.   When a technology is as popular as client-server computing, it seems as if it is the only option for the mid-1990s and beyond: If the organization has a newly developed database, the user probably has to get at it through client-server connections. For many legacy systems, the old way of doing things may be perceived as being so expensive or so hard to integrate with new applications that client-server technology ostensibly appears to be an obvious choice.[5] But does this imply that client-server is the universal answer? In reality, there is a complex process for assessing a multi-dimensional issue; it involves investing the time and effort required to develop rigorous models for testing and evaluating client-server technologies and applying them in those areas where they are appropriate.[16] According to some, IS professionals are discovering that the promise of server-situated applications is a mix of fact and fiction.[11]

Some see flexibility with client-server computing, but note that there is a price to pay for that flexibility. For example, the IS department may have to buy, say, 200 copies of a licensed software application (rather than building it in-house), and then, when the software is upgraded a few months later, obtain the upgrade kits—this can be done for one or two updates, but eventually the applications have to be repurchased. Also, the retraining necessary can be a major cost factor. Hence, there are several challenges associated with client-server architectures, including the following:

1. There are cost and design considerations that have to be taken into account when considering deployment of client-server systems. At this juncture, the time and resources needed to develop client-server applications typically exceed those that would be needed for a traditional monolithic approach.[8] In part that is due to the fact that traditional applications have been designed for over 30 years and there is experience with and understanding of this paradigm, whereas client-server systems are relatively new. Also, as discussed in Chap. 1, there are many hidden cost factors to take into account.

2. Maintenance costs for mission-critical client-server systems can be similar to those for mainframes. For example, critical portions of a client-server system need to be located in a secure environment, and the requirements for backup power, air conditioning, fault tolerance, offsite data vaulting, real-time system management, etc. are similar to those for the legacy systems.

3. Existing computers need to be upgraded to participate in client-server computing. For example, in some environments legacy systems need to be retained in order to maintain volumes of data on disk farms that are too large for smaller systems. In these cases, mainframe costs are reduced but not eliminated, with the cost of the newer client-server systems simply being added.

4. Client-server systems rely to an increased degree on communication. Networks may need to be made more robust and more reli-

able, and have to be carefully optimized for response time. Client-server traffic can degrade a network, particularly when organizations configure client-server networks according to expected usage and not peak usage.[11] The speed of the server is immaterial if the network is the bottleneck; impaired performance (for example, slow response time) can affect an entire department, say 20 or 30 people. In some cases, this author has seen dozens of colleagues dependent on a client-server application idled and disgruntled as the system seems to be going up and down several times a day for stretches of weeks or months, while this author (having chosen not to do his word processing on a server-based system) keeps humming away fearlessly and uninterrupted at his laptop.* This is not to imply that stand-alone or loosely linked systems are better, but if networked systems are to be used, then both the network and the servers must be professionally managed in such a way that they are very reliable and well tuned, so that a single failure does not impair the productivity of dozens of people (communication issues are revisited in Sec. 2.5).

There also are nontechnology challenges: People at all levels have to be trained† in the client-server technology, and, as noted in Chap. 1, human resources can represent some of the greatest costs. As thousands of departments and IS organizations begin to deploy client-server computing and information becomes increasingly more splintered, the corporation runs the risk of losing its information resource as a key strategic asset. In addition, central IS is running the risk of becoming isolated as systems multiply outside the mainframe environment. And while some IS organizations experience success in cutting costs by moving applications off the mainframe, this solution does not address information management as a strategic, enterprise-wide asset.[3]

In many *Fortune* 1500 companies, corporate senior management is forcing the move to a client-server paradigm, claiming that such a paradigm is significantly less expensive and a more effective approach to computing. But there are IS professionals who remain skeptical, pointing out that there is little hard data to support those

---

*This author's dream: clear his two monitor-based computers off his cluttered desk and simply use a laptop; at night pack the laptop away (take it home and continue to work?), and in the morning simply "connect" to the enterprise network for printers, E-mail, communication gateways, etc., through a *wireless LAN*.

†Outsourcing proponents claim that, at times, in-house IT staff may not be able to see the need to move quickly to gain expertise in new technologies; as a result, outsourcing the legacy systems may be a way to create the incentive to learn the new technologies.

benefits and a growing body of evidence that calls them into question. Fuzzy economic models may have been used to justify the decision.[16]

For some applications and/or business environments, client-server technology may not be the best answer. In some such situations, client-server technology could entail more complexity than needed and an investment of resources beyond the value of the benefits that can be derived. An important consideration in assessing the value of client-server computing is the way the work is split between client and server.

A typical client-server application operates as follows: Assume that the user needs to query a database with millions of records (or rows, in relational database terminology) for one record, or at most a few records. This query may be carried out in successive stages, the first of which might yield many possible qualifying records (say, as an example, 50,000). The user does not necessarily want to see these records, but just to be informed that there are that many records. In successive stages, the user adds additional search criteria until the scope has been narrowed to one or a few records, which the user then wants to examine directly. This type of application is well suited to a client-server approach for the following two reasons:

1. There is a need to store and access a large number of database records (millions, in this example). This requires a large disk (or disk farm) and a fast CPU. In turn, this requires more capacity and power than one would normally install on a desktop. Additionally, one does not want to replicate such capacity across the enterprise for hundreds or even thousands of users. Sharing one large server provides economies of scale. Table 2.5 gives the

TABLE 2.5   Cost of Storage at Press Time, Showing Economies of Scale (Actual Products)

Storage capacity (MByte)	Cost ($)	Cost per MByte in $
42	169	4.0
85	195	2.3
127	229	1.8
170	259	1.5
240	339	1.4
525	869	1.6
700	1129	1.6
1000	1249	1.2
1200	1300	1.1
1700	1399	0.8
2400	2449	1.0
3400	3299	0.9

costs of internal PC hard drives (late 1993 prices) to show the economies of scale in storage.

2. The network traffic would be very high without a client-server arrangement, as it would be necessary to transmit a large number (here, millions) of records between the network file server and the desktop workstation. With the client-server arrangement, the user can issue a command to the server; after some computing, the server sends a notification that 50,000 records, in this example, meet the criteria. This is followed by another command and another notification, and finally one last command and the desired record itself. Here, the network traffic is very small.

However, some applications do not work as discussed above. Suppose that a query against the same database consisting of millions of records needs to generate 250,000 records to calculate some statistic, such as the total or mean value of some numeric field within each record. The database query results in a large amount of network traffic. One way to approach this in a client-server environment is to use a RPC, discussed earlier. This is, effectively, a program that runs on the server—in this example, to calculate the total or the average value of a specific field in each of the 250,000 records, and then pass only the summary values back to the client instead of the 250,000 records. This approach is doable, but it has limitations:[5]

1. There is a need for a database server that supports RPCs (not all of them do).

2. The user must be able to create application segments using the server's programming tools, not the client's.

In a case such as this one, traditional systems may actually be better.

To some degree, the client-server debate is framed by two opposite views. Establishments that have decided to retain mainframes are focused on mainframe-based DB2 and the IBM (client-server) products. Their critics say that they are desperately seeking answers to "How do I manage a multivendor environment with the same staffing level that I had with only a single-vendor environment?"[16]

Should on-line transaction processing always be a client-server application? It depends on the nature of the application, the database, and the server in use. OLTP is based on the concept of atomicity—a transaction is an all-or-nothing proposition, since any partial result corrupts the database. For example, in transferring money from a customer's account to another account, one must be sure that both accounts are properly updated; if something fails along the way, one must back off any updates that might have been done and start the entire transaction again. Client-server systems can do this well, since many server back ends support the concept of atomic transactions. The area in which a client-server database can be problematic is that of *referential integrity,* where certain parts of the database have a logical relationship to other parts.* For example, the existence of an accounts receivable record implies that there is a customer record describing who owes the money; when a customer record is deleted, there should not be any leftover receivable records that pertain to that customer. In a client-server environment, it is preferable to enforce this in the back end: When a transaction to delete a customer record is presented, the server checks to make sure that referential integrity is accomplished. But if a client-server back end is not capable of enforcing referential integrity automatically, one must ascertain that every front-end application contains logic for checking all referential integrity conditions. In a large OLTP system, this may be impractical because other users may be updating the database, or because the amount of checking required overwhelms the computing and memory capacity of the client. An alternative approach would be to avoid a client-server-based solution and combine all transaction applications in one unified database management system running on a mainframe, minicomputer, or large server.[5]

How should one approach existing (perhaps old) database applications developed before client-server systems entered the scene? Software development is a labor-intensive effort, even when programmers develop 10 debugged lines per hour. Some estimate the U.S. industry to be a $100 billion a year industry. Assuming a 10-year life cycle (discussed in more detail in Chap. 3), this implies an investment of about $1 trillion in software. Such an investment cannot be ignored in favor of a complete overhaul, particularly in an age of fiscal conservatism. Legacy applications fall into two general categories:

1. Mainframe-resident applications, typically using IBM 3270 terminal emulation as their front end, that do not involve heavy computation, but rather provide traditional data entry and query; ostensibly these applications are good candidates for client-server systems. As discussed in Chap. 1, some organizations have made the decision to reengineer and do away with mainframe technology. In this case it is a given that the mainframe applications have to be migrated. On the other hand, if an organization expects to retain (some of) the main-

---

*Some argue that some applications can gain effective referential integrity with little overhead through the use of partitioned data (i.e., data are stored where they are used) and optimistic locking techniques. Triggers detect conflicts, and stored procedures can deal with them. With this approach, most situations present good performance, and exceptions are handled once by stored procedures, not by the application programmer.

frame environment, it is necessary to examine each 3270 legacy application individually to determine the cost/benefit of converting it to a client-server system. Some of the top mission-critical applications may be converted, while some secondary or tertiary applications may be retained as they are. For example, if the application and its underlying data are poorly documented because the application was developed by programmers of five professional generations earlier (that is, 10 years ago, assuming an average tenure of 2 years), converting it may not be worth the time and trouble.

2. Small XBase applications. Typically these have been developed for private use on a local hard disk of a stand-alone PC and become network applications when the database files are moved to a file server. In theory, these applications are good candidates for conversion to client-server systems. The business (not technical) issue, again, is the cost/benefit consideration. Many XBase applications are small (that is, the database is small or there are just a few concurrent users), and the conversion is not justifiable in measurable economic terms. XBase applications can now use SQL (e.g., FoxPro/ACCESS), so that if the application grows, it can become multiuser or use a large server processor.

Clearly there must be a closer match between technologies and business objectives.[16] One must first look at what the need is and then select the platform, not the other way around. Being in a high-tech field, where technology seems to be all-absorbing, this author has had to develop some common-sense analogies to help shed some light. For example, on Saturday one would not select a tool at random from the toolkit in the garage and then, depending on the tool selected, determine what type of house maintenance he or she would do. Rather, one would say, "I need to hang that painting"; given this need, one would pick a hammer. Pliers are a great tool, but do not try to hang a painting with them. In the early to mid 1980s, when the author was in a *Fortune* 500 company and developed more than 30 major automation systems (on-line order processing, on-line complaint entry and tracking, on-line inventory control, etc.) using fourth-generation languages, he was amazed to find that no matter what the need was, from real-time software on a telecommunication switch, to on-line order processing, to inventory systems, to simulation of erlangian teletraffic models, to econometric systems in support of sales calls, to tariff analysis, the answer from IS was always the same: Regardless of the application, nothing but COBOL would do. That's like selecting the tool before knowing what the job to be done is; it's like packing suitcases without knowing if you are going on vacation to Alaska, New York City, Arizona, or Mount Everest. One should want to make sure that selecting a computing platform is not a knee-jerk reaction.

2.1.5 Making the transition to client-server computing

Enterprise-wide client-server computing empowers organizations to reengineer business processes and distribute transactions in order to streamline operations while providing new and better services to customers. The transition to enterprise-wide client-server computing is an evolutionary effort with three stages (these steps have in fact been used by major organizations that have already made the transition):[3]

1. Deployment of client-server computing for departmental applications

2. Integrating mainframe-based applications with a client-server network

3. Deployment of client-server computing on an enterprise-wide level

(Naturally some progressive companies can go directly to the third step if they so choose; however, the three-phase evolution is more common.)

Deployment of client-server computing for departmental applications. As noted earlier, client-server computing first evolved within work groups and departments as a means of cutting costs, providing alternatives to host systems, and improving performance and access to information. Client-server computing can provide a substantial competitive advantage by enabling departments to work faster and better. When properly implemented, client-server computing can create a more effective environment for line-of-business applications than traditional mainframe computing.

Two illustrative examples (out of thousands of implementations) documented in the literature are CSX Transportation and Breuners Home Furniture.[3] CSX Transportation deployed client-server computing to help streamline its order processing and customer service department. The result was a significant reduction in data entry errors and increased responsiveness to customers, with overall savings of $30 million per year in personnel, paper, and warehouse costs. Breuners Home Furniture created a client-server retail merchandising system to serve more than 20 retail outlets and 2 distribution centers. The result was more responsive customer service, reduced data-processing costs, and lower staff training costs.

Integrating mainframe-based applications with a client-server network. The successful deployment of client-server systems on a departmental

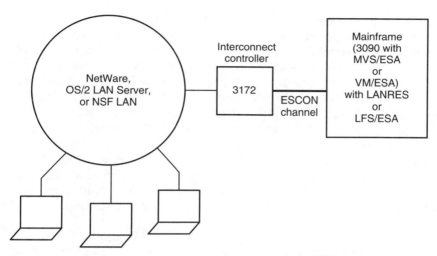

Figure 2.5 Integrating a mainframe as a superserver. LANRES = LAN Resource Extension and Services; LFS/ESA = File Services/Extended Systems Architecture.

level sets the stage for the next phase: End users soon seek to access data outside their existing client-server environment. As the integration occurs, the client-server system interoperates with relational and nonrelational database management systems, indexed files, mainframe data, and other services provided by existing legacy applications. This can be accomplished through gateway products and open interfaces.

An illustrative example (out of thousands of implementations) documented in the literature is Textron Financial Corp. The company deployed a group of gateway and server products to allow a mainframe-based application using the IBM Customer Information Control System (CICS) and DB2 relational database management system to run hundreds of PCs, workstations, and servers (the mainframe became a superserver in a client-server system).[3] The resulting environment maintained and leveraged legacy mainframe applications and databases while delivering data to the desktop.

Mainframe vendors like IBM are beginning to bring out mainframe-LAN software to facilitate the use of mainframes as superservers in client-server networks. Figure 2.5 shows an example.[17] Users are beginning to create "server farms" in secure rooms and letting the IS department manage them; a mainframe-based alternative to a multitude of servers may be cost-effective in specific situations.

Deployment of client-server computing on an enterprise-wide level. With the establishment of successful departmental client-server networks that interoperate with resources outside those networks, organizations are ready to pursue the most strategic stage of client-server development: enterprise-wide client-server computing. This phase goes well beyond departmental client-server and gateway products by providing total integration of departmental and corporate IS applications that span the enterprise. This environment enables the organization to leverage existing central as well as line-of-business systems. With enterprise-wide client-server applications, the IS organization is able to reestablish control over data while at the same time supporting a truly distributed environment. The IS organization now can maximize the value of information by increasing its availability and at the same time maintain central control over data integrity. End users can access data from anywhere in the enterprise from the desktop.

High-end client-server systems: an example.   Client-server applications are now entering a realm once thought to be the exclusive domain of mainframe systems. This section describes one such system, based on published accounts, to illustrate the power of the client-server technology.[18]

In 1993, Delta Airlines launched what was the largest client-server application ever, deploying a network of Sybase relational databases on Unix servers that was designed to match the performance of mainframe databases (three other airlines were slated to install similar systems). The Passenger Revenue Accounting System, developed by Andersen Consulting, holds 100 Gbytes of information and is expected to hold 180 Gbytes by 1996. The original system was developed by Andersen and Northwest Airlines in the 1980s, and relied primarily on IBM mainframes and IBM's DB2 relational database management system to manage the 75 Gbytes of information. For Delta and the other carriers, Andersen recast the application to eliminate the mainframe and to run over networked SPARC servers from Sun Microsystems. Each server acts as a platform for up to 10 physical databases with 2 Gbytes of data per database. Delta initially used Sybase's SQL Server 4.9.1, and later upgraded to the more advanced Sybase System 10 product. For transaction processing, 2 Gbytes of information is the current practical limit, but with the Sybase System 10 the limit is going up by an order of magnitude. The Delta system handles about 500,000 batch transactions per week and supports 250 concurrent users on Sun workstations doing up to 100,000 ad hoc queries per week. The original development of the application of Northwest cost over $50 million and took three years to build, but it paid for itself in less than a year through better accounting for airline ticket revenues. The application filters out all tickets with errors, making them available for on-line correction by clerks at the Unix clients, a capability that has turned a cost center into a profit center; the corrections can return to the airline about 1 percent of gross revenues. By moving the ticket database to multiple networked Unix servers and Sybase, the developer estimated, the two carriers that bought the system would together save $30 million over the 10-year life of their contracts.

2.2 Using SQL

Structured Query Language is a de facto standard language for creating, updating, and querying databases, as discussed earlier. Some of the key design aspects of SQL were

- To provide a data access language that could be proven to manipulate data correctly and reliably

- To remove the physical storage feel-and-look of the data from the user

SQL is a flat-file implementation with extracted indexes to provide direct access to the records (rows) of the file (table) being accessed; each field (columns) can be used as part of the search criteria.

However, there are subtle differences in each vendor's product. Multiple databases using different "dialects" of SQL may well exist in a client-server network. This forces IS managers to retain in-house SQL-trained programmers in order to deal with these differences.

APIs, a type of "middleware," can bring some stability to this environment. APIs provide connectivity between applications and databases. One example of an API is Microsoft's Open Database Connectivity (ODBC); it allows Windows-based clients to access data from multiple relational database management systems (e.g., IBM's DB2 and Digital Equipment's Rdb) and from its own SQL Server. ODBC also links to Apple Computer's Data Access Language. The Integrated Database Applications Programming Interface (IDAPI) initiative is being advanced by Microsoft competitors (such as Borland International, IBM, Novell, and WordPerfect Corp.). IDAPI aims at addressing heterogeneous client implementations at the server; it integrates SQL as well as traditional databases.* Other APIs have been advanced; however, experts recommend a "buyer beware" approach to lesser-known APIs.[11]

Vendors are now bringing to the market more sophisticated client-server software, particularly in the context of networked databases (that is, distributed database systems). The new software aims at pro-

---

*In the view of some observers, ODBC and DRDA have won the war.

viding improved performance, while supporting asynchronous communication between clients and servers; in addition, added administrative and diagnostic features are being introduced.[19] Other features being added include "multiprotocol interchange" to handle protocol conversion without having to tax the database system itself.

Object-oriented database management systems. Object-oriented database management systems (OODBMS) are an extension of SQL. Records are stored as objects (See Table 2.1); this allows more complex data types to be manipulated with a single command or with a few commands. In addition to an object-oriented view of the data, there are, as noted in Table 2.1, objected-oriented languages. The benefits of such an object-based approach are that the objects can be acquired and assembled to create applications. Conceivably, in the future one may not buy entire applications, but rather, applications may be assembled from a collection of objects built by different "construction" firms.

2.3 Distributed Computing Environment

DCE is a set of integrated software modules that provide an environment for creating, using, and maintaining client-server applications on a network (see Ref. 9 for a more extensive discussion). DCE is sponsored by the Open Software Foundation (OSF), which is a not-for-profit organization aiming at delivering an open computing environment based on industry standards. Some see DCE as the most important architecture to be defined for client-server technology.

DCE includes capabilities such as security, directory, synchronization, file sharing, RPCs, and multithreading. One can view DCE as a "black (software) box"* installed by the (major) hardware and software vendors that in theory eliminates their technological barriers; such a black (software) box connects a variety of operating systems, dissimilar hardware platforms, incompatible communications protocols, applications, and database systems in a manner transparent to all concerned (end users, system managers, and application developers).[2] Another way of looking at this is as a bridge between the embedded base of applications and future applications and platforms.

2.4 The Client-Server Market

Table 2.6 provides, for illustrative purposes, a partial list of companies (suppliers) that support client-server technology in one fashion

---

*More exactly, a prepackaged set of integrated interoperability applications (RPCs, presentation services, naming, security, threads, time services, distributed file services, management, and communications) that enables connection of diverse hardware and software systems, applications, and databases.

TABLE 2.6   Partial List of Vendors that Support Client-Server Technology in One Fashion or Another

ADS Systems	META Group
Alantec	MicroFocus
American Management Systems, Inc.	Microsoft
American Software, Inc.	Motorola Corporation
Andersen Consulting	Motorola/Codex
Atre, Inc.	NET
Attachmate Corporation	NetWise
Auspex Systems, Inc.	N Systems
Bachman Information Systems	New Media Associates, Inc.
Banyan	New Sciences Associates
Client/Server Roundtable	Novell, Inc.
Competitive Advantage Group	Object Management Group
CSC Partners	Oracle Corporation
Computer Aid Inc.	ParcPlace Systems
Computer Associates	PeopleSoft, Inc.
Computer System Advisor	Platinum Software Corporation
Control Data Systems	Platinum Technology
Cortex Corporation	Pokin Software & Systems, Inc.
Database Design Solutions	Portia/Powers Communications
DataComm Research Services	Systems
DCA	Powersoft Corporation
Digital Equipment Corp. (DEC)	Professional Computer Solutions, Inc.
Dynamic Information Systems	Raima Corporation
Ecosystems	R&O
ERI	Robert Binder Systems Consulting, Inc.
Ernst & Young	Ross Systems
Fusion Systems, Inc.	SAP America Inc.
Gupta Technologies, Inc.	SES, Inc.
High Tech Resource Inc.	SEEQ Technology
IBM Corporation	SHL Systemhouse
IBM PC Company	SmartStar Corp.
IBM Personal Software Products	Solbourne Computer
IBM APPC Market Enablement	Software Productivity Group
Influence Technologies	Strassmann Inc.
INTERSOLV, Inc.	Sun Microsystems
Information Builders, Inc.	Sybase
Intellicorp	Systems Integration—Martin Marietta
James Martin & Company	Systems Strategies, Inc.
JD Edwards	Technology Insight, Inc.
JYACC	Texas Instruments
KASEWORKS	The Hurwits Consulting Group
KnowledgeWare, Inc.	Trinzic Corporation
Lante Corporation	Uniface Corp.
LBMS	Unify Corporation
Logic Works, Inc.	Villard-Lindsay
Lucus Management Systems	XDB
Martin Marietta	XcelleNet
M. Corby & Associates	ZYGA Corporation

or another (based on exhibitors at a recent Client/Server East Conference and Exposition).

2.5 Communication Systems in Place

Client-server systems rely, by definition, on communication and networks. Client-server computing can be implemented on a number of communication protocol suites, including NetWare IPX/SPX, NetBIOS, TCP/IP RPC, OSI, and SNA LU6.2. IS managers must select the protocol suite that best suits their installed base and applications inventory. One advantage of TCP/IP is that many (if not the majority of) applications support the Internet protocol suite. There is an increased need for multiplatform connectivity, making the problem technically challenging. Table 2.7 gives an indication of the heterogeneity of contemporary IT systems.

Early SQL versions often used a considerable portion of the network's bandwidth by pushing nonessential data onto the network; later SQL versions from Oracle, Sybase, and Gupta Technologies, among others, make better use of bandwidth by storing procedures on

TABLE 2.7   Heterogeneous Communication Requirements

	SNA	DECnet	TCP/IP	OSI	Other
IBM 370,390	High	Medium	Medium	Very low	Medium
PCMs	Low	Low	Medium	Low	Medium
DEC VMS	Low	High	Medium	Very low	Low
IBM AS/400	Medium	Very low	Very low	Very low	Low
Other departmental systems	Low	Very low	Medium	Very low	Medium
Unix	Low	Low	Medium	Low	Low
Weighted (generic system)	Medium	Medium	Medium	Very low	Medium

High: 70–100 percent of organizations with the system at the left employ the protocol shown at the top.

Medium: 20–69 percent of organizations with the system at the left employ the protocol shown at the top.

Low: 5–19 percent of organizations with the system at the left employ the protocol shown at the top.

Very low: 0–4 percent of organizations with the system at the left employ the protocol shown at the top.

the server. This reduces the amount of requested data required from a server to trigger a transaction.[11] Developing client-server applications across a wide area network is even more challenging.

To make distributed computing a reality, one needs a sophisticated network infrastructure that can support not only client-to-server communication, but also server-to-server communication.[19] Server-to-server interactions are complex and resource-intensive. Some distributed database management systems support data replication, which is the process of copying data, distributing them to remote sites, and retaining synchronization as changes are made to the data in real time. However, without an effective underlying network (that is, a network of adequate bandwidth, reliability, flexibility, etc.), replication is of limited value. The need to establish flexible WAN infrastructures is now recognized by many of the network database vendors.[19]

This section examines communication systems at the local and remote level that may be used to support client-server environments.

2.5.1 Local connectivity*

Local connectivity is physically achieved using LANs. LAN technology has encompassed three generations. *First-generation* technology, based on coaxial cable or twisted-pair cable media, spanned the period from the mid 1970s to the late 1980s. Many corporations have or are still deploying these LANs. *Second-generation* technology, based on shared fiber optic cable media, emerged in the late 1980s to early 1990s. *Third-generation* LANs based on ATM are now beginning to become commercially available, and may see major deployment in the mid 1990s to support new high-bandwidth applications such as multimedia, video, desk-to-desk videoconferencing, and high-throughput client-server systems. The transmission speed achievable with LANs is from 4 to 16 Mbits/s for first-generation LANs, 100 Mbits/s for second-generation LANs, and gigabit-per-second rates for third-generation LANs. The need to interconnect colocated and/or remotely located LANs has emerged as a key need of the 1990s. The trend is toward enterprise-wide networking, where all departments of a company are interconnected with a seamless (backbone) network, allowing company-wide access to all information and hardware resources. Enterprise-wide client-server systems rely on these enterprise-wide networks.

---

*Sections 2.5.1 and 2.5.2 are based on Ref. 20.

TABLE 2.8   Key Premises Systems in Support of Client-Server and Other Evolving Business Applications

Traditional LANs with microsegmentation
Switched hubs: dedicated 10-Mbit/s Ethernet to each desktop over twisted-pair cable
IEEE 802.9/"Isochronous Ethernet"*
High-speed token ring (16 to 622 Mbits/s)*
Fiber Distributed Data Interface (FDDI)/Copper Distributed Data Interface (CDDI)
FDDI II
"Fast Ethernet" based on CSMA/CD (100-Mbit/s LAN)*
"Fast Ethernet" not based on CSMA/CD (100-Mbit/s LAN)*
Local ATM at 45 Mbits/s (SMDS mapping)
Local ATM at 52 Mbits/s
Local ATM at 100 Mbits/s: FDDI PHY
Local ATM at 155 Mbits/s: 8B/10B Fiber Channel Standard PHY
Local ATM at 155 Mbits/s: SONET PHY

*Proposed.

After several years of relative stability at the fundamental platform level, LAN technology is now seeing burgeoning activity in several radically new directions. These changes are driven by the increased LAN traffic, not only to support client-server applications, but also to support completely new business applications such as desktop video-conferencing, multimedia, and imaging. Table 2.8 depicts key premises systems either available or under development.

LAN technologies.   First-generation LANs were developed in the early 1970s to provide what was then considered high-speed local connectivity among user devices. The contention-based Ethernet LAN technology was brought to the market by a joint effort of Xerox, Intel, and Digital Equipment Corporation. Ethernet initially employed coaxial cable arranged in a logical bus and operating at 10 Mbits/s; now, thin coaxial and twisted-pair cable are used, usually in conjunction with wiring hubs and physical star arrangements. Extensive standardization work has been done by the Institute of Electrical and Electronic Engineers (IEEE) in the past 15 years, leading to well-known standards such as IEEE 802.2, 802.3, 802.4, and 802.5.

In the early 1980s, a token bus and a token ring technology were also developed, operating at 4 Mbits/s (a 16-Mbit/s system is also available). The token medium-sharing discipline is a variant of the polling method common in traditional data networks; however, instead of centrally controlled polling, the token is passed from station to station in an equitable manner. Only the LAN station possessing the token can transmit. Token ring systems took the approach of using (shielded) twisted-pair wires as the underlying medium, mainly because such a medium is cheaper and simpler to install than coaxial cable [however, unshielded twisted-pair (UTP) is expected to become the dominant LAN medium for traditional LANs]. Over the past decade, the cost of connecting a user to a LAN decreased from about $1000 to less than $200. Ethernet cards costing $100 are appearing on the market; 16-Mbit/s token ring adapter cards range in price from $700 to $900.

Higher network performance is required in order to support the applications that go beyond the movement of just data that are now being put on line by organizations, such as imaging, multimedia, and videoconferencing applications. One way of increasing the bandwidth available to applications is to replace the existing network with one based on FDDI. Efforts on second-generation LANs started in the early 1980s; products began to enter the market in the late 1980s. This token-based backbone/campus technology extends LANs' features in terms of the geographic radius (they now cover a campus) as well as the speed (now reaching 100 Mbits/s). Implementors initially settled on multimode fiber as the underlying medium, although support for single-mode fiber was added in the late 1980s. One factor that has slowed down the deployment of FDDI systems has been the cost of the interface cards. The cost of connecting a user to a FDDI LAN started out at about $8000 and is now around $900 to $1500. Efforts to facilitate the use of twisted-pair copper wires for FDDI have been underway, in order to bring the station access cost down (copper-based interfaces cost in the $500 to $700 range). While standards work in this area has been slow in picking up speed, progress has been made in the recent past.

At publication time there were also suggestions for a new 100-Mbit/s Ethernet technology and for 16- to 622-Mbit/s token ring technology; these would be second-generation systems.

Starting in 1990, efforts have been underway to develop third-generation LANs supporting gigabit-per-second speeds (0.2 to 0.6 Gbit/s) over UTP or fiber facilities.[21] These efforts are based on ATM principles. ATM principles were first developed in the context of wide area networking; the same technology is being applied in the premises networking context using ATM-based hubs and switches. Work along these lines is sponsored by industry vendors under the auspices of The ATM Forum. ATM switches to support high-end workstations have been available commercially since 1993. Workstation manufacturers are developing interface cards to connect their equipment to ATM switches. Initial costs may be around $4000 per port, but these costs should come down considerably (to $1000) in the next couple of years as chipsets emerge.

Table 2.9 summarizes some of the features of these three generations of LAN technology. Given the preceding discussion, one should

TABLE 2.9   Typical Features of LANs

Generation	Speed (Mbits/s)	Equipment	Interconnection speed/services	Applications
First	4–16 (Ethernet, token ring)	Terminals, PCs, workstations;	9.6 kbits/s, 56 kbits/s, T1, frame relay, SMDS	Office automation; decision support; business functions such as accounting (spreadsheets), project management, etc.; mainframe access; manufacturing; some imaging applications
Second	100 (FDDI)	PCs, high-end workstations, high-end servers (CD-ROM and WORM image servers)	Fractional T1, T1, T3, SMDS	Backbone interconnection of LANs, CAD/CAM graphics, imaging
Third	150–622*	High-end workstations, video equipment, high-end servers (CD-ROMs, WORM jukeboxes)	SONET, B-ISDN/cell relay, SMDS	Multimedia, desk-to-desk multimedia conferencing, multimedia messaging, CAD/CAM, visualization, animation, imaging, video-based training over LANs, supercomputer/scientific applications

*Higher in the future.

not assume that traditional LANs will disappear from the business landscape. There will be a continued need for text-based business functions. However, as companies move to image-based operations, multimedia, and desktop videoconferencing, the higher-speed systems will be required.

TABLE 2.10 LAN Topologies

LAN	Early	Recent
First-generation broadband	Bus	Bus
First-generation Ethernet	Bus	Star-shaped bus
First-generation token ring	Ring	Star-shaped ring
Second generation	Fiber double ring	Star-shaped double ring
Third generation	Star-based access segments	—

LAN topologies. There are three major physical (first-generation) LAN topologies: star, ring, and bus. A *star* network is joined at a single point, generally with central control (such as a wiring hub). In a *ring* network, the nodes are linked into a continuous circle on a common cable, and signals are passed unidirectionally around the circle from node to node, with signal regeneration at each node. A *bus* network is a single line of cable to which the nodes are connected directly by taps. It is normally employed with distributed control, but it can also be based on central control. Unlike the ring, however, a bus is passive, which means that the signals are not regenerated and retransmitted at each node.

Other configuration variations are available, particularly when looking at the LAN from a physical perspective: the *star-shaped ring* and the *star-shaped bus.* The first variation represents a wiring methodology that facilitates physical management: at the logical level, the network is a ring; at the physical level, it is a star, centralized at some convenient point. Similarly, the second variation provides a logical bus, but wired in a star configuration using wiring hubs. Table 2.10 summarizes the use of these topologies in the three generations of LANs.

Medium-sharing disciplines. As discussed, in traditional LANs there are two common ways of ensuring that nodes gain orderly access to the network, and that no more than one node at a time gains control of the shared LAN channel. The first is by the contention method; the second is by the token variant of polling.

The contention method is known as *carrier sense multiple access with collision detection* (CSMA/CD). If a node has a message to send, it checks the shared-medium network until it senses that it is traffic-free, and then it transmits. However, since all the nodes in the network have the right to contend for access, the node keeps monitoring the network to determine if a competing signal has been transmitted simultaneously with its own. If a second node is indeed transmitting, the two signals will collide. Both nodes detect the collision, stop transmitting, and wait for a random time before attempting to regain access.

Token-based LANs avoid the collisions inherent in Ethernet by requiring each node to defer transmission until it receives a token. The token is a control packet that is circulated around the network from node to node, in a preestablished sequence, when no transmission is otherwise taking place. The token signifies the exclusive right to transmission, and no node can send data without it. Each node constantly monitors the network to detect any data frame addressed to it. When the token is received by a node, if the node has nothing to send, it passes the token along to the next node in the sequence. If the token is accepted, it is passed on after the node has completed transmitting the data it has in its buffer. The token must be surrendered to the successor node within a specific time, so that no node can monopolize the network resources. Each node knows the address of its predecessor and successor.

Lower-layer LAN protocols.   In a LAN environment, Layer 1 and 2 functions of the OSI Reference Model (OSIRM) have been defined by (1) the IEEE 802 standards for first-generation LANs, (2) ANSI X3T9.5 for second-generation LANs, and (3) industry groups such as The ATM Forum, Alliance for Telecommunications Industry Solutions, and International Telecommunication Union (the last two bodies having standardized the supporting ATM functions) for third-generation LANs.

Using internetworking protocols defined at Layer 3 [such as IP (Internet Protocol)] and connection-oriented (see below) transport-layer protocols [such as TCP (Transmission Control Protocol)], one can build the LAN protocol suite up to Layer 7 in order to support functions like E-mail, file transfer, directory, etc. The use of TCP/IP has been commercially common.

Because LANs are based on a shared medium, the link layer is split into two sublayers. These sublayers are the Medium Access Control (MAC) and the Logical Link Control (LLC). The LLC sublayer provides a medium-independent interface to higher layers. The MAC procedure is part of the protocol that governs access to the transmission medium. This is done independently of the physical characteristics of the medium, but taking into account the topological aspects of the subnetwork. Different IEEE 802 MAC standards represent different protocols used for sharing the medium (IEEE 802.3 is the con-

TABLE 2.11   Functions at Specified Protocol Levels

LLC	■ Reliable transfer of frames
	■ Connection to higher layers
MAC	■ Addressing
	■ Frame construction
	■ Token/collision handling
PHY	(Physical Layer Protocol—explicit only in more recent standards such as FDDI and local ATM)
	■ Encoding/decoding
	■ Clocking
PMD	(Physical Medium Dependent—explicit only in more recent standards such as FDDI, SONET, and ATM)
	■ Cable parameters (optical/electrical)
	■ Connectors

tention-based Ethernet, and IEEE 802.5 is the token-based system). See Table 2.11.

Connectionless versus connection-oriented communication. Two basic forms of communication (service) are possible for both LANs and WANs: *connection-oriented mode* and *connectionless mode.*

A connection-oriented service involves a connection establishment phase, an information transfer phase, and a connection termination phase. This implies that a logical connection between end systems is set up prior to the exchange of data. These phases define the sequence of events ensuring successful data transmission. Sequencing of data, flow control, and transparent error handling are some of the capabilities inherent in this service mode. One disadvantage of this approach is the delay experienced in setting up the connection. Traditional carrier services, including circuit switching, X.25 packet switching, and early frame relay service (discussed later), are examples of connection-oriented transmission; LLC 2 is also a connection-oriented protocol.

In a connectionless service, each data unit is independently routed to the destination. No connection-establishment tasks are required, since each data unit is independent of the previous and subsequent ones. Hence, a connectionless-mode service provides for transfer of data units (cells, frames, or packets) without regard to the establishment or maintenance of connections. The basic MAC/LLC (i.e., LLC 1) transfer mechanism of a LAN is connectionless. In this connectionless-mode transmission, delivery is uncertain because of the possibili-

	LAN environment	WAN environment
Layer 7 to Layer 5	Application-specific protocols such as TELNET (terminal sessions), FTP and SFTP (file transfer), SMTP (e-mail), SNMP (management), and DNS (directory)	
Layer 4	TCP, UDP, EGP/IGP	TCP, UDP
Layer 3	IP, ICMP, ARP, RARP	IP, ICMP; X.25 PLP
Layer 2	LLC; CSMA/CD, token ring, token bus	LAP-B
Layer 1	IEEE 802.3, .4, .5 (PMD portions)	Physical channels

Figure 2.6 TCP/IP-based communication: key protocols. SFTP = Simple File Transfer Protocol; SMTP = Simple Mail Transfer Protocol; DNS = Domain Name Service; ICMP = Internet Control Message Protocol; RARP = Reverse Address Resolution Protocol; IGP = Internal Gateway Protocol; FTP = File Transfer Protocol; SNMP = Simple Network Management Protocol; UDP = User Datagram Protocol; ARP = Address Resolution Protocol; EGP = External Gateway Protocol; PMD = Physical Medium Dependent.

ty of errors. Connectionless communication shifts the responsibility for the integrity to a higher layer, where the integrity check is done only once, instead of being done at every lower layer.

TCP/IP protocol suite. The basic TCP/IP protocol suite is shown in Fig. 2.6 for both LAN and WAN environments (there are about 100 protocols in the Internet suite). A TCP/IP LAN application involves (1) a user connection over a standard LAN system (IEEE 802.3, 802.4, or 802.5 over LLC), (2) software in the PC and/or server implementing the IP, TCP, and related protocols, and (3) programs running in the PCs and/or servers to provide the needed application (the application may use other higher-layer protocols for file transfer, network management, and so on).

Internet protocol. In a TCP/IP environment, IP provides the underlying mechanism to move data from one end system (say, the client) on one LAN to another end system (say, the server) on the same or a different LAN. IP makes the underlying network transparent to the upper layers, TCP in particular. It is a connectionless packet delivery protocol in which each IP packet is treated independently (in this context, packets are also called *datagrams*). IP provides two basic services: addressing and fragmentation/reassembly of long packets. IP adds no guarantees of delivery, reliability, flow control, or error recovery to the underlying network beyond those the Data Link Layer mechanism already provides. IP expects the higher layers to handle such functions. IP may lose packets, deliver them out of order, or duplicate them; IP defers these contingencies to the higher layers (TCP in particular). Another way of saying this is to say that IP delivers on a "best-efforts" basis. There are no connections, physical or virtual, maintained by IP.

Transmission control protocol. Since IP is an "unreliable," best-efforts connectionless network layer protocol, TCP (a transport layer protocol) must provide reliability, flow control, and error recovery. TCP is a connection-oriented, end-to-end reliable protocol providing logical connections between pairs of processes. Some TCP features are

- *Data transfer.* From the application's viewpoint, TCP transfers a contiguous stream of octets through the interconnected network. The application does not have to segment the data into blocks or packets, since TCP does this by grouping the octets in *TCP segments,* which are then passed to IP for transmission to the destination. TCP determines how to segment the data and forwards the data at its own convenience.

- *Reliability.* TCP assigns a sequence number to each TCP segment transmitted, and expects a positive acknowledgment from the receiving peer TCP. If the acknowledgment is not received within a specified interval, the segment is retransmitted. The receiving TCP uses the sequence numbers to rearrange the segments if they arrive out of order, and to discard duplicate segments.

- *Flow control.* The receiving TCP signals to the sender the number of octets beyond the last received TCP segment that it can receive without causing an overflow in its internal buffers. This indication is sent in the acknowledgment in the form of the highest sequence number it can receive without problems. (This approach is also known as a *window mechanism.*)

- *Logical connections.* In order to achieve reliability and flow control, TCP must maintain certain status information for each data stream. The combination of this status information, including sockets, sequence numbers, and window sizes, is called a *logical connection* (also known as a *virtual circuit*).

- *Multiplexing.* This is achieved through the use of a ports mechanism.

- *Duplex communication.* TCP provides for concurrent data streams in both directions.

FDDI and FDDI II.   The FDDI is a set of standards that defines a shared-medium LAN utilizing fiber (single-mode and multimode) and, now, twisted-pair cabling. The aggregate bandwidth supported by FDDI is 100 Mbits/s. It uses a token-based discipline to manage multiple access. FDDI was developed with data communication (rather than, for example, video or multimedia) in mind, particularly for backbone LAN interconnection in a campus or building floor riser environment. FDDI networks are now used both as a backbone (back-end) technology to connect departmental LANs and as a front-end technology to directly connect workstations. As noted earlier, FDDI has experienced slow penetration because the cost of the device attachment has remained high.

Even for traditional applications, there is a recognized potential for network bottlenecks in the near future, not only because of the increased number of users and the introduction of client-server systems (where, as noted, data are not locally located at the PC but must be obtained across a distance), but also because of the increasing deployment of new graphics-intensive and/or image-intensive applications. Therefore, even systems providing an aggregate throughput of 100 Mbits/s, such as FDDI, may be inadequate for high-throughput applications.

The user requirement for the network to carry a mixture of traffic (voice, image, and video, in addition to high-speed data) has led to the development of FDDI-II standards. FDDI-II is an upward-compatible extension to FDDI that adds the ability to support circuit-switched traffic as well as the packet-mode traffic supported by the original FDDI. Proponents of FDDI II claim that FDDI is not suitable for maintaining a continuous, constant-data-rate connection between two devices for applications such as voice, video, and multimedia. Even the synchronous traffic class of FDDI guarantees only a minimum sustained data rate; it does not provide a uniform information stream with no interframe variability. Such a continuous, constant data stream is typical of circuit-switched applications, such as digitized voice or video. However, actual FDDI-II products of any meaningful consequence are yet to emerge, and the commercial outlook for this technology is uncertain.

Up to 15 circuit-switched channels operating at 6.144 Mbits/s are allowed. Each of these channels can in turn be internally allocated as required by the two endpoints utilizing the channel (i.e., it can be further allocated on a time-division multiplexed basis). FDDI-II provides a circuit-switched service while maintaining the token-controlled packet-switched service of the original FDDI. The packet channel controlled by the token discipline can have bandwidth from 768 kbits/s to 99.072 Mbits/s, depending on the number of active wideband circuit-switched channels. Hence, with FDDI-II systems, it is possible to set up and maintain a constant-rate connection between two devices. Instead of using embedded addresses, as was the case with FDDI's frames, the connection is established on the basis of a prior agreement, which may have been negotiated using packet messages or some other suitable mechanism. The technique used in FDDI-II for providing circuit-switched service is to impose a 125-μs frame structure on the FDDI network. A circuit-switched connection consists of regularly repeating time slots in the frame (this mode of transmission is also known as *isochronous*). However, one of the limitations of FDDI-II is that the total bandwidth remains 100 Mbits/s, so that the average per-user bandwidth is still relatively low.

IEEE 802.9 integrated LAN.   The IEEE 802.9 Working Group has developed a specification in support of integrated voice and data at the 10-Mbit/s range. Table 2.12 provides an overview of some key aspects of the integrated voice and data LAN (IVD LAN) this committee has developed.

The IEEE 802.9 standard defines a unified access method that offers integrated voice and data (IVD) services to the desktop for a variety of publicly and privately administered backbone networks [e.g., FDDI, IEEE 802.x, Integrated Services Digital Network (ISDN)]. Such a standard enables IVD terminal equipment (IVDTE) to be attached to IEEE 802.9 LANs and allows them to communicate with other IVD stations as well as data-only stations, voice-only stations, and premises-based networks offering ISDN services. The use of terminal adapter devices permits the attachment of native-mode terminal devices such as data-only modules, voice modules, and ISDN Basic Rate terminals to the IEEE P802.9 interface. The IVD LAN

TABLE 2.12   Highlights of IVDLAN

Defines a standard for carrying voice and data (similar in concept to FDDI II)

Based initially on ISDN concepts; works at 10 Mbits/s total; provides $n \times$ 64-kbit/s channels ($n \leq 30$), plus data channel

Technology represents the integration of IEEE 802 services and ISDN services

Utilizes twisted-pair cabling

Video usage: limited to $n \times$ 64-kbit/s signals; limited to a few users

Standard went through 17 revisions; now complete

Not expected to have major commercial deployment

Potential for multimedia: limited

interface standard is an integrated voice/data interface that provides high-bandwidth packet service and isochronous digital channels on a full-duplex interface to the desktop over unshielded twisted-pair wiring. The principal target of the initial Physical Layer specification is the office environment on premises-based networks. It is intended to be used on unshielded telephone twisted-pair wiring in a physical point-to-point configuration.

isoENET (isochronous Ethernet).   A variant of the 802.9 standard surfaced in late 1992 when National Semiconductor and IBM announced the isoENET proposal for carrying voice and data over a 10-Mbit/s 10BASE-T LAN.[22] It provides a 10-Mbit/s channel for Ethernet, *plus* ninety-six 64-kbit/s out-of-band isochronous subchannels for voice and video. The Ethernet MAC frames coexist over the same physical medium as the isochronous voice and data, but they have a different format. The proposal extends Ethernet to 20 Mbits/s over voice- or data-grade unshielded twisted-pair wire by enabling a single pair of wires to send and receive data simultaneously. Although isoENET would use regular 10BASE-T star wiring, eliminating the need to recable, hubs and PCs need to be (selectively) retrofitted with new adapters. The upgrade can be done on an incremental basis. This approach suffers from the fact that changes to the upper-layer protocols of the PCs and servers are required. Transport protocols, bandwidth management, and channel allocation capabilities must be added. See Fig. 2.7.

isoENET is viewed by its proponents as an evolutionary technology upgrade from standard 10BASE-T Ethernet. isoENET adds a dedicat-

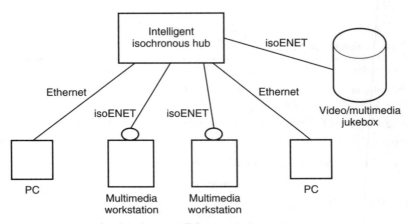

Figure 2.7   Example of isochronous Ethernet environment.

ed full-duplex 6.144 Mbits/s of isochronous bandwidth per node to the existing shared 10-Mbit/s packet bandwidth available from standard 10BASE-T Ethernet. The isochronous bandwidth is divided into ninety-six 64-kbit/s channels (including one designated for signaling and control and one reserved for maintenance).

isoENET uses a 4B/5B encoding scheme originally specified in the ANSI X3T9.5 FDDI standard. This method of encoding provides an 80 percent utilization of the IEEE 802.3 specified 20-MHz clock signal, in contrast to the 50 percent utilization with standard Ethernet's Manchester encoding. This scheme provides the additional 6.144-Mbit/s isochronous bandwidth per node and maintains current line frequency emissions, minimizing FCC-related issues.

Isochronous connections between nodes are made via call setup procedures supported in isoENET node adapter cards and hubs and based on Q.931 extensions. Services such as requesting a variable number of B channels and multiparty connections are supported much as in ISDN wide area networks. isoENET's circuit-switching characteristics, Q.931-based network signaling, WAN and FDDI-II B-channel structure, and 8-kHz clocking lead to more efficient LAN backbone and WAN interconnection.

At press time, isoENET was under consideration by IEEE 802.9. Standards development by the working group could be completed in a year or two. Isochronous Ethernet technology was demonstrated by both National and IBM in late 1992 using National's isoENET adapters. Isochronous Ethernet–based products were anticipated for 1994. These products could include PC adapters, hub blades, and FDDI-II and WAN interconnect through hubs.

Proposed 100-Mbit/s "Ethernet" systems. In early 1993, about a dozen companies announced that they were investigating the possibility of developing "Ethernet" systems operating at 100 Mbits/s using voice-grade unshielded twisted-pair cable. These systems are also called fast Ethernet, but they may or may not be compatible with Ethernet. The goal is to deliver 100 Mbits/s to the desktop cheaper than would be the case with FDDI-based adapters. Some companies are exploring the same signaling scheme used in copper-based FDDI, while other companies are looking at other schemes.

The issues associated with this endeavor are: Does one keep the same CSMA/CD MAC as the 10-Mbit/s system, or does one move to a MAC that is more isochronous in nature? Does one aim for voice-grade unshielded wiring (Type 3), use data-grade unshielded wiring (Type 5), or use shielded wiring (Type 1)? Can one retain two-pair wiring, or will a four-pair system be needed/preferred? In the opinion of a majority of interested parties, the goal is to keep the existing

TABLE 2.13   Goals for 100-Mbit/s Ethernet

100 Mbits/s
100 m to the hub
802.3 MAC frame format
EIA 568 wiring specification (Category 3)
802-equivalent error rates
Consistency with FCC and European radiation emission standards
Simultaneous support of 10 and 100 Mbits/s
Medium-independent interfaces
Support of multiple hubs
Use of RJ-45 connector for UTP

wiring and replace the PC/workstation and hub cards for no more than a few hundred dollars. The target is to deliver 100 Mbits/s (aggregate shared bandwidth) to the desktop for no more than twice the cost of a 10BASE-T system (which is around $250 per user). As a note, 50 percent of the installed wiring is Type 3, 7 percent is Category 4, 18 percent is Type 5, and 25 percent is STP. Because of the invested base, the main focus is on Type 3 wiring; however, it is not clear that all the technical hurdles can be overcome, leading the designers to consider Type 5 wiring. Three key proposals were made to the January 1993 IEEE 802.3 Committee meeting, in addition to other variants. The goals of the effort, as adopted by the IEEE Committee, are shown in Table 2.13.

In some proposals (e.g., the original LAN Media Corp. and Grand Junction Networks proposals), the frame would remain the same as the Ethernet frame, but the signaling [how the frame is transmitted over the medium, as specified in the Physical and Physical Medium Dependent (PMD) sublayers] would have to be changed and then standardized. Because of these changes, new workstation/PC network interface cards and new hubs would be required (note that LLC, TCP/IP, and the applications themselves do not require any modifications). In addition, because of propagation time issues, the diameter of the network (maximum end-to-end cable length) would have to be reduced by an order of magnitude, from the current 2500 m to 250 m. If the Ethernets in question are interconnected over an FDDI backbone (i.e., hubs interface to an FDDI network), then the distance reduction would probably not be a problem; however, if the network hubs are connected over twisted-pair cable supporting a single logical network, then the diameter restriction is likely to be a problem. A way around this problem is to utilize bridges between hubs.

The ability to operate at higher speeds without having to modify major portions of the MAC protocols has been demonstrated for some time in both the Ethernet and the token ring context (64-Mbit/s token ring systems have been prototyped; however, new network interface cards for the PMD would be required in both cases). There was a claim of broad vendor support for this proposal. Dual-speed (10 and 100 Mbits/s) adapters and dual-speed hub ports are envisioned. Bridging between the two systems is relatively easy (as long as the effective speed/throughput is consistent across both networks).

In other proposals (e.g., HP/AT&T), the MAC protocol is also replaced, eliminating the contention scheme (which is in fact the culprit causing variable delays and throughput in the network) and replacing it with a Demand Priority Protocol using a scheme called Quartet Signaling. Four pairs are required with this approach.

2.5.2 Wide area connectivity

There are several factors that characterize wide area services that are of particular relevance to client-server environments. Table 2.14 highlights some of these characteristics; however, not every possible combination shown in this table corresponds to a service which can be

TABLE 2.14   Key Factors for Wide Area Connectivity

Characteristic	Typical ranges
Speed (bandwidth)	$n \times 64$ kbits/s, T1/DS1/E1 (1.544–2.048 Mbits/s), T2/DS2 (6.312 Mbits/s), T3/DS3 (44.736 Mbits/s), STS-1 (51.84 Mbits/s), STS-3c (155.250 Mbits/s), STS-12c (622.08 Mbits/s)
Bearer mode	Connection-oriented or connectionless
Switching type	None (dedicated line), circuit-switched, packet-switched (frame relay, cell relay)
Symmetry	Bidirectional symmetric bandwidth, bidirectional asymmetric bandwidth, unidirectional
Connection type supported (signaling support)	Point-to-point, point-to-multipoint, multipoint-to-multipoint
Geographic scope of coverage	Intra-LATA, inter-LATA, international

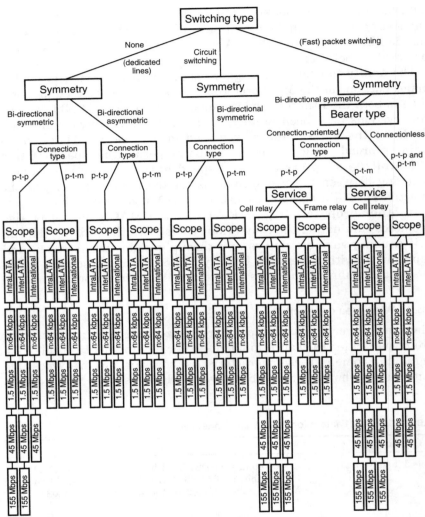

Figure 2.8 Taxonomy of principal WAN services applicable to client-server computing. p-t-p = point-to-point; p-t-m = point-to-multipoint.

secured from a carrier. Figure 2.8 shows some of the more common combinations. Connection-oriented communication, highlighted in both the table and the figure, is similar to the traditional dedicated line or circuit-switched environment, where the user goes through a connectivity setup phase, an information transfer phase, and a connectivity teardown phase (for a circuit-switched call, this is done in real time; for a dedicated line service, the setup is done at service initiation time and the teardown is done at service cancellation time). In

TABLE 2.15   High-Speed Service and Related Terms

Cell relay service	155- or 622-Mbit/s public switched WAN service (service is also possible over a private switch) where user's cells are delivered at high speed to a remote destination (or destinations). Both a permanent virtual connections (PVC) service and a switched virtual connections (SVC) service are evolving. Availability: 1993 and beyond.
Cell switching	A method for multiplexing, switching, and transporting a variety of high-capacity signals, using short, fixed-length data units known as cells. The asynchronous transfer mode is the accepted international standard for the cell structure.
Fractional T1	A point-to-point dedicated service supporting $n \times 64$-kbit/s connectivity (typically, $n = 2, 4, 6,$ or 12).
Frame relay, private	A multiplexed service obtained over a private high-speed backbone equipped with appropriate nodal processors (fast packet switches). Used to interconnect LANs at $n \times 64$ kbits/s or 1.544 Mbits/s.
Frame relay, public	A multiplexed service provided by a carrier. The user has a single access line into the network and can deliver frames to remote users without having to provide dedicated communication links or switches. Used to interconnect LANs at $n \times 64$ kbits/s or 1.544 Mbits/s.
ISDN H0	A switched service providing physical connectivity at 384 kbits/s, using the ISDN call setup mechanism.
ISDN H11	A switched service providing physical connectivity at 1536 kbits/s, using the ISDN call setup mechanism.
SMDS	A public switched service supporting connectionless cell-based communication at 1.544 and 45 Mbits/s access speed, targeted for LAN interconnection.
SONET	A specification for digital hierarchy levels at multiples of 52 Mbits/s. Also, a point-to-point dedicated service supporting $n \times$ 52-Mbit/s connectivity over fiber-based facilities.
Switched T1	A switched service providing physical connectivity at 1.536 Mbits/s.
T1 (DS1)	A point-to-point dedicated service supporting 1.544 Mbits/s aggregate connectivity.
T3 (DS3)	A point-to-point dedicated service supporting 44.736 Mbits/s aggregate connectivity or 28 DS1 subchannels.

a connectionless service, each data unit is treated independently of the previous one, and no connectivity setup/teardown is required, much the same way as an information frame is transferred in a LAN.

Table 2.15 depicts some of the key telecommunication services now becoming available in support of distributed computing. Table 2.16

TABLE 2.16   Classification of Key WAN Services in Support of Client-Server Systems

	Nonswitched	Switched
Low speed	Analog private line	Dialup with modem
	DDS private line	ISDN
	Fractional T1 private line	Packet-switched network
	T1 private line	
	Frame relay (permanent virtual circuit)	Frame relay (switched virtual circuit)
High speed	T3 private line	Switched multimegabit data service (SMDS)
	SONET private line	
	ATM/cell relay service (permanent virtual circuit)	ATM/cell relay service (switched virtual circuit)

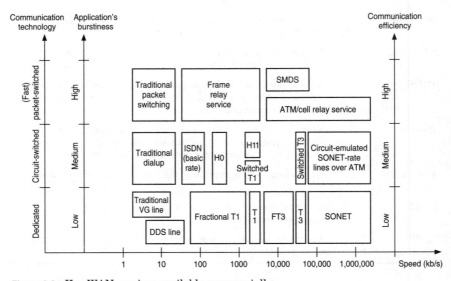

Figure 2.9   Key WAN services available commercially.

groups these services into four types, namely dedicated/switched and low speed/high speed. Figure 2.9 shows the applicability of some of the key interoffice/long distance high-speed services plotted against the burstiness requirement of the application (burstiness is the ratio of the instantaneous traffic to the average traffic).[20] Figure 2.10

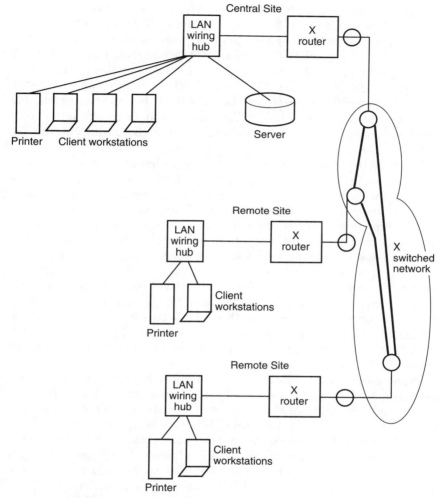

Figure 2.10 Client-server system across a WAN. X = dialup; ISDN; X.25; frame relay; SMDS; cell relay; $n \times 64$, T1, T3 line; switched T1.

shows an example of a client-server system implemented across a WAN.

Cell relay service. Asynchronous transfer mode is a high-bandwidth, low-delay switching and multiplexing communication technology supporting wide area communications; as noted, the same technology is now also being applied to the development of next-generation LANs (to be exact, ATM refers to the network platform, while cell relay service refers to the actual service obtainable over an ATM platform). It is the general industry consensus that ATM is the WAN service of choice for applications requiring high throughput. For readers familiar with the operation of a protocol stack, it is simply a matter of realizing what functional partitioning has been instituted by the designers of ATM and what are the peer entities in the user's equipment and in the network. The cell relay protocols approximately equate to the functionality of the MAC/LLC layers of a traditional LAN, but with the following differences: Random access is not utilized, channel sharing is done differently, and the underlying media may be different.[23]

Two remotely located user devices (say a client and a server) that need to communicate over an ATM network can establish one or more bidirectional virtual (i.e., not hard-wired and/or dedicated) connections between them to transmit cells (fixed-length packets 53 bytes long). This connection is identified to each user by an appropriate identifier, similar in some respects to how virtual channels are identified in a packet-switched network. Once such a basic connection is set up, user devices can utilize the virtual connection-oriented channel for specific communication tasks. Each active channel has an associated bandwidth negotiated with the network at connection setup time. The transfer capacity at the user-network interface (UNI) is 155.52 Mbits/s; other UNIs at the DS1 (1.544 Mbits/s) and DS3 (44.736 Mbits/s) rates are also being contemplated in the United States.

Connections in an ATM network support both circuit-mode and packet-mode (connection-oriented and connectionless) services of a single medium and/or mixed media and multimedia. ATM carries two types of traffic: constant bit rate (CBR) and variable bit rate (VBR). For example, video transmission generates CBR traffic, while data applications (say, router traffic for a traditional LAN) generate VBR traffic. CBR transfer-rate parameters for on-demand services are negotiated at call setup time. (CBR transfer-rate parameters for permanent services are agreed upon with the carrier from which the user obtains service.) VBR services are described by a number of traffic-related parameters (peak rate, sustained rate, maximum burst length, etc.) that are also negotiated at call setup time.

For wide area communication, cell relay involves the following aspects:

1. Specification of the network interface configuration, i.e., the required protocols and procedures that the user must implement in his or her equipment in order to obtain the high-speed, high-quality cell relay service. The user equipment can be composed of a variety of elements (workstations, routers, servers, multiplexers,

etc.). The access speed and other quality of service (QOS) factors can be specified by the user. The interface covers both the information flow and the call control flow (that is, the user has a transmit channel and a signaling channel).

2. A high-speed, typically fiber-based local loop to enable an information stream originating at a user's location to reach the broadband switch at the serving central office or some other hub location, where it is appropriately handled.

3. A high-speed broadband switch that is able to interconnect users at the required bandwidth rates.

4. A call control capability (at the broadband switch or other location) to accept the user's service requests and to allocate network resources to satisfy these requests. The call control capability supports point-to-point, point-to-multipoint, and multipoint-to-multipoint connectivity.

5. A network capability to maintain the requested bandwidth, connectivity, and QOS.

6. An interoffice high-speed network infrastructure supporting wide area connectivity.

7. An interoffice (overlay) signaling network to carry the users' service requests (i.e., signaling information) to the appropriate destination.

The access protocol in the user equipment consists of a Physical Layer at the lowest level and an ATM Layer over it that provides information transfer for all services. Above the ATM Layer, the ATM Adaptation Layer (AAL) provides service-dependent functions to the layer above the AAL. (These layers above the AAL are similar, or in fact identical, to TCP/IP; in fact, TCP/IP may continue to be used by users' PCs and hosts—note that AALs usually go only as high as the Data Link Layer.) The AAL protocols are implemented in the user's equipment. The service data units reaching the AAL consist of user information coming down the protocol stack, e.g., from a TCP/IP stack or from a video codec; the information is segmented/cellularized by AAL into 53-octet cells so that it can be efficiently shipped through the network. The AAL enhances the services provided by the ATM Layer to support the functions required by the next higher layer. The AAL-specific information is nested in the information field of the ATM cell. In order to minimize the number of AAL protocols, a service classification has been defined based on the following three parameters: (1) timing relation between source and destination (required or not required), (2) bit rate (constant or variable), and (3) connection mode (connection-oriented or connectionless). Five classes of applications are then defined, as follows:

Class A: Timing required, bit rate constant, connection-oriented

Class B: Timing required, bit rate variable, connection-oriented

Class C: Timing not required, bit rate variable, connection-oriented

Class D: Timing not required, bit rate variable, connectionless

Class X: Unrestricted (bit rate variable, connection-oriented or connectionless).

Wide area networks providing cell relay services were appearing in 1993–94, with more widespread penetration thereafter. There is keen interest in ATM and cell relay service on the part of local exchange carriers, interexchange carriers, and international carriers. Cell relay service provides both a permanent virtual connection and a switched virtual connection service. A PVC implementation establishes a fixed path through the network for each source-destination pair, which remains defined for a long period of time (weeks, months, or years). In SVC, resources are put in place only for the duration of the actual session (minutes or hours). Early carrier offerings supported only PVC service (SVC service is expected to appear in 1994–95). Cell relay service is expected to be used in large companies.

Switched multimegabit data service. Switched multimegabit data service is a connectionless high-speed, high-quality packet service. It enables access at DS1 and DS3 speeds and supports an end-to-end throughput close to these values. SMDS is defined as a technology-independent service, positioned for LAN interconnection. SMDS enables the reliable exchange of variable-length data units; this allows SMDS to encapsulate entire frames generated by most LANs. At the DS1 rate, the user can access SMDS over twisted-pair or fiber; at the DS3 rate, fiber is employed (the user's access, however, is at the electrical DS1 or DS3 interface). On the 45-Mbit/s interface, the user can elect a 4-, 10-, 16-, 25-, or 34-Mbit/s throughput access class. SMDS specifies the end-to-end delay for large protocol data units traversing two DS3 access lines to be less than 20 ms 95 percent of the time. For data units traversing a DS3 access line at one end and a DS1 access line at the other end, the end-to-end delay is specified to be less than 75 ms 95 percent of the time. For access over two DS1 lines, the delay is specified to be less than 130 ms 95 percent of the time.

SMDS had become commercially available by year-end 1991, with more deployment taking place at this time. A SMDS-configured router is required to access the service. A number of vendors have announced equipment. The SMDS access equipment supports peer-to-peer PHY, MAC, LLC, and IP protocols looking to the local LAN, and it implements an 802.6-based protocol covering the equivalent of the functionality of the MAC layer looking toward the public network. (IP is also implemented router to router, namely, above the SMDS network, end to end.) The end-to-end user protocols run transparently over the carrier's SMDS. In the future, SMDS may be provided over a multiservice ATM-based network platform. SMDS is expected to be used in large companies.

Frame relay service. Frame relay service (FRS) is a connection-oriented service operating at $n \times 64$ kbits/s or 1.544 Mbits/s (2.048 Mbits/s in Europe). It is offered by a variety of carriers, including the Regional Bell Operating Companies and interexchange carriers. It started to be available in early 1991, and by press time it was available in approximately 50 U.S. cities and in key European cities. FRS is positioned for LAN interconnection. Given its relatively low speed, it is only marginally useful for high-speed applications. Compared to X.25-based service, FRS aims at reducing network delays, providing more efficient bandwidth utilization, and decreasing communication equipment cost. The increase in efficiency and reduction in delay are achieved by performing error correction on an end-to-end basis rather than on a link-by-link basis, as is the case, for example, in traditional packet switching. This makes the protocol much simpler. Communication links are now carried in increasing numbers on fiber optic facilities, making them cleaner, as measured by the bit error rate. Because the circuits are much cleaner, performing error management on an end-to-end basis is more effective. Most of the applications to date have been for wide area LAN interconnection where the LANs support traditional data-only applications. Some experimentation in support of videoconferencing has been reported, but with limited success.

A frame relay interface can support multiple sessions over a single physical access line. Frame relay interfaces have been implemented on such products as LAN bridges and routers, as well as on T1 multiplexers. Frame relay provides both PVC and SVC service. In practice, all user implementations and all carrier offerings initially supported only PVC service (SVC service may appear in 1994–95). Frame relay service is expected to be used in medium to large companies.

Digital dedicated line services. In spite of the emergence of other digital services, high-speed dedicated digital lines operating at $n \times 64$ kbits/s ($n = 1, 2, 6, 12$), 1.544 Mbits/s (also known as T1), and 45 Mbits/s (also known as T3) are still a common way to interconnect remote LANs. With a dedicated line, the entire bandwidth can be applied to the interconnection task (unless a portion of the bandwidth is allocated to another application). Since (1) the bandwidth is not generally shared, (2) there is no delay variation, and (3) there is no frame discard over the WAN, dedicated lines are somewhat better suited for high-performance applications than, for example, FRS. This approach, however, does have at least three drawbacks:

1. Relatively high cost
2. A multitude of lines (growing at 0.5 times the square of the number of locations to be connected), implying high communication and network management cost
3. Inflexibility in reaching "off-net" locations, with provided connectivity typically between only two or a few sites

High-speed dedicated services are expected to be used in medium to large companies.

Analog private lines.   The classical interconnection method employed by network designers for the past quarter-century has been to use analog private lines. This approach involves a permanently installed voice-grade line (3000 Hz) between two points. These channels are adapted from voice communication to data communication through the use of a modem. The modem transforms data into an analog signal suitable for transmission over the traditional telephone network. While digital backbones are now becoming popular, a large portion of today's data communications is still carried by voiceband modems over the analog telephone network, particularly for terminal-to-mainframe applications. This approach, although relatively inexpensive, supports only a bandwidth in the 9.6- to 19.2-kbit/s range. (Modems with compression may support speeds up to 38.4 or 57.6 kbits/s; however, this rate may not be sustained for the entire transfer session and may not be achievable with images that are already compressed.) These dedicated services are expected to be used in small to medium companies.

Dialup.   This approach uses modems connected to the LAN server (bridge or router) in order to utilize the analog public telephone network. Circuit switching implies that the communications channel is not dedicated 24 hours per day, but must be brought on line when needed and then taken down when no longer needed. Traditional modems have operated at speeds up to 19.2 kbits/s; however, until recently, speeds of 9.6 kbits/s have been more common. This implies that the throughput across this type of LAN-to-LAN link is fairly small. Consequently, only a small number of users and/or short inquiry/response-like transactions can be supported. Since the link between the two servers is not available on a dedicated basis, the bridge or router would have to dial up the remote device as needed; this implies that a delay of approximately 2 to 5 s would be incurred.

The advantage of this approach is, however, that this type of connectivity is fairly inexpensive; it would be ideal for an environment where there are dozens (or even hundreds) of remote LANs with only occasional need to exchange data. Long distance telephone service can be obtained for 10 to 25 cents per minute depending on distance, time of day, and carrier. If there is sufficient calling volume, bulk rates are available from carriers. A 9.6-kbit/s full-duplex operation modem for dialup lines can be purchased for as little as $300. High-speed modems can now achieve up to 38.4 kbits/s on dialup lines using error correction and data compression; these modems can be purchased for approximately $900 or less. Modems with high-end compression may support speeds up to 57.6 kbits/s. These services are typically used in small to medium companies.

ISDN. This interconnection approach involves the use of switched *digital* facilities between the LAN routers. ISDN provides end-to-end digital connectivity with access to voice and data services (for those users that need integrated access) over the same digital transmission and switching facilities. It provides a range of services using a limited set of connection types and multipurpose user-network interface arrangements. ISDN provides three channel types: B channels, D channels, and H channels. The *B channel* is a 64-kbit/s access channel that carries customer information, such as voice calls, circuit-switched data, or packet-switched data. The *D channel* is an access channel carrying control or signaling information and, optionally, packetized customer information; the D channel has a capacity of 16 or 64 kbits/s. The *H channel* is a 384-kbit/s, 1.536-Mbit/s, or 1.920-Mbit/s (Europe) channel that carries customer information, such as video teleconferencing, high-speed data, high-quality audio or sound programs, and imaging information.

ISDN defines *physical user-network interfaces*. The best known of these interfaces are

2B + D	Two switched 64-kbit/s channels, plus a 16-kbit/s packet/signaling channel
23B + D	Twenty-three switched 64-kbit/s channels, plus a 64-kbit/s packet/signaling channel
H0 + D	Switched aggregated 384-kbit/s links
H10 + D	Switched aggregated 1.544-Mbit/s links

As can be seen, ISDN provides considerably more bandwidth on a circuit-switched connection than is possible with standard analog circuits. ISDN is now available in the top 100 markets, and is expected to be increasingly available in other areas. ISDN services are initially likely to be used in medium to large companies.

References

1. T. E. Bell, "Jobs at Risk," *IEEE Spectrum,* August 1993, p. 26.
2. P. Smith, *Client/Server Computing,* Sams Publishing, Carmel, Ind., 1992.
3. Promotional Material, *Network Computing,* Client-Server Supplement, May 1993.
4. R. Graff and D. Minoli, *Client/Server Solutions,* Van Nostrand Reinhold, New York, 1995.
5. S. Morse, "Client/Server Is Not Always the Best Solution," *Network Computing,* Client-Server Supplement, May 1993, pp. 7 ff.
6. A. Freedman, *Electronic Computer Glossary,* The Computer Language Co., 1993.
7. H. Newton, *Newton's Telecom Dictionary,* 1993.
8. R. Moskowitz, "What Are Clients and Servers Anyway," *Network Computing,* Client-Server Supplement, May 1993.
9. D. Minoli, *1st, 2nd, and Next Generation LANs,* McGraw-Hill, New York, 1994.
10. "Sharing the Load: Client-Server Computing," *Data Communication,* Mar. 21, 1989, pp. 19–29.
11. J. C. Panettieri, "How to Break Through the Logjam," *Network Computing,* Client-Server Supplement, May 1993.
12. L. Berg, "Implementing Client/Server Computing," COMNET 92, Washington, D.C., January 1992.
13. K. Myhre, "Please Explain Client/Server," COMNET 92, Washington, D.C., January 1992.
14. D. Ferris, "Client-Server Database Models Are Emerging," *Network World,* May 11, 1992.
15. D. Minoli and B. Keinath, *Distributed Multimedia: Through Broadband Communication Services,* Artech House, Norwood, Mass., 1994.
16. J. Cox, "Users Urge: See Client-Server Clearly," *Communications Week,* June 21, 1993, pp. 11ff.
17. T. Wilson, "IBM Continues Client-Server Shift," *Communications Week,* June 21, 1993, p. 4.
18. J. Cox, "Delta Launches Mega-Database on Servers," *Communications Week,* May 31, 1993, pp. 1ff.
19. J. Cox, "Oracle to Cast SQL*Net at Distributed Apps," *Communications Week,* Aug. 2, 1993, pp. 1ff.
20. D. Minoli, *Imaging in Corporate Environments,* McGraw-Hill, New York, 1994.
21. D. Minoli, "Third Generation LANs," Proceedings of TEXPO 1993, San Francisco, Apr. 6–8, 1993.
22. D. Minoli, "Isochronous Ethernet: Poised for Launch," *Network Computing,* August 1993, pp. 156ff.
23. D. Minoli, "ATM Makes Its Entrance," WAN Connections—Supplement of *Network Computing,* August 1993, pp. 22ff.

3

Financial Techniques

Outsourcing can be expressed as a make-versus-buy or own-versus-lease decision facing the organization. In its generic form, outsourcing has been studied in a number of settings, including the manufacture of parts in the automobile industry, the sales function in the electronics industry, the procurement of components or services in the naval shipbuilding industry, and the distribution of equipment, components, and supplies across a set of industrial firms.[1] In the IT industry, outsourcing is the significant contribution by external suppliers in the physical and human resources associated with the entire IT infrastructure,* or specific components of it, in the user organization. In the context of IT outsourcing, the outsourcer may contribute computer assets for the organization; alternatively, the ownership of certain computer assets of the organization may be transferred to the outsourcing company. In terms of human resources, the outsourcer may utilize its own personnel to support the required services, or it may utilize existing staff of the organization who are transferred to the outsourcer.

For both the physical and human resources, classical financial modeling plays a key role. The purpose of this chapter is to discuss basic financial mechanisms that the organization should employ in its decision making. Today financial planning is typically done using either a PC program such as Lotus 1-2-3 or Excel, or some more sophisticated decision support system. Yet, it is important to understand some of the basic principles involved so that the IS professional does not sim-

---

*The IT infrastructure can be defined as the "internal organization of people and resources devoted to computer-based systems involving both tangible equipment, staff and applications, and the intangible organization, methods and policies by which the organization maintains its ability to provide system services."[2]

ply enter data into a system blindly without having some intuitive appreciation of what the package might be doing. The reader may refer to Ref. 3 or other references, including Refs. 4 and 5, for a more extensive treatment.

3.1   Financial Terminology

Basic concepts that an IS manager should be familiar with are identified in this section. The concepts are presented from a tangible asset point of view. Outsourcing deals may or may not involve tangible assets. The organization in question is willing to pay a certain recurring fee to a provider for services that have been defined at contract signing time. The analytical methods described below are equally applicable to the outsourcing environment as long as the appropriate terminological substitutions for assets (services) and cash flows (payments) are made. In particular, "buy" can mean develop or keep your own IS infrastructure, and "lease" can mean outsource.

3.1.1   System life cycle

Although many managers give heavy weight to the initial cost of a given solution, true financial analysis corroborates the conclusion that what initially costs more may turn out to be the cheapest solution in the long run. Apparent savings in equipment, planning, or R&D may be wiped out by future high operating and maintenance costs; conversely, what may appear at deployment time as expensive features may prove to be valuable over time, reducing operating/ maintenance costs and revenue loss resulting from outage or service unavailability.

In evaluating business alternatives, one must consider not only the first costs, but all the expenditures and income derivable over the decision's life cycle. Viewed from another perspective, the capital expenditures for a particular system may come at various points in time. These observations imply that

1. The financial measures must be assessed over the entire life cycle of the investment.
2. Money has a time value, and this must be explicitly considered in the decision process.

3.1.2   Capital assets

A capital asset is a physical asset used by a firm in producing goods or services.

3.1.3 Capital budget

The capital budget is a statement of the organization's planned investments, generally based upon estimates of future income (e.g., corporate outlay slated for IS/IT), production needs, and availability of capital.

3.1.4 Expense budget

The expense budget is a statement of the organization's planned expenses during the time interval in question, typically a year. It covers many of the IT items listed in Table 1.3, except for hardware. Payroll, training, software, insurance, rent, fees, etc., all have to come out of the expense budget.

3.1.5 Depreciation

Depreciation is a deduction of part of the cost of an asset from the company's income in each year of the asset's life. Some typical (minimal) depreciation intervals are: for modems, PCs, and other "small" equipment, five years; for front-end processors, PBX, and other "large" equipment, seven years. Recently an accelerated depreciation schedule has been enacted into law, allowing firms to fully depreciate a piece of equipment before the end of its useful life. The motivation was to permit some segments of the manufacturing industry to retire older (but still functioning) equipment and retool in preparation of anticipated foreign competition.

3.1.6 Cash flow

Cash flows represent the money coming to the firm or paid by the firm as a result of making an investment: in other words, the difference between the cash inflows generated by the project—say, an outsourcing decision—(new sales, products, benefits, etc.) and the necessary outflows (equipment costs, labor, etc.). The decision models discussed below call for the net after-tax cash flows CF_1, CF_2, CF_3, etc., to be used in the appropriate formulas; if these flows are incorrectly assessed, the models will not provide accurate results. It is important that the decision maker undertake a real effort to quantify the associated costs and revenues as precisely as possible. In particular, costs go well beyond equipment, as discussed in Chap. 1.

3.1.7 Amortization

Amortization is the process of paying off the principal of a loan over a period of time. The term is also used for writing off tangible assets by prorating their initial cost over a fixed period of time.

3.1.8 Cost of capital

The cost of capital is the rate of payment required to finance a given project—for example, the prime rate or the average rate on all the securities (bonds and stocks) issued by the company. Also called the *cost of money*, it represents, for example, the borrower's payment to the lender for the use of capital in the form of a loan. Interest has been charged since antiquity. Invested capital will provide a gain or benefit for the original owner; interest is a measure of that financial benefit. It therefore represents the minimum acceptable rate of return on an investment or project—such as outsourcing—undertaken by the company.

Determining the amount of gain achievable from invested capital is crucial to any economic decision analysis. If a firm needs to borrow the money to finance a conversion, say, from a mainframe-based to a client-server-based IS environment, and the interest rate charged by the lender (bank) is, say, 8 percent a year, then the benefit derivable from that conversion must at least be the equivalent of 8 percent, or there is no advantage in the undertaking. For example, no one would invest $1000 in equipment to achieve a reduction in the cost of some function of $1/month if he or she had to pay $80 a year to the lender to finance the change. Even if the organization had the money and did not have to borrow, it still should not undertake such a project; it could lend that money out (say to a bank) and realize an interest-based return (say $80 a year if the interest rate was 8 percent).

3.1.9 Principal

Principal is the amount of money on which interest is paid by the borrower. It decreases according to the amortization schedule.

3.1.10 Interest

Interest is the same as the cost of capital. Interest can be demanded as simple interest or compound interest. In the former, the borrowing charge is a linear function of the initial loan; in the latter, the charge is an exponential function of the original loan. Compounding always makes the amount due (much) larger than under the simple interest case. In business, compounding is the norm.

There are a number of ways in which a loan can be repaid. Three common ways are

1. Pay the interest due at the end of each period, and repay the entire principal at expiration. For example, $100,000 borrowed at 9 percent for 3 years would result in payments of $9000 for the

first year, $9000 for the second year, and $109,000 in the third year.

2. Do not pay interest and principal until the expiration. In the above example, the first-year disbursement would be $0, the second-year disbursement would be $0, and the third-year disbursement would be $129,503 (interest due for the first year, but not paid: $9,000; interest due for the second year, but not paid: $9,810; interest due for the third year: $10,693).

3. Interest and principal are recovered through a number of equal installment payments. This is the familiar "home mortgage" type. For the above example, the installment payment due at the end of each year is $39,506.

It should be noted that all three methods yield the same equivalent compensation to the lender. The amount of cash flowing to the lender is different under each approach, yet, financially, all three are identical. The formulas employed to calculate these payments assure the lender of this internal consistency. This is done via the *present value* concept.

3.1.11 Present value

Present value is the value of money at the present time, even if the money is due at some future point. Because of (1) inflation, (2) the opportunity to invest the money and earn interest, and (3) the uncertainty of the future, a sum of money today is more valuable than that same sum a year down the road. For example, the present value of a pension is very small: the participants in a pension plan do not know if they will live long enough to collect, or if they will quit before they are vested, or if the company will go out of business before they are vested; thus money in the participants' hands today would be more valuable and sure. The same concept applies to business cash flows. Money is normally discounted at the cost of capital. Hence, given the same financial climate (prime rate, inflation rate, etc.), a network enhancement which promises to return $1 million in one year is better than an alternative that promises to return $1,050,000 in two years.

3.1.12 Future value

The future value is the value of money at some future point. For example, $1 invested at a compound rate of 10 percent would be worth $2.59 in 10 years (its purchasing power then will be the same as at the present time if the rate of investment equals the rate of inflation).

3.1.13   Leases

A lease is a contract between a lessor and a lessee, under which the lessee pays a fee for the use of a resource owned by the lessor. The fee is usually paid monthly and involves a prenegotiated fixed charge.

A net lease is a lease under which the lessee pays all maintenance and upkeep of the asset.

A third-party lease is an arrangement under which the lessor borrows funds to cover part or all of the purchase price of the asset. The third party who secures the funds owns the equipment. Sometimes a firm buys the equipment, sells it to the third party, and then leases it back.

Sale and leaseback is an arrangement under which the user of the asset sells an asset and then leases it back from the new purchaser.

3.1.14   Salvage value

The salvage value, also called residual value, is the price, if any, that the firm can receive for an asset after it has used the asset for an extended period of time, normally the "useful life" of the equipment.

3.1.15   Payback period

The payback period is the interval required for an asset to generate enough cash flow to cover the initial outlay for that asset. For example, an asset costing $15,000 and generating an after-tax cash flow of $5000 has a payback period of three years.

3.1.16   Breakeven point

The breakeven point is the level of cash inflow at which the firm is just breaking even, or earning a zero profit on a given project/investment.

3.1.17   Capital gains (losses)

Capital gains and losses represent the difference between the original cost of an asset and its selling price. Capital gains or losses are realized when the asset is sold and not before.

3.2   Decision Models

This section identifies four decision-making methods.

3.2.1   Net present value method

This is generally considered to be the best of the four methods discussed here. The first step is to calculate the net cash flow generated by the project, starting with project revenues and subtracting expenses (other than depreciation), capital expenditures, and taxes. (Taxes are obtained by multiplying revenues minus all project expenses including depreciation by the tax rate.)

The net present value is the benefit that accrues to the firm from buying the specific equipment (servers, bridges, routers, departmental systems, etc.). It is the sum of the present values of all future cash flows minus the initial cost. A positive net present value means that the project yields a rate of return that exceeds the cost of capital; a negative net present value means that the project earns less than the firm could obtain by keeping the money in the bank. The method is thus summarized as follows:

In an accept-reject decision, the project is selected if the NPV is positive; the project is not undertaken if the NPV is negative.

In comparing mutually exclusive alternatives (buy modem A or modem B; deploy a private network or use a carrier), determine the alternative that has the greatest NPV, and select that alternative as long as the NPV is positive.

3.2.2   Internal rate of return (IRR) method

The IRR is the rate of return on a project. If the rate of return is high (if it exceeds the cost of capital or some higher value), then the project or alternative is selected. If the IRR is low, then the project is not selected.

The IRR method can be explained two ways. The technical explanation is that the IRR is that rate which makes the NPV exactly zero. A more intuitive explanation is as follows: A manager has I. This money, if put into the intended project, will earn cash flows CF_1 at time 1, CF_2 at time 2, etc. What interest rate would the manager have to receive from a bank to obtain the same cash flows? If this rate is low, do not proceed with the project, because the bank could easily match that rate; if the rate is high, then undertake the project, because you will not find a bank giving that high a rate of return.

Thus, if the IRR exceeds the cost of capital, one would opt for the project.

The IRR method is not as good as the NPV method. In particular, when comparing alternatives, it is not correct to simply pick the alternative with the highest IRR. If one project has an internal rate of return of 20 percent and another has a rate of 50 percent, which is better? The 20 percent case may be better. Consider a project which costs $2000 and has a 50 percent IRR, and another project which costs $2 million and has a 20 percent IRR. The former will return only $1,000, the latter $400,000; thus, the second project is better even though the IRR is lower. A quick verification by way of the NPV will support this conclusion. In the 50 percent case, the manager is effectively investing $2 million (assuming that he has this amount at his disposal) as follows:

$$\$2,000 \text{ at } 50 \text{ percent}$$

$$\$1,998,000 \text{ at } 5 \text{ percent (say in a bank account)}$$

After a year, he would have

$$(\$2,000 + \$1,000) + (\$1,998,000 + \$99,900) = \$2,100,900$$

Under the 20 percent IRR case, the entire sum of $2 million is invested at 20 percent, so that he would have $2,400,000, which is better.

Also, it may be algebraically impossible to find the IRR, as there are projects which do not yield a meaningful IRR (this has to do with "imaginary roots" of a polynomial).

3.2.3 Payback period method

The payback period is the length of time it takes to recover the initial investment. The payback period method postulates acceptance of a project/equipment only if the payback period is less than some specified value, such as 36 months. When comparing two options, the one with the shortest payback period would be selected.

This method is not as good as the NPV method because it does not include cash flows beyond the payback period. These cash flows are still relevant to the issue, and should be considered.

3.2.4 Accounting rate of return method

The accounting rate of return, also called the return on investment (ROI), is defined as the average annual after-tax accounting profit generated by the investment/equipment divided by the initial expense. This method is also inferior to the NPV because it does not evaluate cash flows or take into account the cost of money. While these last two methods may have been used prior to the general availability of computing power, being arithmetically simpler, the better method should now be used. With PC and mainframe spreadsheet packages now in wide use (Excel etc.), it is simple to apply the correct methodology.

3.3 Examples

Consider the example of either buying some equipment for $20,000,000 or leasing it for $800,000 a month ($9.6 million per year) for 36 months. Assuming a revenue benefit from having installed the new equipment of $18,000,000 for each of 3 years, a cost of capital of 10 percent, an amortization period of 36 months, a salvage value of $1,000,000, a tax rate of 35 percent, and an initial vendor discount of 8 percent, one finds with the NPV method that the buy option is better.* The NPV in the purchase case is $15,360,005; the NPV in the lease case is $13,578,210. Only when the equipment cost exceeds $22,510,040 does the lease option become better. The lessor needs to make a profit and must charge accordingly; this drives the decision to the buy option. Tables 3.1, 3.2, and 3.3 depict in a methodical way the calculation steps that went into the decision.

The same techniques can be employed when assessing the NPV of an outsourcing deal. Naturally, all the appropriate cash flows have to be adequately accounted for.

---

*This consideration does not take into account risk—for example, that the configuration was wrong and had to be replaced later, in which case the lease option might have been better in the end.

TABLE 3.1   Economic Study for Lease Option ($9,600,000 per Year)

Cost of capital	10%	
Initial purchase cost	$0	
Company's tax rate	35%	
Salvage value	$0	
Fixed yearly revenue without project	$0	
Depreciation without project	$0	
Expense without project	$0	
Fixed yearly revenue with project	$18,000,000	
Depreciation with project	$0	
Expense with project	$9,600,000	

	Without	With	Difference
Revenues	$0	$18,000,000	
Expenses other than depreciation	$0	$9,600,000	
Taxes			
Revenues − expenses	$0	$8,400,000	
Depreciation	$0	$0	
Taxable income	$0	$8,400,000	
Tax	$0	$2,940,000	
Net cash flow for a generic year	$0	$5,460,000	$5,460,000

	Year 1	Year 2	Year 3
Net cash flow	$5,460,000	$5,460,000	$5,460,000
Present values	$4,963,636	$4,512,396	$4,102,178
NPV	$13,578,210		

TABLE 3.2 Economic Study for Buy Option

Cost of capital	10%
Initial purchase cost	$20,000,000
Company's tax rate	35%
Salvage value	$1,000,000
Fixed yearly revenue without project	$0
Depreciation without project	$0
Expense without project	$0
Fixed yearly revenue with project	$18,000,000
Depreciation with project	$6,333,333
Expense with project	$0

	Without	With	Difference
Revenues	$0	$18,000,000	
Expenses other than depreciation	$0	$0	
Taxes			
Revenues − expenses	$0	$18,000,000	
Depreciation	$0	$6,333,333	
Taxable income	$0	$11,666,667	
Tax	$0	$4,083,333	
Net cash flow for a generic year	$0	$13,916,667	$13,916,667

	Year 1	Year 2	Year 3
Net cash flow	$13,916,667	$13,916,667	$14,916,667
Present values	$12,651,515	$11,501,377	$11,207,112
NPV	$15,360,005		

3.4 Analytical Machinery

Some additional financial machinery is presented in this section to provide a skeletal foundation of financial mathematics for the interested reader. Readers who are satisfied with the discussion given above or who do not possess sufficient analytical background can skip this section. For a more detailed treatment, refer to Ref. 3, on which this discussion is based, or any other economic analysis book.

3.4.1 Cash flows, single payments

Money has a time value, as already indicated—$20,000 now is more valuable than $20,000 a year from now. At 10 percent interest, $20,000 now and $22,000 a year from now are equivalent. A way to grasp this equivalence is to plot cash flows on a time line. Figure 3.1 depicts two simple monetary transactions: borrowing $20,000 for one year at 10 percent and lending $20,000 for one year at 10 percent.

TABLE 3.3   Equivalence of Two Options at the Calculated (New) Price

Cost of capital	10%
Initial purchase cost	$22,510,040
Company's tax rate	35%
Salvage value	$1,000,000
Fixed yearly revenue without project	$0
Depreciation without project	$0
Expense without project	$0
Fixed yearly revenue with project	$18,000,000
Depreciation with project	$7,170,013
Expense with project	$0

	Without	With	Difference
Revenues	$0	$18,000,000	
Expenses other than depreciation	$0	$0	
Taxes			
Revenues − expenses	$0	$18,000,000	
Depreciation	$0	$7,170,013	
Taxable income	$0	$10,829,986	
Tax	$0	$3,790,495	
Net cash flow for a generic year	$0	$14,209,504	$14,209,504

	Year 1	Year 2	Year 3
Net cash flow	$14,209,504	$14,209,504	$15,209,504
Present values	$12,917,731	$11,743,392	$11,427,126
NPV	$13,578,210		

The time line is a good way to depict monetary transactions graphically. Given a single repayment F to be made n years (or interest intervals) in the future for an initial loan P at interest rate i, such repayment must be

$$F = P \times (1 + i)^n$$

At $i = 10$ percent (and $P = 1$), for $n = 10$, $F = 2.59$; for $n = 20$, $F = 6.72$; for $n = 50$, $F = 117.4$; and for $n = 100$, $F = 13,780$. This means (for example) that an IRA deposit of $1,000 at age 20 will be worth $117,400 at age 70.

The so-called rule of 72 can provide as a good approximation for future (single-payment) transactions: A loan P at interest i will have to be repaid with the amount $2 \times P$ in $72/i$ years (for relatively low values of i, say $i \leq 10$ percent).

The concept of present value is key to financial decision making. Turning the above formula around, the present value P of a future (single payment/repayment) sum is

$$P = F \times \frac{1}{(1+i)^n}$$

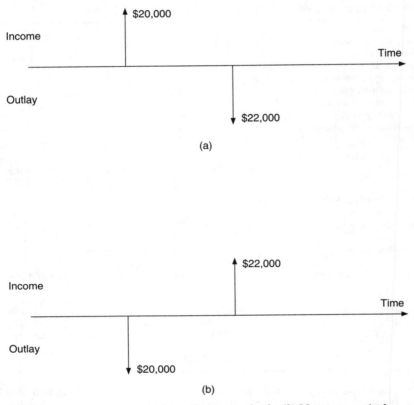

Figure 3.1 (*a*) Monetary equivalence, borrowing funds. (*b*) Monetary equivalence, lending funds.

That is, $117,000 to be received 50 years from now is worth $1,000 right now; the two figures are financially equal. The present value can be viewed as the amount of money to put in the bank now to be able to meet a future expense F a specified number of years from now.

The two basic terms involved in future value/present value calculations are found in tables or can easily be obtained with a PC (until 15 years ago, tables were the easiest route). However, in formulas and analytical expressions, two symbols are employed to identify these quantities:

$$(F/P, i, n) = (1 + i)^n$$

$$(P/F, i, n) = \frac{1}{(1 + i)^n}$$

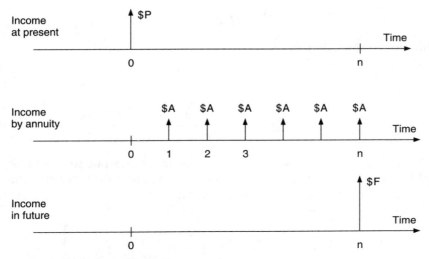

Figure 3.2 Equivalence of annuity payments.

3.4.2 Cash flows, annuity (several equal payments)

Financial terms normally involve making several payments over a number of years. This is the so-called annuity or mortgage plan. Payments resulting from an annuity are financially equivalent to a single payment (up front or at the end of some period), as shown in Fig. 3.2. For example, depositing $1000 a year at 10 percent for three consecutive years will yield a future value (at the end of three years) of $3152.50.

The future value of these multiple payments (deposits) is obtained from the formula

$$F = A(1 + i)^n + A(1 + i)^{n-1} + A(1 + i)^{n-2} + \cdots + A(1 + i)^1 + A$$

where A is the annual deposit; this is written in abbreviated notational form as

$$F = A \times (F/A, i, n)$$

with

$$(F/A, i, n) = (1 + i)^n + (1 + i)^{n-1} + (1 + i)^{n-2} + \cdots + (1 + i)^1 + 1$$

Again, this term can be obtained from a standard financial table.

The sinking term factor is the reciprocal of this annuity fund. It represents the annual savings required to meet a future obligation of F. The amount to be deposited is (reversing the annuity equation just listed)

$$A = \frac{F}{(F/A,\, i,\, n)}$$

This can be rewritten as

$$A = F \times (A/F,\, i,\, n)$$

Clearly,

$$(A/F,\, i,\, n) = \frac{1}{(F/A,\, i,\, n)}$$

Another typical question is: How much must one put in the bank right now to be able to receive an annuity of value A for n years? This is the present value of the annuity. See Fig. 3.3.

It can be shown that the present value P is

$$P = A \left[\frac{1}{(1 + i)^1} + \frac{1}{(1 + i)^2} + \frac{1}{(1 + i)^3} + \cdots + \frac{1}{(1 + i)^n} \right]$$

which can be rewritten as

$$P = A \times (P/A,\, i,\, n)$$

For example, installing a client-server system will provide net income of exactly \$20,000 for each of three years. What is the present value of these cash flows? How much is this worth to the manager right now, at 5 percent prevailing rates?

$$P = 20{,}000 \times (P/A,\, 5,\, 3)$$

Consulting a table (or programming the first three terms of the $(P/A, i, n)$ equation above), one obtains

$$P = 20{,}000 \times 2.7232 = 54{,}464$$

Note that this calculation resembles that for the net present value

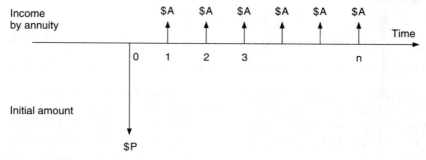

Figure 3.3   Present value of an annuity.

method described earlier (except that all cash flows are assumed to be equal).

One last concept is the capital recovery factor (also called loan repayment factor). This is the amount of money which can be withdrawn every year for n years, given an initial deposit of P. Reversing the above equation for the annuity net present value, one obtains

$$A = \frac{P}{(P/A,\, i,\, n)}$$

which can be rewritten as

$$A = P \times (A/P,\, i,\, n)$$

For example, depositing $5446.40 right now at 5 percent would allow one to withdraw $2000 for three years, since

$$A = 5446.40 \times 0.367 = 2000$$

with $(A/P, 5, 3)$ obtained from a table, or directly by dividing $(P/A, 5, 3)$ into 1 (the equation for this last term was given above). The reason for the term "capital recovery" stems from the fact that this formula can be used to determine what income is necessary to recover a capital investment given the rate of interest on the investment.

Until recently, the terms discussed above had to be obtained from tables. When the specific values could not be located on the table (for example, if the interest was 8.35 percent and one had only an integer-valued table), interpolation methods were used. Today, almost any PC can be programmed (or software is available) to calculate these terms. The only concern would be one of rounding off for large values of the horizon n; in reality, very few people need to calculate values for n exceeding 20, and hence standard calculation techniques should be adequate.

3.4.3   Cash flows, variable quantities

So far we have obtained present values (and future values) of cash flows which were of the same value. In a real-life IS problem, cash flows will probably be different each year. For example, installation of a 20-site private ATM network connecting several regional client-server systems may cost $10,000,000, with a *net* cash flow of − $8,000,000 in the first year (namely, the expense in year 1 was $10,000,000, but $2,000,000 which otherwise would have gone to a long distance carrier was now saved), − $1,500,000 in the second year (tuning and refinements), $35,000 in the third year, $3,000,000 in the fourth year, $5,000,000 in the fifth year, and −$1,000,000 in the sixth year (because of technological obsoles-

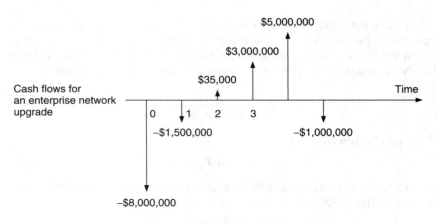

Figure 3.4   Variable cash flows.

cence, numerous network components have to be upgraded at that time). See Fig. 3.4.*

Let CF_1, CF_2, CF_3, etc., be the cash flows for years 1, 2, 3, etc. Net present value is now calculated as follows:

$$P = CF_1 \times (P/F, i, 1) + CF_2 \times (P/F, i, 2) + CF_3 \times (P/F, i, 3) + \cdots$$

where the $(P/F, i, j)$ terms, for any year j, were defined above.

3.4.4   Cash flows in an outsourcing case

In an outsourcing case, the organization typically receives an infusion of cash at the inception of the contract. Then the organization pays monthly charges, which may be constant or (more likely) variable, for the duration of the contract. This is somewhat similar to a home-equity loan, where the consumer gets an infusion of cash at the time of the transaction by "selling" the property to the bank and then buying it back through regular monthly payments; however, the organization is not required to pay back the exact amount (as would be the case with a third-party lease on equipment). Figure 3.5 is an example of a cash flow diagram for a company with $100 million per year revenue and a 5 percent investment in IS. As discussed in Chap. 1, a budget of $5 million a year typically equates to about $5 million of embedded IT infrastructure. An outsourcer could buy out that embedded base of

*The reader should note that the NPV of this project is negative; hence, this project would not be implemented in real life.

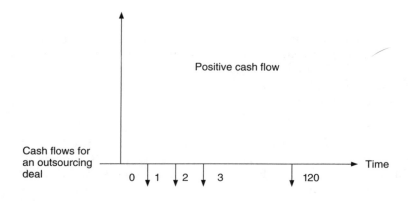

Figure 3.5 Cash flows for an outsourcing deal.

equipment. In this example, it is assumed for simplicity that the entire base of equipment is transferred, so that the organization gets $5 million at project inception. Then it would make 120 payments to the outsourcer at some negotiated level.

3.4.5 Computing net cash flows for capital budgeting

For the purpose of capital budgeting and selection of alternatives, the net cash flow of a project is

Net cash flow from project = cash inflows − cash outflows

= project revenues − expenses other than depreciation

− capital expenditures − income taxes

with

Income taxes = tax rate × (project revenues − project expenses other

than depreciation − depreciation)

1. All revenues and expenses must be appropriately identified.
2. Depreciation affects the cash flow only through its impact on income taxes. (Depreciation is not a cash expense; it is a way to spread the cost of an asset over the asset's life.)
3. Taxes are computed as though the project were financed entirely with equity funds. Interest on debt is not included as an expense in determining taxable income.
4. Tax rates depend on current tax law and on the company's rev-

enues.

5. The method of determining the cash flow from a given data processing, telecommunications, or outsourcing project is to compare the firm's cash flow *with* and *without* the implementation of the proposed project. The difference between the two is the additional cash flow attributable to the project.

Consider a client-server system serving 200 users that costs $1,200,000, has a life of 10 years, has a salvage value of $200,000 at the end of 10 years, and is depreciated on a straight-line basis at $100,000 per year (the difference between the initial cost and the salvage value, divided by the project lifetime). The corporate tax is taken at 50 percent. At acquisition time, the cash flow is the initial project expense, − $1.2 million. The computation of the cash flow for subsequent years follows the layout of Table 3.1. Note that one must compute the various measures (revenues, expenses, etc.) for the status quo (no investment) as well as for the investment. What one is after is the *net cash flow* resulting from the investment compared to that if there is no change or if another alternative is pursued. Note that the no-change case has its own intrinsic revenues and expenses (here this could be an existing mainframe-centered system).

For the example at hand, the net cash flow as compared to the status quo is $175,000 for years 1 through 9, and $375,000 in the 10th year (because of the salvage value). These cash flows can now be employed in the variable cash flow formula given earlier to determine the net present value:

$$\text{NPV} = \text{CF}_1 \times (P/F, i, 1) + \text{CF}_2 \times (P/F, i, 2) + \cdots$$
$$+ \text{CF}_{n-1} \times (P/F, i, n-1) + \text{CF}_n \times (P/F, i, n) - I$$

where I is the initial outlay.

3.5   Other Relevant Concepts

This section defines other financial concepts that are used in the rest of the text.

Return on equity (ROE).   ROE is the ratio of profit to equity. The financial markets view a high ROE as desirable. Outsourcing the entire IS operation will improve the ROE, since the computers and telecommunication equipment are no longer on the organization's balance sheet.

Profit margin.   Profit margin is the ratio of profits to sales.

Transaction. A transaction is an exchange between two or more parties. A transaction may be for specific goods (e.g., the purchase or lease of a client-server or mainframe system) or for a service (e.g., hiring an outsourcer).

Contract. A contract is an agreement between two or more parties. Contract theory is based on the classical work of R. Coarse.[6,7] In this view, a firm exists because the firm lowers the costs of certain transactions; for example, the cost of negotiating and concluding a contract is lower when a firm uses a single contract (that is, a transaction) instead of a series of contracts (that is, a series of transactions). The existence of a firm may be based on the optimal length of a contract: the longer the contract, the more difficult and costly it is to specify the parties' functions and tasks in detail; when such contracts are unacceptable, firms are likely to be established.

A complete contract specifies every possible contingency. Most business contracts are not complete; they are incomplete, and the contracting parties must get together and resolve possible conflicts. In outsourcing, the contract may specify the response time, the cost per CPU second, the cost per gigabyte of storage, etc. (This topic is treated in more detail in Chaps. 4 and 8.)

Incomplete contracts, common in outsourcing environments, have been studied from a *transaction cost economics perspective* and from a *property rights perspective*. (The reader is referred to Ref. 6 for more information on these concepts.)

Transaction cost economics examines the implications of different organizational forms when the parties to the transaction make specific investments (specific investments are those investments that are most valuable in one specific setting or relationship). Specific investments may include investments in specific physical capital, specific human capital, site-specific capital, dedicated capital, or brand-name capital. For example, the time that an outsourcer spends learning about an organization's specific operating procedures, business priorities, decision-making approaches, etc., is a specific investment. This specific investment increases the outsourcer's value when the outsourcer continues to support this organization or one just like it (say, in the same industry). It will be of less value when the outsourcer develops, at a later time, systems for other organizations or for organizations that are different (i.e., employ different procedures, have different business priorities, etc.). Nonetheless, vendors that want to be effective outsourcers need to make specific investments, as must the organization contemplating outsourcing. These specific investments help dissipate organizations' concerns that many outsourcers in general, and systems integrators in particular, do not really understand the needs of the users. In general, specific investments may be advantageous to both parties in the short term, but they could be detrimental in the long term: they can lead to a situation of organizational dependency on a specific vendor, or to a situation where some parties or individuals are stuck with highly selective knowledge that is of interest to few people.

From a property rights perspective, organizational form is defined by the ownership of productive assets. Ownership of these assets gives the owner certain privileges, including use of the asset, denial of the use of the asset to someone else, or ability to lease out or sell the asset. The owner of the asset may voluntarily (or for a fee) transfer some rights (for a time-defined limit or indefinitely) to another party; rights not transferred in the contract are called residual rights. Asset ownership brings bargaining power, thereby affecting the division of the surplus of the trade (the value of the trade minus the cost of the trade).

References

1. L. Loh and N. Venkatraman, "Determinants of Information Technology Outsourcing: A Cross-Sectional Analysis," *Journal of Management Information Systems,* 9(1):7–24, 1992.
2. M. L. Markus, *Systems in Organizations,* Pitman, Marshfield, Mass., 1984.
3. D. Minoli, *Broadband Network Design and Analysis,* Artech House, Norwood, Mass., 1993.
4. J. B. Barney and W. G. Ouchi, *Organizational Economics,* Jossey-Bass, San Francisco, 1986.
5. R. Schmalensee and R. D. Willig, *Handbook of Industrial Organization,* North-Holland, Amsterdam, 1989.
6. W. B. Richmond, A. Seidmann, and A. B. Whinston, "Incomplete Contracting Issues in Information Systems Development Outsourcing," *Decision Support Systems,* 8(5):459–477, 1992.
7. R. H. Coarse, "The Nature of Firms," *Economics,* 4:386ff, 1937.

4

Outsourcing Principles: An Analytical Perspective

Under contractual arrangements, called outsourcing in the trade press, organizations are increasingly shifting specific components of their IT infrastructure from the techno-wander mindset endemic in institutions dominated by technicians uninterested in monetary metrics, to a more rational market-based paradigm of surrendering the operation to the lowest bidder in an optimized manner, whether that bidder is an in-house group (insourcing) or an outside group (outsourcing). Such enlightened efforts have been called *rationalizing the management* of the IT infrastructure.[1] In this context it is worth noting that studies have shown that technology in a vacuum rarely gives businesses a competitive advantage; rather, it only reduces the cost of doing business.[2] Ultimately, outsourcing seeks to establish incentives* for delivering and using information successfully—that is, offering higher quality at lower cost.[3]

The increased press that outsourcing is receiving, both in industry publications and in business magazines read by CEOs, CIOs, etc., is beginning to heighten awareness of the need to quantify its efficacy in an analytical manner. Almost a thousand articles on outsourcing have

---

*Internally, the possibility of outsourcing may motivate the organization's IS staff to improve the service they deliver, in terms of cost and timeliness, to avoid the risk of being out of a job. Externally, IS services provided by an outsourcer are generally under explicit quality metrics.

been published in the past five years. Most of these articles focus on a specific company's decision to utilize outsourcing. Few papers take a more fundamental view of this trend, particularly from an analytical perspective.[1–10] Despite the significant implications of outsourcing and the corporate interest in it, there has been almost no theoretical research addressing it in a rational manner. This chapter examines general aspects of outsourcing from an analytical point of view, under the assumption that it is important to first establish some fundamental principles of a discipline, and only then look at the application implications (Chaps. 5 to 8). It synthesizes the results from Refs. 1 to 3 and 7 to 10, to which the reader is referred for more detail. Besides the specific results that are identified, the purpose of the chapter is to reinforce the need for quantitative modeling and to show some examples of the type of analysis that has already been undertaken.

The conventional wisdom is that outsourcing is a key strategy that enables organizations to improve return on equity. Often this statement is taken for granted. This chapter aims at giving some analytical* credence to this assertion. In particular, as part of an analytical assessment of outsourcing, the IS manager should develop performance measures in order to quantify and parametrize the productivity of the IS function. "What you cannot measure, you cannot control" is a good description of the situation; it has been estimated that 90 percent of all IS operations do not employ any measures of productivity.[2] Therefore, a key part of the evaluation process to support an outsourcing decision is the building of a framework for the measurement of IS quality, productivity, products, and processes. Outsourcing decisions should properly be cast as questions in economic theory of organizations and markets. Given an organizational form and a set of required IS functions, the delivery of services can be studied in the context of contracts and incentives. Unfortunately, within an organization these contracts and incentives are usually implicit; one of the characteristic features of outsourcing is that it enables an organization to establish explicit contracts and incentives.

Outsourcing can be applied to a variety of company functions, as seen below. The chapter is not exclusively tied to IT at the technological level; however, IT is used throughout as an example of the principles being discussed.[†]

---

*In this discussion, "analytical" refers to the use of actual data to test and validate assumptions, rather than a closed-form model as the term often implies. Since the outsourcing field appears to be so full of anecdotal evidence, any generalized mathematical analysis (e.g., chi-square tests, Snedector's F test, Student's t test—see, for example, Ref. 11) qualifies, in our opinion, for the label "analytical."

†Refer to the next chapter for a more technology-based discussion.

Readers who do not have the adequate analytical background in statistics and differential equations may choose to skip portions of this chapter on first reading.

4.1 Overview

Outsourcing, originally an outgrowth of professional services and timesharing in the 1960s, now covers nearly all areas of IT, as follows:[7]

- Information processing services, such as data entry, transaction processing, and back-office clerical tasks; these well-defined production tasks require little interaction between the organization and the outsourcer.

- Contract programming, such as application development and maintenance, systems analysis, design, programming, testing, implementation, training, and possibly system porting and conversion.

- Facilities management, that is, the responsibility for operation and support of a computer system or data center, including support of all hardware, software, networking, and human resources.

- System integration, that is, the development of a fully integrated system (hardware, software, and communication) from the design phase through the implementation and handoff phase.

- Support operations, such as maintenance, disaster recovery, training and education, help desk, PC support, etc.

As can be seen from this list, outsourcing covers the spectrum of IS: from leasing an entire IS department, to having a few programmers develop applications, to having contract clerks enter non-real-time corporate data. A 1992 study conducted at MIT's Sloan School of Management, using data supplied by CIOs at 200 *Fortune* 500 manufacturing and service firms, showed the following three results:[12]

1. Cost remains a primary factor in the outsourcing decision.
2. Outsourcing follows an "emulative pattern" after a large deal is announced.
3. Investors generally react favorably to outsourcing plans, especially when cost considerations are high.

Two concepts come into play in a discussion of outsourcing: markets and hierarchies. Markets coordinate the flow of materials or services through *supply and demand forces* and external transactions between different firms: When goods or services are to be bought, the available offerings from many sources are compared.[10] However, many large organizations, which are hierarchical in structure, often own the resources to produce what they need: goods or services come from a predetermined supplier, not from a group of suppliers. With regard to data processing, in the past, large organizations have operated primarily using hierarchies, since applications have been developed largely by a predetermined supplier, the data processing group. This bureaucratic approach may not engender the type and amount of cooperation needed to reach goals efficiently, accounting for part of the slowness with which in-house-developed systems come about.[13]

Technology has changed organizations in such a way that fewer layers are necessary: Information no longer needs to go through management channels, since it is readily accessible to all over an E-mail or similar system. Now there are *cluster organizations* within companies. Cluster organizations are groups of people who get together for the purpose of solving business problems or defining processes together; once they are done, the group disbands. There is also an evolution to a *flatter structure* with knowledge at the bottom, where the specialists are situated. One sees *value-adding partnerships,* which consist of groups of independent companies working together to deliver a final product. There are *spider's web organizations* which have independent or coordinated nodes, depending on the problem, all of which are connected because of the need to be in touch with information or resources of other nodes.

Outsourcing is part of these reengineering trends. In effect, outsourcing is a shift towards the market in order to get work done. Because organizations have existing systems and their corresponding IS groups, eliminating everything and rebuilding from the ground up to meet the need for rapid systems development is unrealistic. Besides the expense of such a change, there would be resistance from IS personnel who have established power bases derived from traditional centralized computing; therefore, companies have continued with their fundamental transaction processing systems and have gone to the market for certain types of work. This means getting work developed by people outside of the company.[10]

An organization's success at major IS outsourcing depends on a variety of factors. Among these one can list corporate structure and philosophy, corporate culture, IS strengths and weaknesses, the position of the IS function in Nolan's stage model and in Dickson's hierarchy (discussed later), the extent of end-user computing, and the contract that is envisioned. Given these normative factors, an ideal outsourcing situation is one in which the organization itself is not vertically integrated and can be characterized as being closed/stable/mechanistic. The specific application to be outsourced should be nonstrategic, mature (in the control stage in Nolan's model), at the clerical or information reporting level, and not directly involved in end-user computing.[9] These concepts are explained below. (Contract aspects are covered in Sec. 4.5.)

Corporate structure and philosophy.   A vertically integrated organization is one that owns or (closely) controls the entire development of the product and its constituent elements. An organization that is vertically integrated may be philosophically unable to give up control of a large portion of the IS function. This type of organization depends on the symbiotic integration of all departments of the organization. A management's decision to outsource IS functions in a vertically integrated firm should include a careful review of the implications.

Corporate culture.   Organizations have intrinsic cultures. Two cultures at polar extremes can be characterized as follows[9]:

- *Open/adaptive/organic (OAO) culture.*   The organization is oriented toward problem solving and frequent change.
- *Closed/stable/mechanistic (CSM) culture.*   The organization carries out rigid activities as efficiently as possible.

OAO culture is typical of small companies, while CSM culture is typical of large, bureaucratic companies. IS functions in a CSM organization can be outsourced relatively easily, since such functions are presumably unchanging and require efficiency. IS functions in an OAO organization will change frequently, and outsourcing may be too expensive because of these frequent changes. Most organizations fall between these two extremes. The IS manager should assess, to the extent possible, where the organization fits on the OAO/CSM continuum and proceed accordingly.

IS strengths and weaknesses.   Outsourcing is a solution to a corporate IS efficiency/cost problem; for outsourcing to be effective, the IS area being outsourced should not be related to a strategic business area. The risk of "missing out on a potential competitive advantage through outsourcing is great."[9] Areas that hold strategic promise need to be correlated with IS strengths so that the IS organization has the technology and the expertise to enable the organization to move ahead of the competition. The IS manager considering outsourcing should determine which are the organization's areas of strategic business strength (and where are the weaknesses), and proceed accordingly. Effectively, the organization must decide what is the optimal degree of outsourcing: 100 percent outside, 0 percent outside (that is, 100 percent inside), or an appropriate mixture of the two.

Nolan's stage model. Nolan's stage model can be a useful device for planning information systems.[13] It postulates three stages, initiation, contagion, and control, which are followed by a technology shift. Initiation is characterized by the development of initial applications of a technology; it requires intimate knowledge of both the technology and the organization where the technology is to be deployed. Contagion is characterized by the spread of these technologies/applications throughout the organization and the introduction of some controls over the technology; it requires knowledge of the organization and its peculiarities. Control is characterized by little new development or spread; at this stage, applications are simply used in production mode and rules are followed. The IS manager considering outsourcing should first determine which of Nolan's stages best represents the function to be outsourced. Of the three stages, it should be clear that the control stage is the least organization-specific; hence, these functions are the ones that can be most easily and effectively outsourced.

Dickson's hierarchy. Dickson's hierarchy provides yet another way of looking at systems in an organization.[14] The hierarchy describes a progression of information systems, from the lowest-level clerical systems, through information-reporting systems and decision support systems, to expert systems at the highest level. Systems at the lowest two levels, clerical and information-reporting, are the easiest to outsource, being stable and well-defined; in fact, clerical systems such as payroll have been outsourced for many years. Decision support and expert systems are more difficult to outsource because they require more extensive knowledge of the particular group or organization. The IS manager should classify the systems under consideration, determine where they fit in the hierarchy, and proceed accordingly.

Extent of end-user computing. An organization that has a lot of end-user computing may have difficulty in trying to outsource such systems. The IS manager may want to concentrate on those systems that are centrally run and maintained. If the decision is made to outsource systems that directly cross the end-user computing boundary, the IS manager should ensure that these changes are transparent to the user.

4.2 Generic Modeling

Outsourcing can be examined analytically at three levels: the economy, the industry, and the organization.

- *Economy.* The temporal effects of trends and cycles may motivate organizations to rationalize the management of resources via outsourcing.

- *Industry.* Competitive pressures may motivate organizations to establish partnerships with industry vendors.

- *Organization.* The search for a competitive advantage may serve as a critical decision for outsourcing.

The analysis that follows focuses on organizational dynamics. This is important because some managers like to build empires by accumulating control over corporate resources, and the association of information with power may inhibit a process of global optimization (for example, through outsourcing) rather than local optimization.[1,15]

Since outsourcing is a multidimensional problem, it is possible to construct a variety of models to attempt to study it. Here we present a framework based on two variables:[1]

1. The degree of internalization of physical resources by the organization

2. The degree of internalization of the human resources the organization requires to support the physical resources

See Fig. 4.1. It is immediately clear that points in this two-dimensional space have associated cost metrics (some of which were identified in Chap. 1 at the component level): high internalization of physical resources implies costs in physical maintenance, power, air conditioning, physical security, etc.; high internalization of human resources implies direct payroll, benefits, training, office space, etc.

Figure 4.2 depicts four possible scenarios of resource management for a given corporate task, say IT. In strategy S1, the organization basically runs its own operations in a "business-as-usual" manner. This necessitates the acquisition of physical resources to support the task (say, mainframes) and the availability of an internal staff to manage the corporate resources. The other three strategies represent various outsourcing approaches.

In strategy S2, the organization retains its own resources, but uses a staff that is not part of the organization to run the function, say a data center operation. For example, the staff could be supplied by a "temp" agency or an outsourcer. The advantage of this approach is that the organization still has physical ownership of the equipment; this implies that it has greater control of how the equipment is used, and it may be able to benefit from factors such as depreciation, salvage value, etc. However, employee issues (salary administration, benefits, hiring/firing, training and retraining, etc.) are offloaded. The

Degree of internalization
of human resources

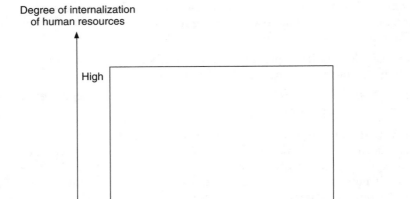

Figure 4.1   A two-dimensional model of outsourcing.

disadvantage of this approach is the continued management of the physical resources: daily well-being (security, power, air conditioning, space, etc.), mid-range planning (capacity planning, equipment acquisition, vendor negotiations, integration, etc.), and longer-term technology transition planning.

Strategy S3 is a complete outsourcing arrangement in which both the physical facilities and the human resources are surrendered to the outsourcing vendor. The advantages result from relinquishing most of the oversight functions (some oversight is still required to assure conformance to stipulated performance metrics). The complete lack of direct control may have some disadvantages, particularly in the longer term, when the business climate might change to some degree.

In strategy S4, the organization has given up the physical resources but has kept the people to run these resources. This is typical of a lease situation in which the equipment is owned, on the books, by a third party; however, for all intents and purposes, the organization maintains the equipment (consider, for example, a consumer car lease).

In addition to these clear-cut strategies, there will also be hybrid arrangements: perhaps only a portion of the physical resources will

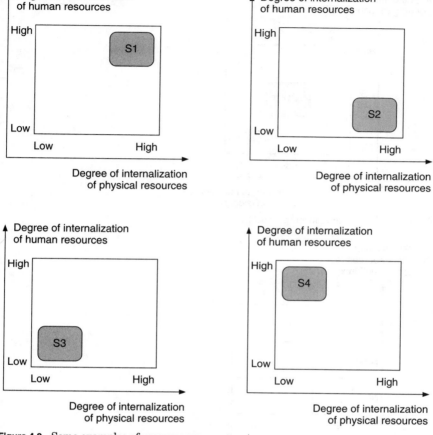

Figure 4.2 Some examples of resource management.

be taken over by an outsourcer (say, the outsourcer will take over the mainframe but not departmental and/or client-server systems). See Fig. 4.3.

This discussion leads to a tripartite decision space, as shown in Fig. 4.4.

Although various functions within a larger function (say, network management within the umbrella of IT) are not totally independent of one another, the decision that the corporate manager is called to make will be a multidimensional one, as seen in Fig. 4.5.

Even looking at just two functions (say, data processing and telecommunications), there are four variables (see Fig. 4.6) and 81 possible strategies (see Table 4.1). S01 is no outsourcing at all; S81 is complete outsourcing.

Degree of internalization
of human resources

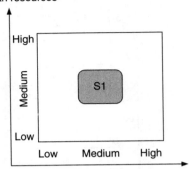

Degree of internalization
of physical resources

Figure 4.3 Hybrid outsourcing strategy.

Retention of
human resources to
support function x

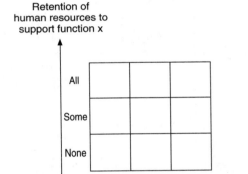

Retention of
physical resources to
support function x

Figure 4.4 Tripartite decision space for outsourcing
a given organizational function.

It is also possible to look at outsourcing in another way. First recall that outsourcing of a function may entail outsourcing of a number of subcomponents. For example, if one has the equation

$$IT = \{mainframe\ operations\} \cup \{client\text{-}server\ operations\}$$

$$\cup \{LAN\ networking\} \cup \{WAN\ networking\}$$

$$\cup \{application\ development\} \cup \{system\ integration\} \cup etc.$$

one can outsource any combination of one or more components. These components have different domains of influence within the organiza-

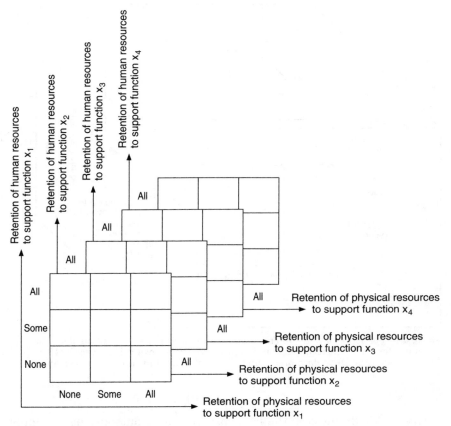

Figure 4.5 Multidimensional decision making for outsourcing.

tion. *Domain of influence* refers to the extent to which a component is inherent in the core business activity of the organization, as well as the administrative and functional coordination involved. For example, outsourcing the WAN usually affects the corporation to a large degree—that is, at a "general domain" level—while outsourcing application development affects only a specific department of the organization—that is, at a "specific domain" level. (Note, however, that given a specific component, this variable is not something that the IS manager must make a decision about; hence, it is not like the two outsourcing variables discussed above or the one discussed next.) Different contractual terms exist for outsourcing. For example, application development outsourcing may be project-based, and data center operations outsourcing may be period-based. Figure 4.7 depicts how typical IT components map to this coordinate system.

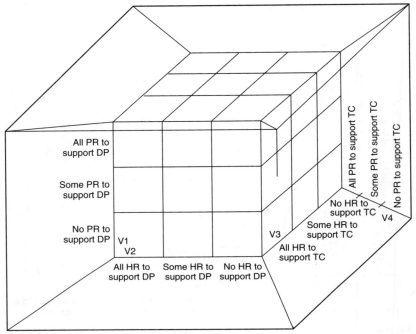

Figure 4.6 Portion of a four-dimensional cube (hypercube) showing four decision variables for a two-function outsourcing problem. PR = physical resources; HR = human resources; DP = data processing; TC = telecommunications; V = variable.

Given this discussion, the basic premise of IT outsourcing is simple enough: An organization should periodically reassess its corporate IT processes to determine if they are still relevant and effective. If a task is found to still be relevant, then it should be determined if this task is better done in-house or by an external firm that specializes in the task. The major decision factors are relative cost advantage (using, for example, the techniques discussed in Chap. 3) given economies of scale and outsourcer's specialization, and the nonmonetary impact on the organization. Tasks that have a more general corporate domain will be more difficult to analyze, implement, and manage from an outsourcing perspective. Contractual modes and degree of reallocation of human and physical resources need to be included in the decision process. In principle, outsourcers provide increased efficiency because of economies of scale and improved knowledge, skills, and capacity based on the fact that they pool resources and serve multiple clients. However, these potential advantages need to be analytically demonstrated in the specific organization in question.

TABLE 4.1   Decision Points for a Two-Function Outsourcing Decision

Strategy	PR retention for DP	HR retention for DP	PR retention for TC	HR retention for TC
S01	All	All	All	All
S02	All	All	All	Some
S03	All	All	All	None
S04	All	All	Some	All
S05	All	All	Some	Some
S06	All	All	Some	None
S07	All	All	None	All
S08	All	All	None	Some
S09	All	All	None	None
S10	All	Some	All	All
S11	All	Some	All	Some
S12	All	Some	All	None
S13	All	Some	Some	All
S14	All	Some	Some	Some
S15	All	Some	Some	None
S16	All	Some	None	All
S17	All	Some	None	Some
S18	All	Some	None	None
S19	All	None	All	All
S20	All	None	All	Some
S21	All	None	All	None
S22	All	None	Some	All
S23	All	None	Some	Some
S24	All	None	Some	None
S25	All	None	None	All
S26	All	None	None	Some
S27	All	None	None	None
S28	Some	All	All	All
S29	Some	All	All	Some
S30	Some	All	All	None
S31	Some	All	Some	All
S32	Some	All	Some	Some
S33	Some	All	Some	None
S34	Some	All	None	All
S35	Some	All	None	Some
S36	Some	All	None	None
S37	Some	Some	All	All
S38	Some	Some	All	Some
S39	Some	Some	All	None
S40	Some	Some	Some	All
S41	Some	Some	Some	Some
S42	Some	Some	Some	None
S43	Some	Some	None	All
S44	Some	Some	None	Some
S45	Some	Some	None	None
S46	Some	None	All	All
S47	Some	None	All	Some
S48	Some	None	All	None
S49	Some	None	Some	All
S50	Some	None	Some	Some

TABLE 4.1   Decision Points for a Two-Function Outsourcing Decision (*Continued*)

Strategy	PR retention for DP	HR retention for DP	PR retention for TC	HR retention for TC
S51	Some	None	Some	None
S52	Some	None	None	All
S53	Some	None	None	Some
S54	Some	None	None	None
S55	None	All	All	All
S56	None	All	All	Some
S57	None	All	All	None
S58	None	All	Some	All
S59	None	All	Some	Some
S60	None	All	Some	None
S61	None	All	None	All
S62	None	All	None	Some
S63	None	All	None	None
S64	None	Some	All	All
S65	None	Some	All	Some
S66	None	Some	All	None
S67	None	Some	Some	All
S68	None	Some	Some	Some
S69	None	Some	Some	None
S70	None	Some	None	All
S71	None	Some	None	Some
S72	None	Some	None	None
S73	None	None	All	All
S74	None	None	All	Some
S75	None	None	All	None
S76	None	None	Some	All
S77	None	None	Some	Some
S78	None	None	Some	None
S79	None	None	None	All
S80	None	None	None	Some
S81	None	None	None	None

4.3   A Factor Analysis of Outsourcing

Because of the high dimensionality of an outsourcing decision, it would be desirable to have a macro model that would provide some generic guidance to the organization contemplating outsourcing. While a complex financial analysis based on the principles discussed in Chap. 3 is possible, and ultimately necessary, a macro model can provide a more intuitive tool for the early stages of decision making. Although outsourcing can affect tens of billions of dollars a year (say, a quarter of a trillion dollars in the next seven years, from press time to 1999), as already noted, the analytical literature is scant at best. Factor analysis can be employed to study the problem. This section provides a synopsis of one of the few analyses that have been reported;[1] the reader is referred to the paper itself for more details.

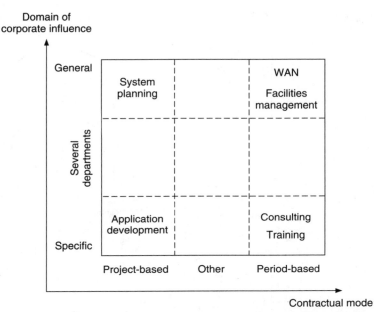

Figure 4.7 Mapping IT components. *Note:* The domain dimension is not the decision variable upon which the IS manager must decide; the contractual mode is.

The model studied is shown in Fig. 4.8. Table 4.2 lists key questions that a senior manager may be asking and that the model can answer using actual data. Answering questions such as these in a manner that has statistical credibility requires both valid data and analytical modeling. Reference 1 documents the extensive data that went into the analysis.

The measure of interest is

$$Y = \beta_0 + \beta_1 X_1 + \beta_2 X_2 + \beta_3 X_3 + \beta_4 X_4 + \beta_5 X_5 + \beta_6 X_6 + \beta_7 X_7 + \varepsilon$$

where
Y = degree of outsourcing (ratio of IT outsourcing expenditures to total expenditures)
X_1 = business cost structure (sum of cost of all goods sold and associated expenses divided by sum of net sales and total assets)
X_2 = business performance (return on assets and earnings per share)
X_3 = financing leverage (ratio of long-term debt and total liabilities to shareholder equity)
X_4 = IT cost structure (ratio of IT expenditures to both gross property, plant, and equipment before depreciation and net property, plant, and equipment after depreciation)
X_5 = IT performance (ratio of net income and sales to IT expenditure)

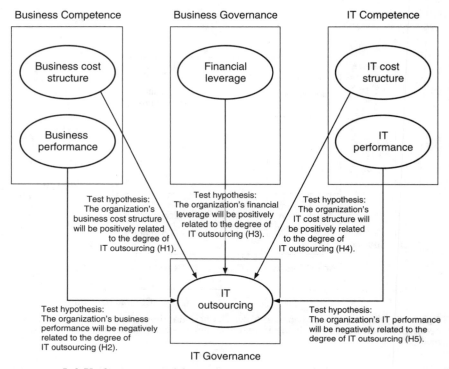

Figure 4.8 Loh/Venkatraman model.

X_6 = business size (control variable)
X_7 = industry (control variable)
ε = error

The detailed analysis shown in Ref. 1, based on actual data on 200 U.S. corporations, shows that Q1, Q4, and Q5 are answered empirically in the positive (the hypotheses are accepted), while Q2 and Q3 cannot be answered empirically in the positive (the hypotheses cannot be accepted). The results are interpreted as follows:

Q1.   There is a demonstrable positive relationship between the organization's cost structure and outsourcing. In other words, high costs usually motivate an organization to review its infrastructure in an effort to improve its business efficiency.

Q2.   There was no demonstrable negative relationship between business performance and outsourcing. Business performance is therefore not a primary factor in outsourcing, being too "remote" a factor.

TABLE 4.2 **Key Macro Questions about Outsourcing**

Key question	Observations
Q1: Will the organization's business cost structure be positively or negatively affected by the degree of IT outsourcing?	An organization's business cost structure affects its profitability. Companies are continuously challenged to increase output and reduce costs. IT is now central to an organization's ability to produce; however, it also has a major cost impact, as discussed in Chap. 1. Outsourcing can often reduce IT costs.
Q2: Will the organization's business performance be positively or negatively affected by the degree of IT outsourcing?	When business performance is low, management is under pressure to streamline the organization's operations, including divesting or redeploying assets. Business restructuring to improve profitability is driving the movement to IT outsourcing (as well as other types of outsourcing) or, better yet, reengineering.
Q3: Will the organization's financial leverage be positively or negatively affected by the degree of IT outsourcing?	The desire or need to reduce debt has been identified as one of the drivers for outsourcing. Debt and equity are two business governance paradigms: Debt is more appropriate for financing redeployment of assets, while equity is more appropriate for nonredeployable assets. IT assets are generally nonredeployable; therefore debt is not the optimal strategy in the IT context, and high company debt has given rise to the need to reduce nonredeployable assets through outsourcing.
Q4: Will the organization's IT cost structure be positively or negatively affected by the degree of IT outsourcing?	Because of the high outlays associated with IT (as discussed in Chap. 1), organizations are searching for better cost control. In turn, organizations have restructured IT by altering the paradigm of in-house operation in an attempt to free up capital that is tied up in data center hardware and reduce (or eliminate) operating costs.
Q5: Will the organization's IT performance be positively or negatively affected by the degree of IT outsourcing?	Organizations are making IS a profit/loss center. In turn, profit-based operation has put pressure on IS to show measurable payback. Given the vital importance of IT in most organizations, redesign (such as moving to client-server arrangements) and restructuring are taking place.

Q3. There was no demonstrable positive relationship between financial leverage and outsourcing. Financial leverage is therefore not a primary factor in outsourcing, being too "remote" a factor.

Q4. There is a demonstrable positive relationship between IT cost structure and outsourcing. Since IT costs keep increasing, organizations are finding it necessary to consider cost-management strategies such as outsourcing. This finding is consistent with the prevailing view about the need to rationalize IT costs (see the introductory paragraph of this chapter) in order to improve competitive posture. As mentioned in Chap. 1, savings in the 15 to 20 percent range are generally feasible.

Q5. There is a demonstrable negative relationship between IT performance and outsourcing: Low economic returns on IT investments affect the likelihood of organizations' outsourcing.

Additionally, neither the business size nor the industry segment, which served as control variables, emerged as a significant factor. This is somewhat surprising, since the trade press would seem to imply (at the superficial level) that mid-size companies and certain industry segments are more prone to outsourcing; however, a rational review of the data included in Ref. 1 did not support these hypotheses. Figure 4.9 depicts the resulting relationships. As a final note,

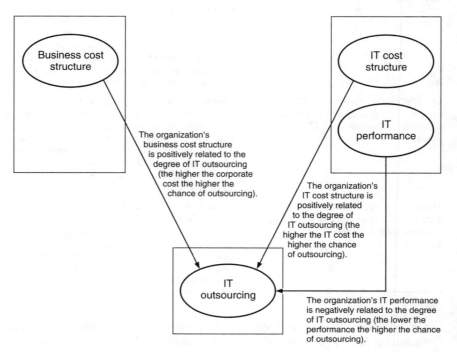

Figure 4.9 Empirical relationships affecting outsourcing.

Ref. 1 proposes possible extensions of this analysis to provide additional insight.

4.4 A Success Factors Model for Outsourcing Assistance

For the purpose of illustrating the type of modeling that can be undertaken in assessing outsourcing decisions, this section provides a path analysis of the behavior of organizations and external consultants. The model looks at interactions which influence project success in selecting an IS system. The supporting study included a pilot case study, a cross-sectional analysis of five firms, an a-priori model, and a quantitative survey of 49 applications to validate the model.[8] This type of analysis is applicable to system integration and application development outsourcing. Again, the goal is to reinforce the need for analytical methods in decision making.

Figure 4.10 depicts the consultant-engagement model. Table 4.3 lists the questions that the model aims at answering analytically.[8] Intuitively, the answer to all these questions would seem to be yes; however, analytical support adds strength to the associated decisions. Ultimately, the organization needs to focus on these classical aspects of the consultant/outsourcer relationship, among others:[16]

- Learning to engage consultants/outsourcers more effectively

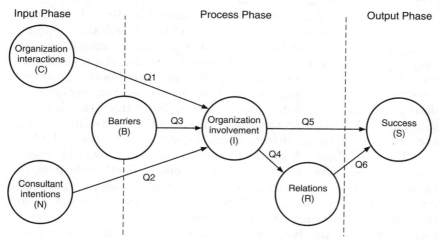

Figure 4.10 Gable/Sharp model for analytical analysis relating to consultation-based outsourcing.

TABLE 4.3   Questions for Analytical Analysis Relating to Consultation-Based Outsourcing

Q1: Will the organization's involvement be higher if the organization's intention to be involved is stronger?

Q2: Will the organization's involvement be higher if the consultant's intention to facilitate organization involvement is stronger?

Q3: Will the organization's involvement be lower when there are barriers to the organization's involvement?

Q4: Are organization-consultant relations positively associated with organization involvement?

Q5: Will engagement success be positively associated with organization involvement?

Q6: Will engagement success be positively associated with organization-consultant relations?

- Assessing the appropriateness of the level of the organization's dependence on the consultant/outsourcer
- Justifying further use or curtailment of the use of the consultant/outsourcer
- Assessing the impact of the engagement on the organization

It turns out that when it comes to application selection (and sometimes even system integration), a fairly large percentage of the organizations is found to terminate the consultation relationship after the initial selection process for reasons such as the following: Vendor support is found to be adequate and the task is completed, better understanding of the application/system is developed by direct involvement with the implementation phase, the cost of the consultant is found to be high, or the organization is dissatisfied with the consultant. The model can be used to study methods of improving the organization-consultant (outsourcer) relationship. It is presented here primarily to illustrate the type of analysis that is advocated in studying organization/outsourcer relationships, and secondarily for the intrinsic results that can be derived from the data. (The data themselves may change over time, but the analytical machinery may continue to be valid.)

As Fig. 4.10 shows, there are six constructs in the model: (1) organization's intentions to be involved; (2) consultant's intentions to involve the client organization; (3) barriers to organization's involvement; (4) organization's involvement; (5) organization-consultant relations; and (6) engagement success. The model is composed of three stages: the involvement stage, the relations stage, and the success stage.

The data for the study originated from the Small Enterprise Computerization Program (SECP), which is a Singapore government program to encourage and assist local businesses to become more competitive through the introduction of IT. Valid data from 35 registered consultants pertaining to 49 projects are used in the model.

Organization and consultant intentions are measured using the theory of reasoned action, a widely employed model of human behavior.[17] The model is tested using hierarchical regression and path analysis (regression employs stepwise selection of independent variables). The analysis is reported in a tabular form that lists appropriate statistics (R^2, adjusted R^2, the standard error, and significance of the F statistic) and details of the independent variable contained in the regression equation (the regression coefficient, b; the standard error of the regression coefficient, SE b; the standardized regression coefficient, ß; the Student's t statistic for the standardized regression coefficient, t; the observed two-tailed significance level of the t statistic, Sig t; the Pearson correlation coefficient between the independent variable and the dependent variable, r; and the significance of r, Sig r.[16] Normal probability plots of the standardized residuals and standardized scatterplots of predicted values against residuals are part of such analysis. A discussion of regression analysis can be found in most college-level texts on statistics.

Regression analysis

Organization involvement. Referring to Fig. 4.10, one has

$$I = b_0 + b_1C + b_2N + b_3B + \varepsilon$$

The study indicated that $b_0 = 3.79$, $b_1 = 0.28$, $b_2 = 0.22$, $b_3 = 0.48$; the standardized ßs are 0.30, 0.35, and 0.26, respectively; and the correlation terms are 0.38, 0.38, and 0.36, respectively. Taken together, organization intentions, consultant intentions, and barriers account for 35 percent of the variance in involvement (this corresponds to the adjusted R^2 term).

Organization-consultant relations. Referring to Fig. 4.10, one has

$$R = b_0 + b_1I + \varepsilon$$

The study indicated that $b_0 = -0.20$, $b_1 = 0.95$; the standardized ß is 0.84; and the correlation term is 0.84. Involvement accounts for 70 percent of the variance in relations.

Engagement success. Referring to Figure 4.10, one has

$$S = b_0 + b_1I + b_2R + \varepsilon$$

The study indicated that $b_0 = 2.06$, $b_1 = -0.07$, $b_2 = 0.55$; the standardized ßs are -0.09 and 0.88, respectively; and the correlation terms are 0.64 and 0.80, respectively. Involvement has a nonsignificant beta coefficient of -0.12, while the beta coefficient for relations is 0.88. Together they contribute 63 percent of the variance in success.

Path analysis. A path analysis enables one to decompose correlations between the model variables into direct and indirect effects.[18] The ability to quantitatively distinguish direct from indirect effects enhances the interpretation of relations as well as interpretation of the pattern of the effects of variables on one another. The path coefficients p_{ij} represent direct effects, where the first coefficient represents the effect (the dependent variable) and the second coefficient represents the cause (the independent variable). An indirect effect is the effect of one variable on another via a mediating variable. The sum of the two effects is called the total effect.

The independent variables are defined to be organization intentions, consultant intentions, and barriers. The dependent variables are involvement, relations, and success (these correspond to the three stages of the regression model discussed above). Figure 4.11 depicts the path coefficients for the model of Fig. 4.10. The path values p_{ij} correspond with the normalized beta values of the regression analysis. Within the circle representing each of the dependent variables in Fig. 4.11, one finds the value R^2 from the regression analysis. Path coefficients are indicated by solid arrows (correlation coefficients between independent variables are shown by dotted arrows).

As an initial step, one must verify that the model fits the empirical data. This is done in Ref. 8 using Specht's Q statistics. The next step is to decompose the correlations between the model variables. The correlations are decomposed into direct, indirect, spurious, and unexplained effects. Direct and indirect effects are summed to yield total effects. The reader is referred to Ref. 8 for more details of the statistical techniques used in the study.

Answer to questions. The analysis summarized above enables one to answer numerically the questions posed in Table 4.3. The analysis shows that the answers to all questions except Q5 are in the affirmative. Hence, the organization's involvement will be higher, the stronger the organization's intention to be involved. The organization's involvement will be higher, the stronger the consultant's intention to involve the organization. The organization's involvement will be lower where barriers to organization involvement exist. These observations are not just common sense but are "proved" in Ref. 8 using empirical data.

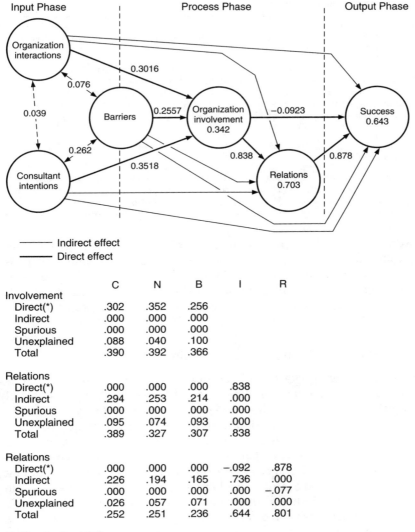

	C	N	B	I	R
Involvement					
Direct(*)	.302	.352	.256		
Indirect	.000	.000	.000		
Spurious	.000	.000	.000		
Unexplained	.088	.040	.100		
Total	.390	.392	.366		
Relations					
Direct(*)	.000	.000	.000	.838	
Indirect	.294	.253	.214	.000	
Spurious	.000	.000	.000	.000	
Unexplained	.095	.074	.093	.000	
Total	.389	.327	.307	.838	
Relations					
Direct(*)	.000	.000	.000	−.092	.878
Indirect	.226	.194	.165	.736	.000
Spurious	.000	.000	.000	.000	−.077
Unexplained	.026	.057	.071	.000	.000
Total	.252	.251	.236	.644	.801

(*) Standardized β terms.

Figure 4.11   Path analysis.

The implications of these findings are that while the organization's proactive intentions do lead to an increased level of involvement, the consultant/outsourcer has an equally important role in making the relationship work; barriers also have a significant impact on the organization's ability to get involved in the project. Table 4.4 further expands on the results of this study.

TABLE 4.4 Analytically Demonstrated Results

Organizations need to develop an appreciation of the ways in which a consultant/outsourcer may consciously or unconsciously exclude them from the project and respond accordingly.

Organizations must attempt to maximize compatibility with the consultant/outsourcer (or avoid major incompatibility) by involving appropriate organization staff to work with specific consultant staff. Efforts need to be made to develop and maintain workable relationships throughout the contract's life. Since the initial contract may not cover all possible contingencies, good relations are needed to reach an appropriate understanding and/or compromises.

Organizations should, to the degree possible, maximize involvement, as this builds good relations.

The consultant/outsourcer needs to assess the intentions of the organization—a low level of intentions may suggest that inappropriate individuals (or staff, e.g., unmotivated staff) may have been selected to represent the organization's interest in the project.

Besides the fairly intuitive results, this discussion points to the desirability of using analytical tools to provide some rational justification for what may be a billion-dollar corporate decision. It appears to us that a basic analytical examination should not be omitted for lack of resources in a decision of such monetary scope and deep corporate influence.

4.5 Contracting Modeling for Outsourcing

Contracting frameworks have been developed to examine the merits of outsourcing IS application development tasks. Such an analysis of incomplete contracts (see Chap. 3) is undertaken in Ref. 3; the analysis is summarized in this section to reinforce the need for quantitative assessments of outsourcing.* Contracts, or agreements between the organization's IS department and the outsourcer, play a critical role in outsourcing, as they specify the terms of the transactions among the parties. For new system development, the contract specifies the developer's responsibilities, the system completion date, the system's cost, and the organization's responsibility. However, these contracts are often incomplete; they do not specify every possible contingency a priori.

Application development can be seen as a series of exchanges between the development group and the user group. These exchanges represent interactions supporting the definition, design, or delivery of a particular subsystem; other transactions include enhancements and modifications to an existing application. The development group can

---

*Material from Ref. 3 was included in this section with permission of Prof. A. Whinston, University of Texas at Austin.

be the organization's IS department or an outside firm; correspondingly, the user group can be a client department in the organization (when insourcing) or the IS organization (when outsourcing). In what follows, the design group is equated with the outsourcer and the user group is equated with the organization's IS department.

The modeling effort investigates the effects of information asymmetry (where the organization and the outsourcer may not have the same data on which to evaluate the process), and the effects of different rules for profit-sharing between the organization and the outsourcer, on the decision of whether to outsource or to use an internal development team. The analysis indicates that the advantage generated from outsourcing an application development effort comes primarily from the specific investments (Chap. 3) made by the external group (the outsourcer), and that outsourcing dominates internal development (insourcing) when these investments are relatively more important than investments by the organization in order to do the job in-house. This type of analysis provides an explanation for the coexistence of both internal development teams and various outsourcing services.

4.5.1 Contract theories, IS context

Using contract theory, briefly covered in Chap. 3, as a foundation for studying the issues facing IS in general and application development in particular affords the following benefits:[3]

1. Contract theory can form a basis for creating models that provide insights into the outsourcing issues facing the IS manager. These models can help one understand why a firm outsources its facilities management but may insource some of its application development functions. Contract theory enables one to focus on the incentive issues involved in managing the IS function: Incentives are necessary for motivating the people involved in executing the IS functions, and these incentives play a significant role in facilitating the interaction between the organization and the outsourcer's development group.

2. The models, theories, and predictions can be tested by empirical studies and data, as was done in the previous sections. Combining the analytical models with empirical validation provides reliable decision methodologies for corporate and IS managers. (Related theoretical models have been subject to empirical tests for other areas of the firm, e.g., outsourcing accounts receivable functions.)

Contracting issues come about when a firm must decide whether to undertake a function as part of its internal operations or to outsource it. For IS, tasks under possible scrutiny include developing, maintaining, and operating various hardware and software systems, all of which can be either outsourced or undertaken internally. Drivers for such an investigation include technological economies, market imperfections, and transaction economies. In economic theory parlance,[3]

1. Technological economies occur when the production frontier is greater. It is possible to achieve economies of scale for hardware, software, management, and other IS functions. (This topic is reexamined in the next chapter.)

2. Market imperfections arise from imperfect competition, externalities, and imperfect and/or asymmetric information.

3. Transaction economies occur when the cost of the exchange process is lower internally than in the market. These costs include those of writing and enforcing the contract, communication, coordination, and monitoring.

The treatment below takes the transaction cost economics perspective discussed in Chap. 3. The model from Ref. 3 discussed here assesses the role of transaction economies in the development of customized applications, where there is a series of interrelated transactions and associated investments. These transactions are carried out under a contractual arrangement. One wants to examine the effects of asymmetric information and different sharing rules when determining the optimal amount of specific investment (zero specific investment would imply outsourcing). It was also mentioned elsewhere in this text that there is a general concern about the outsourcer's lack of specific knowledge regarding an organization; consequently, a contracting policy for application development that is aimed at inducing the software developer and the organization to make specific investments is needed.

4.5.2 Model

Application software development often requires a substantial amount of resources. Such applications can be developed in-house or outsourced. In many cases, software development becomes a source of dispute between the organization commissioning the software and the developers.

An application development project implies a series of exchanges between the development group and members of the organization. These exchanges must be properly managed to minimize costs associated with the effort. Consider a user group contemplating the installation of an application for a new business function. The contract between the user organization (or the IS organization) and the development group must specify the initial scope of the application and the terms for compensating the development group. The contract must also contain provisions for specifying how to decide whether to implement future modifications and for sharing the gains from the implemented enhancements. As is generally the case for decision support applications, design changes can be expected after the contract for the initial system has been written. These changes can occur during the development period or after system deployment. At the early stages of the system development process, it is impossible to identify all these changes, their value, and their cost. Therefore the organization cannot contract for the complete application (that is to say, the application resulting from the initial deployment plus all future enhancements). For example, the development group may be reluctant to agree to a fixed time or price contract that allows the organization to specify future enhancements or modifications loosely.[3]

Enhancements to applications frequently account for a significant portion of the applications' life-cycle cost. Specific investments made by the user group and the development group can raise the chances of identifying high-value enhancements and lower the cost of implementing these enhancements. However, the organizational form and the sharing rule both affect whether an enhancement will ultimately be implemented. The organizational form determines who can control a design change. There are (at least) two options: (1) employ a salaried, organization-controlled, in-house development team or (2) outsource the development effort (i.e., contract with an independent software developer). Under organization-controlled, in-house development, the organization decides unilaterally whether to implement an enhancement. Under outsourcing, both the organization requesting the enhancement and the outsourcer must agree on the nature of the enhancement. The external development team is assumed to be incentive-driven. If the organization perceives that the value of the enhancement is too low, it can forgo its implementation; similarly, if the outsourcer feels that the costs are too high, it can refuse to implement the enhancement. The sharing rule specifies the division of any monetary surplus for enhancements to the application between the organization and the outsourcer.

The model assumes a normalized case in which the initial cost of having an internal IS group develop the system is the same as that of outsourcing the system development. The analysis presented below examines how the sharing rule affects whether an enhancement will be implemented by influencing the level of specific investments made by both the organization and the outsourcer. Additionally, when there is asymmetric information, the sharing rule affects the expected value to the outsourcer and to the organization of concealing the true cost or value of the enhancement.

The value to the organization of implementing an enhancement is denoted by v, and the cost to the outsourcer of implementing an enhancement is denoted by c. The gross surplus is $v - c$. The enhancement's value v may turn out to be either high, v_H, or low, v_L. The cost c of implementing the enhancement may turn out to be either high, c_H, or low, c_L. By investing added effort, the organization's personnel can increase the probability that an enhancement will have the higher value, v_H. Similarly, the outsourcer can make specific investments to increase the probability that any future enhancement will entail a low cost, c_L. The organization's investment costs are given by $f(x)$, where $x = $ Prob $(v = v_H)$. The developer's investment costs are given by $g(y)$, where $y = $ Prob $(c = c_L)$. $f(x)$ and $g(y)$ are assumed to be strictly increasing convex functions; this implies that increasing the probability of a high enhancement value or a low enhancement cost turns out to be increasingly expensive. One can further assume that $f(x)$ and $g(y)$ are independent, so that the total cost of the specific investment to support an enhancement is $f(x) + g(y)$.

A two-stage model (contracting and development) can be employed to capture the sequential nature of the development process, as follows:[3]

- In period 0, the parties determine the sharing rule and the organization form. The model assumes that the developer and the organization know the functional form of $f(x)$ and $g(y)$ and the values v_H, v_L, c_H, and c_L; however, they do not know the cost of any specific enhancement.

- Next, the IS development process starts, and each party makes specific investments to increase the expected value of future enhancements to the system. In the next period, period 1, the organization identifies an enhancement opportunity and decides whether to implement that enhancement. The "gross surplus" from implementing any enhancement is then divided between the developer and the user.

The sharing rule allocates α portion ($0 \le \alpha \le 1$) of the resulting gross surplus $v_i - c_j$ to the organization, and the remaining $1 - \alpha$ to the outsourcer. This sharing rule leads to the following contract:

$$\text{Organization share} = \alpha (v_i - c_j) \quad \text{with } i, j \in \{H, L\}$$

$$\text{Outsourcer share} = (1 - \alpha) (v_i - c_j) \quad \text{with } i, j \in \{H, L\}$$

This sharing rule embodies incentives for the outsourcer. α is a measure of the organization's bargaining power. α close to 1 implies high bargaining power (in fact, for in-house development, $\alpha = 1$).

With outsourcing, the bargaining power is more evenly distributed between the two parties. Under these contractual arrangements, the organization should outsource when its net payoff (its share of the gains minus the cost of its specific investment) is higher under outsourcing than under internal development. Two cases can be examined:

1. Common knowledge of v and c
2. Asymmetric information

Common knowledge. This base case postulates that in period 1 the actual cost c_j and value v_i of the enhancement, with $i, j \in \{H, L\}$, are known to both parties. Such information is used to determine whether to implement a particular enhancement. Common knowledge of the cost and value precludes obfuscation by either party. The base case can be used to study the impact of minimizing information asymmetry, that is, improving communication. The gross expected gain from implementing an enhancement is[3]

$$E\{G(x, y)\} = \max [0, (v_H - c_L)]\, xy + \max [0, (v_L - c_L)](1 - x)y +$$
$$\max [0, (v_H - c_H)]\, x(1 - y) + \max [0, (v_L - c_H)](1 - x)(1 - y)$$

The organization's portion of the expected surplus minus its investment costs is given by

$$OS = \alpha E\{G(x, y)\} - f(x)$$

The developer's portion of the expected surplus minus its investments is given by

$$DS = (1 - \alpha)E\{G(x, y)\} - g(y)$$

The "local" optimized specific investment levels are obtained by solving the differential equations

$$\left(\frac{\delta}{\delta x}\right) OS = 0$$

or

$$\left(\frac{\delta}{\delta x}\right)[\alpha E\{G(x, y)\}) - f(x)] = 0$$

and

$$\left(\frac{\delta}{\delta y}\right) DS = 0$$

or

$$\left(\frac{\delta}{\delta y}\right)[(1 - \alpha)\, E\{G(x, y)\} - g(y)] = 0$$

The solutions are indicated as $x_\alpha{}^*$ (the organization's optimal investment level for α) and $y_\alpha{}^*$ (the outsourcer's optimal investment level for α).

Outsourcing is desirable (feasible) if it generates a positive surplus for the outsourcer and if the organization's surplus is greater than it would be under internal development; that is

$$DS \geq 0 \quad \text{and} \quad OS_{at\,\alpha < 1} \geq OS_{at\,\alpha = 1}$$

With an internal development group, all gains from implementing an enhancement accrue to the organization. This is the reference point that can be used by the organization to make the decision about outsourcing and/or bargain with an external developer.

The feasibility space can be partitioned into six subcases as follows:

Subcase 1: $c_L < c_H < v_L < v_H$

Subcase 2: $c_L < v_L < c_H < v_H$

Subcase 3: $v_L < c_L < c_H < v_H$

Subcase 4: $v_L < c_L < v_H < c_H$

Subcase 5: $c_L < v_L < v_H < c_H$

Subcase 6: $v_L < v_H < c_L < c_H$

Although it is possible to obtain closed-form solutions, they tend to be complex and do not offer any readily visible insight. Numerical methods can be employed to examine the effect of different parameter values on the outsourcing decision process.

Subcase 1: $c_L < c_H < v_L < v_H$ In this case, an enhancement will always be made because the value of an enhancement will always exceed its cost. As an example, if $f(x) = ax^2$ and $g(y) = by^2$, then one has[3]

$$E\{G(x, y)\} = (v_H - v_L)x + (c_H - c_L)y + (v_L - c_H)$$

$$OS = \alpha[(v_H - v_L)x + (c_H - c_L)y + (v_L - c_H)] - ax^2$$

$$DS = (1 - \alpha)[(v_H - v_L)x + (c_H - c_L)y + (v_L - c_H)] - by^2$$

$$x_\alpha{}^* = \min\left[1, \frac{\alpha(v_H - v_L)}{2a}\right]$$

$$y_\alpha{}^* = \min\left[1, \frac{(1 - \alpha)(c_H - c_L)}{2b}\right]$$

The level of α that leads to the highest total surplus (OS + DS) is

$$\alpha^* = \frac{2b(v_H - c_H)^2}{2b(v_H - c_H)^2 + 2a(c_H - c_L)^2}$$

Finally, one would choose outsourcing when the following condition is met:

$$\frac{(v_H - v_L)^2}{2a} + \frac{c_H - c_L}{2b} + (v_L - c_H) < \frac{(c_H - c_L)^2}{b}$$

As noted from these expressions, x_α^* grows linearly on α, which represents, by definition, the share of the organization's gain. The organization's specific investment also increases linearly on $(v_H - v_L)/2a$, which represents the value of its investment relative to the cost. The outsourcer's specific investment grows linearly on $(1 - \alpha)$ and on the relative cost of its investment, $(c_H - c_L)/2b$. Looking at the outsourcing criterion, it depends on v_H, v_L, a, c_H, c_L, and b: Outsourcing becomes desirable when the value of the outsourcer's investment relative to the cost of the investment is larger than the value of the organization's investment relative to its cost. For the chosen $f(x)$ and $g(y)$, the larger $c_H - c_L$ is relative to $v_H - v_L$, the more likely it is that the outsourcing decision will produce a larger surplus. For given values of c_H, c_L, v_H, and v_L, a function $g(y)$ such that $g(y) << f(x)$ (for equivalent values of x and y) will produce a larger organizational surplus with outsourcing than with internal development.

Figures 4.12 and 4.13 illustrate two examples. In the situation in

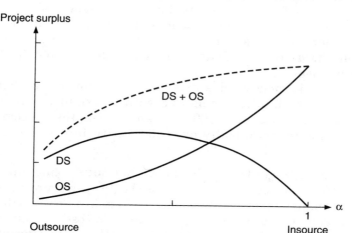

Project surplus

Figure 4.12 Internal development is always superior to outsourcing. $f(x) = 100x^2$; $g(y) = 500y^2$; $v_L = 210$; $v_H = 310$; $c_L = 150$; $c_H = 200$. *Notes:* (1) Organization surplus for internal development—35.00. (2) Internal development is optimal strategy since OS grows (monotonically) as α grows. (3) Outsourcer surplus grows to a maximum at $\alpha = 0.38$, then decreases. (4) $g(y) \geq f(x)$ for the same value of x and y. (5) Outsource—never; OS maximized at $\alpha = 1$.

Project surplus

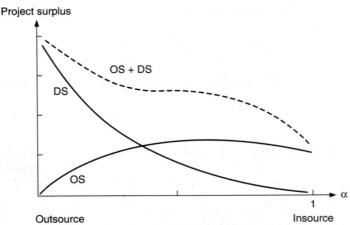

Figure 4.13 Outsourcing can be more beneficial than insourcing. $f(x) =$ $100x^2$; $g(y) = 100y^2$; $v_L = 300$; $v_H = 310$; $c_L = 190$; $c_H = 290$. *Notes:* (1) Organization surplus for internal development—10.25. (2) Outsourcing with right contract ($\alpha = 0.60$) is optimal strategy since OS is largest for that value. (3) Outsourcer surplus decreases monotonically. (4) $g(y) = f(x)$ for the same value of x and y.

Fig. 4.12, internal development (insourcing) is always superior to outsourcing. DS first increases even though the developer's (i.e., outsourcer's) share of the gains goes down because the organization's investment is increasing, making the gross surplus grow faster than the decrease resulting from the decreased share. At higher values of α, although the organization's investment is still increasing, it does not compensate for the decrease in the developer's (i.e., outsourcer's) investment and its decreasing share of the gains that are obtained with the enhancement.

In Fig. 4.13 there is some surplus with insourcing, but the surplus can be maximized with outsourcing and with the right contract arrangement (that is to say, $\alpha = 0.60$). As can be seen, the developer's surplus drops monotonically over the entire interval as α increases.

Subcase 2: $c_L < v_L < c_H < v_H$. The study shows that outsourcing often predominates. However, for a given $v_H - v_L$ and $c_H - c_L$, insourcing is more likely to dominate outsourcing when the organization's specific investment is relatively lower than the outsourcer's cost of making specific investments (this occurs when the organization's investment is low). As α increases, the organization's share of the gain increases faster than the total payback decreases, so that it is better for the organization to develop the application in-house.

Subcase 3: $v_L < c_L < c_H < v_H$. The study shows that in this case the enhancement is implemented if and only if it has a high value, that is, $v_i = v_H$. Insourcing often dominates. This follows from the fact that the organization must make specific investments for any surplus to occur, and to induce a high specific investment, the organizational share of the gain must be high (i.e., α is high). However, outsourcing was better when (1) $c_H - c_L$ was large relative to $v_H - c_H$ and (2) both parties' costs of making specific investments are low.

Subcase 4: $v_L < c_L < v_H < c_H$. In this case an enhancement is made only when its cost is low, that is, $c_j = c_L$. It follows that it is always advantageous for the organization to outsource, since the developer must make some specific investment for any surplus to occur.

Subcase 5: $c_L < v_L < v_H < c_H$. In this case an enhancement is made only when its cost is low and its value is high, that is, $c_j = c_L$ and $v_i = v_H$. It follows that it is always advantageous for the organization to outsource, since for $\alpha = 1$, the outsourcer will not have to make specific investments.

Subcase 6: $v_L < v_H < c_L < c_H$. In this case enhancements will not be made, since the cost of the enhancement always exceeds the value derived from that enhancement. Therefore the outsource/insource issue is moot.

Asymmetric information. Situations may exist in which there is a condition of asymmetric information. For example, both parties know the potential value of v_L, v_H, c_L, and c_H in the initial period (period 0); however, in the next period (period 1), the organization knows the actual value v_i (that is, if $v_i = v_L$ or $v_i = v_H$) but does not know the actual cost c_j, whereas the outsourcer knows the actual cost c_j (that is, if $c_j = c_L$ or $c_j = c_H$) but does not know the value v_i of the enhancement to the user. It is assumed that the a posteriori cost to the outsourcer and the a posteriori value to the organization are not verifiable, and therefore cannot be included as part of the contract. Yet, in spite of the uncertainty, a decision to implement the enhancement or not must be made.

One is interested on the impact of asymmetric information between the organization and the outsourcer on the decision to outsource and on OS and DS. In particular, the sharing rule will be more difficult to establish. The same six subcases listed earlier apply. This discussion is based again on Ref. 3.

Subcase 1: $c_L < c_H < v_L < v_H$. In period 0 both parties already know that $c_H < v_L$; hence an enhancement will always be implemented. For insourcing ($\alpha = 1, y = 0$, implying that $c_j = c_H$), one obtains

$$E\{G(x, y)\} = \max [0, (v_H - c_L)] \, xy + \max [0, (v_L - c_L)](1 - x)y$$
$$+ \max [0, (v_H - c_H)] \, x(1 - y) + \max [0, (v_L - c_H)](1 - x)(1 - y)$$
$$OS = \alpha E\{G(x, y)\} - f(x)$$

or

$$OS_{\alpha = 1} = (v_H - c_H)x + (v_L - c_H)(1 - x) - f(x)$$
$$= (v_H - v_L)x + (v_L - c_H) - f(x)$$

For outsourcing,

$$OS_{\alpha < 1} = \alpha(v_L - c_H) \, xy + (v_H - v_L)xy + \alpha(v_L - c_H)(1 - x) \, y + \alpha(v_L -$$
$$c_H)x(1 - y) + (v_H - v_L)x(1 - y) + \alpha(v_L - c_H)(1 - x)(1 - y) - f(x)$$
$$= (v_H - v_L)x + \alpha(v_L - c_H) - f(x)$$

In the outsourcing case, both the organization and the outsourcer may be tempted (i.e., have an incentive) to misrepresent their parameter values. For example, the organization may claim that the value of the enhancement is low (or lower than in reality), and the outsourcer may claim that the cost of the enhancement is high (or higher than in reality). This enables the organization to capture $v_H - v_L$ when $v_i = v_H$, and the development group to capture $c_H - c_L$ when $c_j = c_L$. In this case one gets

$$OS_{\alpha = 1} > OS_{\alpha < 1}$$

Hence, internal development dominates outsourcing.

Subcase 2: $c_L < v_L < c_H < v_H$. In this case, the decision to outsource an enhancement will depend on the values of v_i and c_j *declared* by the organization and by the developer (these values may or may not be the actual values). An enhancement will not be implemented if the declared values are $c_j = c_H$ and $v_i = v_L$. The organization has an incentive to declare $v_i = v_L$ if the value of an enhancement is high ($v_i = v_H$), the organization believes that the cost of the enhancement is low ($c_j = c_L$), and the organization believes that the outsourcer will tell the truth with regard to the cost of the enhancement. In this case the organization confiscates $v_H - v_L$ of the gains. The outsourcer has an incentive to declare $c_j = c_H$ if the cost of an enhancement is low ($c_j = c_L$), the outsourcer believes that the value of the enhancement is high ($v_i = v_H$), and the outsourcer believes that the organization will tell the truth with regard to the value of the enhancement. In this case the outsourcer confiscates $c_H - c_L$ of the gains.

The value of outsourcing depends upon the strategies that the organization and the outsourcer employ for revealing their parameter values; such determination requires solving a single-stage two-player game where the payoffs for the strategies depend on c_j, v_i, α, x, y, a, and b. Closed-form solutions are very complex, but the problem can be studied numerically. Such studies indicate that

- When insourcing was the optimal strategy under symmetric information, it is also optimal under asymmetric information.
- When outsourcing was the optimal strategy under symmetric information, it may also be optimal under asymmetric information.

Subcase 3: $v_L < c_L < c_H < v_H$. The development group has the incentive to declare the cost to be high ($c_j = c_H$). In this case an enhancement will be implemented only if it has a high value ($v_i = v_H$). For insourcing ($\alpha = 1$, $y = 0$, implying that $c_j = c_H$), one obtains

$$OS_{\alpha = 1} = (v_H - c_H)x - f(x)$$

For outsourcing,

$$OS_{\alpha < 1} = \alpha(v_L - c_H)x - f(x)$$

One has

$$OS_{\alpha = 1} \geq OS_{\alpha < 1}$$

Therefore, insourcing dominates outsourcing.

Subcase 4: $v_L < c_L < v_H < c_H$. In this case an enhancement will be implemented only when the cost is low ($c_j = c_L$). The outsourcer does not have the incentive to misrepresent the actual costs, whereas the organization has the incentive to claim that the enhancement has a low value ($v_i = v_L$). For insourcing ($\alpha = 1$, $y = 0$, implying that $c_j = c_H$), one obtains

$$OS_{\alpha = 1} = 0$$

For outsourcing,

$$OS_{\alpha < 1} = (v_H - v_L)xy + \alpha(v_L - c_L)y - f(x)$$
$$DS_{\alpha < 1} = (1 - \alpha)(v_L - c_L)y - g(y)$$

One has

$$OS_{\alpha < 1} > 0 \quad \text{and} \quad DS_{\alpha < 1} > 0$$

so that outsourcing dominates internal development.

Subcase 5: $c_L < v_L < v_H < c_H$. In this case an enhancement will be implemented only when its costs is low and its value is high ($c_j = c_L$ and v_i

$= v_H$). In this case neither the outsourcer nor the organization has the incentive to obfuscate the actual parameter values. Since both groups tell the truth, this case is similar to the one with symmetric (common) knowledge. As discussed in the appropriate subcase above, outsourcing dominates.

Subcase 6: $v_L < v_H < c_L < c_H$. No enhancements will be implemented.

4.5.3   Conclusion of the contract modeling analysis

The discussion above shows studying outsourcing in a truly analytical manner is fairly complicated. This situation is further complicated by the fact that few models have been developed. Nonetheless, analytically based decision making is of critical importance.

The different sharing rules and the reliability of the information play a role in the decision-making process. The modeling shows that the benefits to organizations derived from outsourcing are neither uniformly negative or uniformly positive—in some cases insourcing is better; in other cases outsourcing is better. These results should reinforce the need for the CIO and the IS manager to study the problem to the extent possible. It is clear that a misjudgment in a multibillion-dollar decision can have profound negative effects for the organization and for the people involved.

References

1. L. Loh and N. Venkatraman, "Determinants of Information Technology Outsourcing: A Cross-Sectional Analysis," *Journal of Management Information Systems,* 9(1):7–24, 1992.
2. C. Benko, "Outsourcing Evaluation: A Profitable Process," *Information Systems Management,* 10(2):45ff, 1993.
3. W. B. Richmond, A. Seidmann, and A. B. Whinston, "Incomplete Contracting Issues in Information Systems Development Outsourcing," *Decision Support Systems,* 8(5):459–477, 1992.
4. V. Gurbaxami and C. F. Kemere, "An Agent-Theoretic Perspective on the Management of Information Systems," *Proceedings of the 22nd Annual Hawaii International Conference on System Sciences,* (IEEE, Piscataway, N.J., 1989, pp. 141–150.
5. H. Mendelson, "Pricing Computer Services: Queueing Effects," *Communications of the ACM,* 28(3):312ff, 1985.
6. W. Whang, "Alternative Mechanism for Allocating Computer Resources Under Queueing Delays," *Information Systems Research,* no. 1, pp. 71ff, 1990.
7. U. Apte, "Global Outsourcing of Information Systems and Processing Systems," *The Information Society,* 7:287–303, 1990.
8. G. G. Gable and J. A. Sharp, "Outsourcing Assistance with Computer System Selection: A Success Factors Model," *Proceedings of the 25th Hawaii International Conference on System Sciences,* IEEE, Piscataway, N.J., 1992, pp. 556ff.
9. J. L. Wagner, "Issues in Outsourcing," *1992 IRMA Conference Proceedings,* Idea Group Publishing, 1992, pp. 214ff.

10. M. Buck-Lew, "To Outsource or Not?" *International Journal of Information Management,* 12(1):3–20, 1992.
11. W. H. Beyer, *Handbook of Tables for Probability and Statistics,* The Chemical Rubber Co., Cleveland, 1966.
12. J. P. McPartlin, "A More Selective Service," *Information Week,* Nov. 16, 1992, p. 88.
13. J. L. King and R. L. Nolan, "The Nolan Stage Model: A Debate," *12th International Conference on Information Systems, Proceedings,* New York, 1991.
14. G. W. Dickson and J. C. Wetherbe, *The Management of Information Systems,* McGraw-Hill, New York, 1985.
15. H. Mintzberg, *Power In and Around Organizations,* Prentice-Hall, Englewood Cliffs, N.J., 1983.
16. D. Shwartz and G. Lippett, "Evaluating the Consulting Process," *The Journal of European Training,* 4/5, 1975, pp. 17ff.
17. M. Fishbein and I. Azjen, *Belief, Attitude, Intentions and Behavior: An Introduction to Theory and Research,* Addison-Wesley, Boston, 1975.
18. S. Wright, "The Method of Path Coefficients," *Annals of Mathematical Statistics,* no. 5, pp. 161–215, 1934.

Outsourcing of
Data Processing
Functions

Outsourcing is the subcontracting of some or all of the IS functions by one firm (which we consistently refer to here as the "organization") to another firm (which we refer to here as the "outsourcer"). IT has gone from its initial administrative support role in the 1960s to playing a central role in business operations in the 1990s. But as noted in Chap. 1, outsourcing has become a way of life for an increasing number of corporations. About 20 percent of all companies were outsourcing some or all of their IS functions at press time, and a much larger percentage of companies are reported to be looking into it. Also as noted in Chap. 1, for an increasing number of companies, outsourcing has become part of a process of reexamining and reengineering the basic business structure and the IT infrastructure that supports it (some call this *strategic planning*). Outsourcing vendors, in turn, have begun to emphasize their ability to support organizations in these business reengineering efforts. In addition to traditional IS operations, recent outsourcing agreements have involved such diverse activities as network installation and management, software development, and desktop equipment acquisitions.

Proponents claim that *all* organizations should evaluate the feasibility of outsourcing; these proponents take the position that the answer is almost always yes, and that much can be gained simply from the evaluation process, even if the ultimate decision is not to outsource. The evaluation can itself be an agent of change. The process may serve as a catalyst for performance assessments and quality improvements. If nothing else, executive management can become more knowledgeable and aware of the organization's IS posture, and IS managers can become more sensitive to financial issues, realizing that technology is not deployed in organizations just for pure intellectual gratification or career advancement.[1]

Some view outsourcing as another form of delegation.[2] Data center operation is often the first area in an organization where outsourcing is considered, since it is seen as the least strategic of all IS activities. Given that the data center itself is not strategic (although it is certainly tactical: disrupt it for a week and the organization may be out of business, an issue that is well understood by disaster-recovery planners), the organization may feel that it should not have to dedicate its most creative corporate minds to the task of managing the data center, but should instead use these minds for more creative functions.

The previous chapter covered some general outsourcing principles that can be demonstrated using a number of modeling techniques. This chapter looks at a variety of approaches, methods, techniques, aspects, issues, advantages, and disadvantages of data processing outsourcing at the practical IT level; chapters that follow look at other areas of outsourcing.

5.1   Overview

In the 1990s, businesses are placing emphasis on rationalizing their operations. Outsourcing has become a competitive alternative to in-house procurement of the IS function because it is a means of increasing efficiency and cutting costs.[1] The practical rationalization for outsourcing is as follows:[3]

> As an organization we are not in the business of operating computer centers, any more than we are in the business of generating our own electricity, purifying our own water, or building our own transportation infrastructure. Hence, why not arrange for another company, one that is expert at running computer facilities or telecommunication networks in the most optimized manner, to manage and operate our facilities on our behalf? All we have to do is to establish performance standards, negotiate a contract, and pay the outsourcing company for running our operations, preferably having them use our own computers and what used to be our IS staff.

The idea of letting an expert company run the computer facilities was already being put into practice in the 1960s and 1970s. At that time this was known as facilities management. In the mid to late 1980s, the concept was broadened to include new aspects, such as system programming, application development, IS reengineering, introduction of new technology (e.g., client-server systems), network management, help desk, document imaging, and system integration (especially for desktop systems). The term *outsourcing* has now entered the language, replacing the term *facilities management*. Outsourcing vendors are professional IS service providers.

No one knows for certain whether in the long term outsourcing is the right corporate strategy to follow. Only a handful of analytical studies have been published (see Chap. 4), pointing to a certain follow-the-leader approach to outsourcing. Two opposite views are as follows:[3]

- Some view outsourcing as the wave of the future, driven by the need to reduce overhead, shed peripheral activities, and focus on core competencies.

- Others view outsourcing as a refuge for organizations that lack talent, money, and vision; they see it as contributing to a hollowing out of the company, with potentially disastrous consequences down the road.

The truth is probably somewhere in the middle, as there are both advantages and disadvantages to outsourcing, as discussed in Sec. 5.2. Outsourcing is increasingly being viewed as a process of identifying the best way to work with one or more external partners who may provide complementary, useful sources of IT competencies for the organization.[4]

A rule of thumb that has been advanced is as follows: If an organization uses between 10 and 50 MIPS (million instructions per second) of *mainframe* power, then it may be more effective to outsource than to run the operation in-house.[3]* This is related to the fact that there are intrinsic inefficiencies at low utilization (more on this issue later). Customers are increasingly asking for nontraditional solutions that require special expertise; organizations cannot afford to acquire such expertise, whereas an outsourcer can spread it out over a number of accounts.[2] Whether it involves traditional IS functions or other computer functions that can be outsourced, the outsourcing decision is increasingly subject to the following test: How does this decision help a company's core business? Although a few companies have out-

---

*For less use, the IS operation is fairly small and the savings may be trivial in absolute terms. If the organization uses more power, it may have sufficient economies of scale to achieve an effective operation. If a company using more than 50 MIPS decides to outsource, it can certainly do so. Note that mainframe MIPS costs (in hardware) in the range of $50,000 to $100,000 per MIPS; therefore, 50 MIPS range between $2.5 and $5 million in mainframe costs. This figure can in turn be used with the numbers provided in Chap. 1 to obtain an estimate of the total IS cost. The yearly hardware cost would be 25 percent (see Table 1.5) or $0.6 to $1.2 million. Since the mainframe hardware is 3 percent of the total expenditure (see Table 1.4), the yearly IS budget would be $20 to $40 million.

sourced the entire data center and laid off their IS department en masse, the diverse outsourcing agreements that are being established at this time include many options besides total facilities management, so that such drastic occurrences are relatively rare.[5] Some companies do take that course: Eastman Kodak is an example of a company that has outsourced its *entire* IS operation; another example is the Farm Credit Bank of St. Louis, where the IS staff went from 60 to zero in one day.

IS managers who are considering outsourcing should first develop an IT service management strategy in order to properly evaluate the variety of available options. Outsourcing pursued without such a plan or without the involvement of the company's board of directors is likely to be unsuccessful.[6] In the process of developing a strategy, the organization should set service objectives consistent with business goals. The next steps are to generate proposals, evaluate options, identify potential benefits and risks, and make recommendations. When complete, the strategy should define what services are to be delivered, specify which aspects are to come from internal and external sources, and identify the skills and controls required to manage the internal activities and external suppliers.[6–10] This topic is revisited in Sec. 5.3.

5.2 Reasons to Outsource

IS expenditures represent the third largest corporate expense in American business, and nearly 40 percent of U.S. capital is invested in information technology. Senior executives are reportedly dissatisfied with the returns on their IS investments: They perceive IS to be out of control, unable to deliver what the business needs, when it needs it, and with economics that make sense.[1] For many companies, the primary reason for investing in IT (to achieve productivity gains) has not materialized.

Several reasons why IS may not be achieving the desired returns can be identified. First, the diversity of technology platforms and architectures complicates the computing environment, driving up cost, creating challenging conditions in which to introduce and maintain standards and methodologies, and forcing a large portion of the IS effort to be allocated to the integration of these diverse elements. Some organizations have dozens or even hundreds of vendors involved in their IS/communication functions. This high degree of fragmentation complicates the coordination of vendor relations and technology management programs. Second, critical business objectives are not effectively integrated or mapped into IS requirements and plans. In many organizations IS projects are justified on an individual basis rather than being assessed within a common IS infrastructure. Additionally, the IS function may not be placed properly in the organization structure so as to be most effective in the strategic planning of business goals. To resolve these issues, the use of outside IT services to meet corporate data processing requirements—that is, outsourcing—is being chosen by a growing number of companies.[1,11]

5.2.1 Potential advantages

Figures 5.1 and 5.2 depict two algorithms that an organization can employ, at a high level, to determine if some of its IS functions should be outsourced (the percentages in Fig. 5.2 show the share of companies that have selected the indicated paths in a number of surveys, including Ref. 12).

Some view the question "Under what conditions do you outsource?" as now being too simplistic. The issue is not in-house versus outsourcing, but determining how to best manage relationships—some in-house, some outside, and some hybrid. A study recently conducted at MIT's Sloan School of Management shows CIOs moving to adopt the "portfolio management" view, an approach that balances strategic internal and external relationships to determine which best benefit or add value to the company as a whole.[13] A "portfolio manager" handles the disparate relationships with internal development teams and external outsourcers that best fit a particular function.

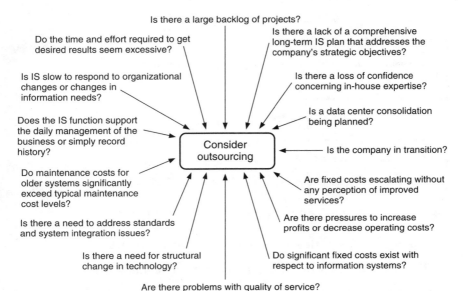

Figure 5.1 Reasons to outsource, according to proponents (Ref. 1): The higher the number of positive answers to these questions, the greater the likely benefit from outsourcing.

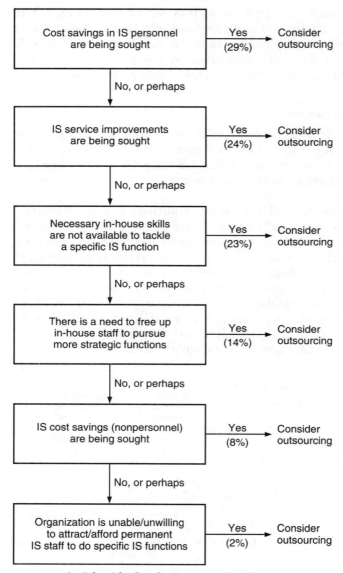

Figure 5.2   An "algorithm" to determine applicability of outsourcing.

At a general level, three key reasons to outsource are

1. To reduce IS costs by offloading nonstrategic functions

   - Ongoing IS (personnel) costs
   - Major capital expenditures

2. To acquire needed new skills in more strategic (new) technologies

- Client-server computing
- New communication technologies (e.g., cell relay, frame relay, SMDS)
- New video/image-based technologies

3. To reengineer the IT and/or the business function(s)

(There are also several ancillary reasons to outsource, as seen in Fig. 5.2.) For years outsourcing vendors have given an almost irresistible punchline: "You can cut your costs by 20 percent."[14] Ostensibly these claims are accurate: Because of their size, outsourcers can generally obtain economies of scale in processing. These same economies are not available to the average organization because its operation is not as large—they may be available only to companies such as the *Datamation* 100 (a list of the top 100 data processing shops in the United States, published annually). Another economy-of-scale advantage is that outsourcing vendors can spread their software development costs among a number of customers. However, along with the cost savings there are some limitations. (These are discussed in the next subsection.)

As implied above, outsourcing may help* an organization avoid major capital investments, such as those needed because of growth; the investments are replaced with recurring charges.† Some organizations may have the problem of overinvestment in IT; i.e., they have built a larger infrastructure than they need. Here outsourcing can potentially recoup the excess investment.

In a well-designed contract, the organization may be able to adjust its computing costs up or down based on actual transaction volumes (perhaps related to seasonal or life-cycle changes). Given their larger base of operations, outsourcers are able to retain spare capacity (for either growth or restoration purposes) more effectively and shift this surplus among their customer base more rapidly (naturally this can be done only within limits, since even the largest outsourcer cannot drastically increase its total capacity in a very short period of time).

In principle, outsourcing vendors bring a broad case of experience, a greater skill set, and greater knowledge to an organization. They can achieve critical mass of staff with expertise in some new or esoteric technical area so as to be effective in finding solutions for an

---

*Also see Fig. 1.1.

†The principles discussed in Chap. 3 come into play in comparing the two alternatives and/or computing the appropriate charges.

organization's computing challenges. Usually, professionals can better sharpen their skills when they are in contact with other professionals in the same field. For example, an organization might have a need for WANs based on cell relay; perhaps only one individual with such an acquired skill is on staff. However, this individual is not able to be technically challenged or challenge others, a process that invariably leads to better understanding of new complex and evolving technologies. Also, the individual may not be able to keep up with *all* the literature that is generated on a topic or attend technology-specific meetings held by primary entities (that is, entities that actually create the technology, as contrasted to downstream seminar providers that may or may not have access to the most authoritative information). Critical mass alleviates this problem: there are more people scanning the literature, the issues can become topics of lunchroom conversations, and because there are several people around to run things, a professional may be able to take a week off every couple of months to attend the primary (or premier) meetings on an evolving technology. Critical mass enables the outsourcers to be better trained and up to date, and thereby bring these technologies to their clients in a more expeditious and hassle-free manner. Bugs and pitfalls are identified once; each organization does not need to find out about them the hard way.

Additionally, there are economies of scale. To illustrate this point, consider a classical arrangement of a help desk (the same argument applies to other aspects of IS, but the help desk example is more intuitive). Assume that there are 10 companies in a certain locality and that each company generates 100 calls per hour (at the busy hour), each 6 minutes long, to its individual help desk. Also assume that the help desk is supporting some mission-critical task, so that no more than 1 call in 100 should receive a busy signal or find the phone unanswered. Then the designer can use a queueing model called Erlang B (and associated table) to compute* the number of positions required to support this "offered load" of $(100 \times 6)/60 = 10$ erlangs. The Erlang B table shows that 18 people are needed to staff the help desk. This is related to the fact that calls arrive randomly—if all calls were perfectly scheduled, then 10 people would suffice, but that is not the case in real life. (See Table 5.1 for a portion of an Erlang B table.) For the 10 companies, this means 180 people. The cost per company (assuming a hypothetical salary of $50,000 per

---

*More sophisticated modeling could also be used (e.g., Erlang C); however, the Erlang B approach is adequate for the discussion at hand.

TABLE 5.1   Abbreviated Erlang B Table

Number of resources needed	Erlangs to be supported		
	Blocking = 0.1%	Blocking = 1%	Blocking = 10%
1	0.00	0.01	0.11
2	0.05	0.15	0.60
3	0.19	0.46	1.27
4	0.44	0.87	2.05
5	0.76	1.36	2.88
6	1.15	1.91	3.76
7	1.58	2.50	4.67
8	2.05	3.13	5.60
9	2.56	3.78	6.55
10	3.09	4.46	7.51
11	3.65	5.16	8.49
12	4.23	5.88	9.47
13	4.83	6.61	10.5
14	4.45	7.35	11.5
15	6.08	8.11	12.5
16	6.72	8.88	13.5
17	7.38	9.65	14.5
18	8.05	10.4	15.5
19	8.72	11.2	16.6
20	9.41	12.0	17.6
30	16.7	20.3	28.1
40	24.4	29.0	38.8
50	32.5	37.9	49.6
60	40.8	49.6	60.4
70	49.2	56.1	71.3

Use: After selecting a desired blocking, scan down that column until the offered traffic is found, then obtain the number of required resources from the *leftmost column*.
See Ref. 16 for techniques to calculate these terms.

employee per year) is $900,000 per year. Now assume that an outsourcer becomes available and that all 10 companies utilize the outsourcer for the help desk. The traffic arrival at the busy hour is now 100 erlangs. The Erlang B table shows that 117 people are sufficient, and yet each organization receives the exact same coverage that it had before.† Assuming a 20 percent profit markup by the outsourcer, the per company cost would be

$$\text{New cost} = \frac{1}{10}*(117*50,000)*(1.2) = \$702,000$$

---

†Table 5.1 only goes up to 70 resources—a full table is required to verify this statement.

which is a saving of over 20 percent. Note that by spreading the costs over a wider base, the outsourcing vendor is able to make a profit and yet charge each organization less than it would otherwise pay. If the process is set up correctly, each organization derives the same exact level of service as if it had its own dedicated staff. The same argument can be made about mainframe operators, programmers, network managers, planners, etc., if these functions are consolidated. The economies of scale in human resources do not apply only to the head count; the outsourcer may be able to provide up-to-date training for its large workforce at a much lower cost than would apply if an organization were to send just a few individuals.[15]

Reliance on a carrier, system integrator, or outsourcer may be good for the organization as a whole, but may not ultimately be good for the IS/telecom professional. Suppose that 10 companies are contemplating cell relay services. As noted in the discussion above, 10 full-time or part-time individuals would be required, one in each company. Now, if an outsourcer or carrier establishes a reputation in that niche and grabs market share, only four individuals might be required because of the efficiencies and economies of scale discussed above. In the final analysis, the service to the organization could be cheaper than if the user had to have the expertise on payroll. In addition, the 10 people may be "home grown," having learned the subject matter on their own and perhaps attended a course or two; as a result, their knowledge may be limited (basic), and they may not be up on the latest events, standards meetings, product announcements, etc. In this case, the organization gets a second-rate knowledge base. When a provider has decided to support a given function, such as cell relay, it may choose the best available set of people, and it has the capability (and motivation) to keep these individuals up to date by having them attend conferences, product announcement meetings, standards meetings, and so on. In terms of the "expert" industry, however, there will be an obvious contraction, unless the economy as a whole expands.

Table 5.1 helps to explain the issue of efficiency discussed earlier. Consider, for example, the column for 10 percent blocking. Look at the ratio

$$e = \frac{\text{number of resources}}{\text{offered load}}$$

tabulated on the following page. As can be seen, the efficiency (third column) is low for small values of the offered load (second column). For example, to support 2 erlangs of load, 4 people are required (51 percent efficiency). To support 25 times that load (that is, 50 erlangs), only 50 people are needed (100 percent efficiency), not $4 \times 25 = 100$. Hence, theoretically, a 50 percent saving can be achieved.

Resources needed	Offered load	Efficiency
1	0.11	0.11
2	0.60	0.30
3	1.27	0.42
4	2.05	0.51
5	2.88	0.58
6	3.76	0.63
7	4.67	0.67
8	5.60	0.70
9	6.55	0.73
10	7.51	0.75
11	8.49	0.77
12	9.47	0.79
13	10.50	0.81
14	11.50	0.82
15	12.50	0.83
16	13.50	0.84
17	14.50	0.85
18	15.50	0.86
19	16.60	0.87
20	17.60	0.88
30	28.10	0.94
40	38.80	0.97
50	49.60	0.99

In summary, studies indicate the outsourcing savings are primarily gained from economies of scale, which occur because the vendor is able to amortize the fixed costs of the technology over a broader base than the organization is able to. These savings can range from 10 to 50 percent (although 15 to 25 percent savings are more common); on average, large outsourcing providers realize a 30 percent cost savings over user expenditures. If properly negotiated, an outsourcing contract could pass half that savings back to the organization.[1] Many contracts are based on unit pricing for the term of the contract, indexed to changes in the Consumer Price Index.

Another advantage of outsourcing is that it facilitates the transfer of risk from within the organization to another firm.* Risks include

---

*Some take an opposite view, arguing that if a system does not do what it is supposed to do, is late, is nonfunctional, or does not meet user needs, the fact that the outsourcer does not get paid is no comfort; in this case, the organization may have to slow down or stop some business function, jeopardizing revenue.

but are not limited to project failure (e.g., capital is invested but the project cannot be successfully completed), capital investment risks (e.g., the risk of incurring a high-interest loan), technological changes (e.g., the risk that the current technology will rapidly become obsolete or will decline in processing efficiency), and staffing (e.g., the risk that the changed technologies will require new expertise, making the organization's workforce "obsolete").[15]

The concept of focusing on core competencies has received considerable attention since the *Harvard Business Review* covered the topic.[17] Indeed, computing is seen by many as a utility function; it follows that an organization should treat it the same way as other utilities, without unnecessarily high corporate investments. Through outsourcing, senior managers of the organization will be better able to concentrate on their core businesses, rather than on IS.[15] This also works in reverse: Because the outsourcer is not burdened with other aspects of the organization's business, it is able to concentrate exclusively on IS/IT. This could mean that the time between the user's or the organization's request for a service and the response would go down substantially, improving delivery of service to the users of IS.

In order to maintain a good reputation, the outsourcing vendor should strive, by design, to provide the client organization with excellent service. To accomplish this, the outsourcer will find it in its interest to use the latest technology and well-trained personnel. As a result, the organization may now have access to new technologies and to a large staff of well-qualified system analysts (or network specialists, database designers, or client-server specialists), rather than just the few that it was previously able to hire. These specialists are better utilized, instead of being fully used only on a sporadic basis.[15]

Another advantage of outsourcing is increased return on equity. ROE is defined as the ratio of profit to equity. Organizations seeking to improve their ROE will find that outsourcing the entire IS operation will help them achieve that goal, since the computers and telecommunication equipment will no longer be on the organization's balance sheet, reducing its equity. Financial analysts and investors view a high ROE as desirable. Given the definition of ROE, a reduction in equity through a sale of equipment to an outsourcer, while maintaining the same profit, will increase the ROE. The cash received from the transaction can be used to pay off some of the corporate debt. Everything else being equal, the profit should stay the same and even increase, since the costs of undertaking specific functions (e.g., the processing associated with clearing a check, producing a credit card bill, etc.) are decreased as a result of the computing efficiencies discussed earlier.

Other inherent advantages of outsourcing over the internal IS operation include the following:[1]

- Service levels are established at the outset of the relationship, forcing the organization to define what is and what is not acceptable.

- Continuing lack of performance can be confronted more immediately and effectively (action against internal underperformance usually requires more time, and problems may be more difficult to resolve).

- Through contractual obligations, accountability is better defined (in many cases, internal accountability is less definitive and therefore less effective).

- Outsourcing costs are more clearly defined in a stable IS/business environment, and therefore are predictable and controllable (in some situations it may be more difficult to estimate and control internal costs).

- User support can be centralized.

- Remaining IS resources can be freed up and used to provide value by focusing on more innovative rather than commonplace tasks.

5.2.2   Potential disadvantages

Although there may appear to be short-term advantages to outsourcing, there may be longer-term disadvantages.* Figure 5.3 shows some reasons why an organization may choose *not* to outsource. For an additional perspective, Figure 5.4 shows a conservative "algorithm" encapsulating issues advanced by those who tend to favor the status quo, or insourcing; the issues raised by this kind of algorithm should be given proper consideration even by those organizations that have already made their decision in favor of outsourcing, as organizations should want to err on the side of caution.

Danger of losing control over the IS function is often mentioned as the principal concern when considering outsourcing. If the entire IS staff or a large majority thereof is severed from the organization, it may be difficult for the organization to have the strategic IS vision needed to face the future. It is clear that automation is going to continue to play an important, ever-increasing role in the business climate of the late 1990s and into the next century. Organizations need to be on top of technological developments in computing and telecommunications in order to determine at an early stage the competitive advantages of these developments. Of course the trade press, technology books, seminars, computer-based training, etc., all aim to facilitate this information transfer. However, these developments are increasingly more complex, and a well-informed and competent staff is need-

---

*Also see Fig. 1.1.

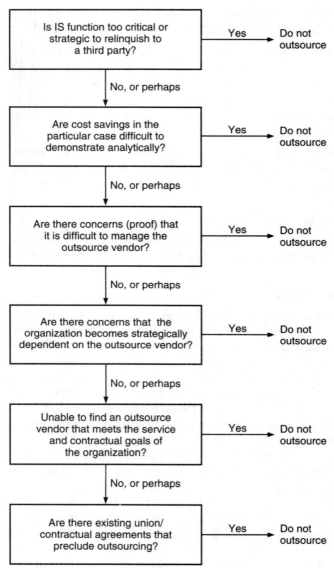

Figure 5.3 Issues working against outsourcing.

ed to appreciate their significance and their latent or patent nuances. Another reported problem is that of attracting quality IS people to an organization when they are simply performing an oversight function.[3] It was mentioned earlier that outsourcing facilitates transfer of risk. However, risk can foster the search for new solutions, thereby possibly providing some competitive advantage. Technological advances devel-

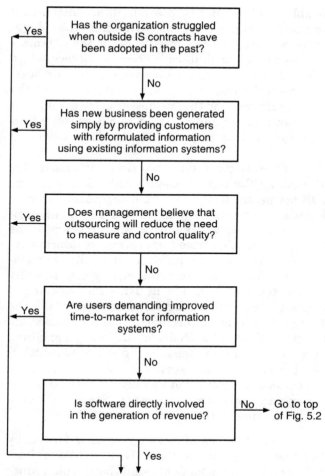

Examine the decision to outsource carefully
(insourcing or status quo may be a short-term answer).

However, realize that the IS/IT infrastructure of an
organization cannot stand still, and there is no long-term
advantage in a technological status quo.

Outsourcing is one of the possible ways to introduce a
new generation of technology (e.g., client-server) to the
organization.

Figure 5.4 A conservative algorithm pertaining to outsourcing
decisions.

oped by a knowledgeable staff will not be possible in an outsourcing situation, since the staff does not have access to the technology. Additionally, there may no longer be any incentives for the organization to find innovative uses of IS capabilities.[15] Forecasting technology spending patterns into the future is an inexact science, at best. The problem is not so much the underlying statistical model, but the confidence levels for the data and for the business environment. The average length of a large outsourcing contract is 8.8 years, which may be too long a period of time to project technology spending accurately.[13]

The potential loss of corporate continuity as a result of outsourcing may be detrimental, making the organization a collection of loosely related parts. Since IS permeates today's way of doing business, some business breakthroughs may be achieved only through a strong symbiosis with IS. It is conceivable that only a close interaction with the IS experts can help an information-based organization improve its business stance. Whether or not to outsource depends on the organization's individual situation: What works for one company operationally rarely works for another; the real danger is in using the outsourcing alternative as a universal solution to managing operating costs.[13] The so-called megadeals (e.g., Kodak) are in decline, as CIOs have become concerned about the irreversibility of such deals; they want something more short-term, more fluid, easier to manage, and easier to switch.[13] There is anecdotal evidence, based on a survey of 250 CIOs, that the long-term economics of outsourcing may not be fully understood by the senior managers who approve such arrangements.[13] Some of the conclusions that emerged at the time of the survey were as follows:

- Some IS organizations run the risk of mortgaging their futures by cutting jobs rather than inefficiencies. Faced with additional budgetary pressures, 52 percent of respondents said they would reduce head count further in the years ahead; given that 64 percent of the respondents have already downsized, IS organizations may find themselves understaffed by the mid-1990s.

- IT expenditures are growing, and total costs far exceed formal budgets. IT costs are migrating beyond the data center utility—and more quickly than most executives think. Over half the respondents said that total IT expenditures for their companies exceed the formal budget by 150 to 500 percent; this makes the outsourcing process hard to manage.*

---

*Some outsourcing proponents actually see this as an opportunity: Since budgets have a tendency to grow so much, outsourcing could, in theory, be used to try to cap the growth.

Many IS problems are related to the large number of diverse participants and activities that are required for the effective delivery of services.[18] Outsourcing may or may not help this situation. A Fortune 1500 company may typically have 100 to 200 vendors* that support its data processing/communication function. If the outsourcing arrangement can somehow reduce that population of vendors, it is conceivable that the complexity of the operation can be reduced. Sometimes organizations seek to buy the cheapest possible solution to each of their computing problems (e.g., buy the cheapest server, the cheapest router, the cheapest modem, the cheapest communication service, etc.). Some consider this to be an irrational move, since, in real life, no manager would buy the cheapest car, the cheapest suit, the cheapest shoes, the cheapest home, etc. This drive for the cheapest equipment usually means bringing in a plethora of new vendors. Such an approach does not take into account the fact that the apparent saving in equipment cost is likely to be offset by higher costs for integration, protocol conversion, multivendor-management, complexity-management, and maintenance. Outsourcing may enable the organization to transfer to the outsourcer the high complexity that has been created by bringing in a multitude of equipment vendors; however, this is not always the case.

For many years there has been a desire to move to multisupplier environments, since the competitive forces reduce costs and enhance features and capabilities. The entire philosophy of open systems (e.g., OSI, TCP/IP, and other systems) is to be able to buy services from multiple providers. With outsourcing there is the risk of become increasingly dependent on one outsourcer. Some organizations have found that dependency to become more onerous as time goes by. One approach is to distribute the outsourcing function among several providers (e.g., one for operations, one for software development, and one for telecommunications). This, however, increases the complexity of the relationship. For example, to add a new application, many or all vendors need to become involved, in addition to the organization itself.

Some companies seem to have realized less savings through outsourcing than they had expected, according to a 1993 survey of 1250 U.S. corporations undertaken by Frost & Sullivan.[19] Asked to rate on a scale of 1 to 10 how strong the outsourcing motivation is in terms of reduced IS costs, the factor was rated an 8 over this large sample space. However, the question on actual cost benefit that has been

---

*That is, the organization may have purchased equipment and services from as many vendors, all of which may have maintenance contracts with the organization, system integration inputs, marketing pitches to encourage the organization to move up to their next-generation equipment, etc.

realized produced a value of 6. Hence, there is some evidence to conclude that the cost advantages of outsourcing are not fully realized by user organizations.

There are also risks in terms of the contract that is signed. First, the contract may be a fixed-price arrangement that is not indexed to the organization's profitability or (possibly) decreased computing load. If the outsourcer believes that it is not making an appropriate rate of return, it may surreptitiously lower the level of service. Second, the contract probably will not take into account the continued decrease in computing and communication costs over time, particularly if the contract is long (say 7 or 10 years), which the user ought to be able to benefit from. These reductions are due to technological breakthroughs that have taken place and that can be expected to continue to take place (e.g., introduction of fiber, increased miniaturization, and so on). Two examples will illustrate this. (1) In 1986 a 386 PC cost $6,000; just seven years later, that machine costs only $1,400 (see Table 2.3). (2) The cost of a T1 line has gone down between 40 and 80 percent (depending on carrier and location) between the late 1980s and the early 1990s. These numbers do not even consider inflation—$6,000 in 1986 is equal to roughly $8,000 in 1993, making the reduction even more conspicuous.

It is not uncommon for organizations to find that after 2 to 4 years of a 10-year contract, their computing needs change; this could be due to a variety of reasons, including acquisitions and new business ventures. IS applications and supporting systems have to be dynamic in order to meet the new business requirements. When the Yankee Group analyzed 30 long-term outsourcing contracts in 1993, it found that every single one had been renegotiated or was being renegotiated, and that part of the impetus was the movement to new technology.[20] Changes in computing needs are often interpreted by outsourcers as an opportunity to raise fees. In fact, when outsourcers book their internal revenue projections, they often book them at 30 percent over what the organization projects because the outsourcers are sure that there will be requests for changes, which they can turn into increased revenues.[14] Particularly in the context of application development, often one finds disputes between the organization and the outsourcer, caused by the fact that a high level of resources is required to make downstream changes.[7]

Some industry observers feel that the outsourcers are keeping too great a share of the savings and that companies would be better off hiring a consultant to find the same savings. Some outsourcers keep 50 percent of the savings, which could amount to $5 million of a $10 million savings; the claim is that a consultant could discover the same savings for $200,000.[21] Some CIOs take the position that if the operations managers are really doing their jobs, they should be able to manage costs and implement new technologies as well as the out-sourcers can.[4]

Two other risks are control over disaster recovery and reversibility. The loss of computing capabilities as a result of fire, flood, terrorism, environmental hazards, etc., can cripple an organization in a matter of days, as several studies have shown. Some industries (e.g., banking and financial services) are mandated by law to have auditable disaster-recovery plans and supporting infrastructure. The issue is how good a disaster-recovery capability the outsourcer provides. Reversibility refers to the ability to change course after some (or all) steps toward outsourcing have been taken. Generally, reversibility is hard to achieve. This problem is somewhat mitigated when the organization does not outsource the entire IS function but only a subset. Although some companies outsource extensively based on the absolute value of the contract (e.g., $35 to $50 million per year worth of service), they only outsource selected services to people that can provide them better than the organization can.[4]

There are risks associated with excessive reliance on economies of scale. The outsourcer will find that increased consolidation, using as few resources as possible, decreases its costs. This, however, can have negative implications for availability and reliability, including aspects of disaster recovery just mentioned. This applies to computing as well as communication. Also, an outsourcer may attempt to impose a particular technical solution in order to retain (or improve) its economies of scale.

Some even claim that there are no economies of scale for facilities management and information processing.[7,22,23] Although this hypothesis is not accepted in this text, such questions deserve to be posed. For example, this author has argued over the years that just because solution X (e.g., client-server computing, connectionless communication, TCP/IP systems, etc.) to a given problem works well in company C_i for 1, 11, or 111 i's in the range $1 \leq i \leq 6,666,666$ (where the upper bound represents an approximation of the number of firms in the United States) is absolutely no guarantee that such a solution will work well for company C_y. One finds a recurring reluctance to study a problem in appropriate depth with the appropriate set of intellectual tools—it is much easier to say, Company Z has outsourced (or brought in client-server, service multiplexers, ATM hubs, etc.), as we read in article Q in magazine R; therefore we shall do the same, and it shall be good for us too.

Because the outsourcer serves many organizations, the business needs of one specific organization may not always necessarily be its highest priority. A new opportunity that the organization perceives as urgent may not be dealt with by the outsourcer in an expedited manner. Also, although there may be many IS specialists, they may not have experience in the organization's line of business, and hence they may not appreciate certain business imperatives. Attempting to bring the work back in-house is an important leverage factor in outsourcing renegotiations.[20] There also is a small risk that some expertise or business information may (inadvertently) be shared with the organization's competition.[15] The less creative functions, such as computer operations, are where organizations can realize the biggest savings. Functions where there is a potential loss of control, such as applications development, are where the biggest risks are posed.[1]

Occasionally there may be labor-related issues affecting outsourcing, particularly in the government sector. For example, the United States Postal Service (USPS) had to place a $1.2 billion outsourcing program for remote bar coding systems on hold following an arbitrator's decision on a grievance filed by members of the American Postal Workers Union. The workers filing the grievance claimed that the award of 25 outsourcing contracts for remote bar coding equipment and services violated an agreement that requires the USPS to give its employees new jobs created by automation.[24]

There may also be problems related to decreased profit margin. As discussed earlier, the sale of computer assets to an outsourcer leads to an improved ROE *if* the profit remains the same or increases. However, outsourcing can also be used to move up to the next generation of technology (e.g., from mainframe-based operations to client-server operations, as discussed in Chap. 2); this may result in higher payments to the outsourcers, and hence decreased profits. For example, an individual may have an old car that has almost no book value but that gets him or her between point A and point B essentially free; if the individual wants to trade up to a new car, he or she will be paying much more for the service of going between point A and point B. In theory, even if the profit went down, the ROE could still go up if the equity term went down enough. (For example, if $P = 50$ and $E = 100$, then ROE $= 0.5$. If E goes to 80, then ROE $= 0.625$, which is desirable; but if P went to 30 as E went to 80, then ROE would go down to 0.375. Finally, if P went to 30 but E went as low as, say, 55, then ROE would still go up to 0.55.) However, the profit margin, which is the ratio of profits to sales, will decrease, and this may not be well received by the investment community.[15]

Finally, there is the issue of the staff. Although many organizations attempt to have the outsourcer hire the existing IS staff (because that makes for better service to the organization—these people are familiar with the company, the business, and the information systems), there is a period of uncertainty that can last for months. Usually the better people are able to get jobs elsewhere, leaving behind mediocre people. Managers realize that when it is all said and done, it is better to tell people up front what the employment situation is going to be.[14]

One of the decision-making restrictions with regard to outsourcing is that often outsourcing scenarios are compared only to the organization's current costs. Such analysis tends to favor a decision to outsource. Preferably one should compare what the tradeoffs would be if the organization ran the best-tuned internal operation it could. This approach suggests that perhaps the organization can restructure its internal operations by way of insourcing, if it has the resources, and obtain many of the same benefits as if it elected to outsource. Such an approach can result in many of the advantages of outsourcing without many of the disadvantages. Some vendors have developed simulations running on both PCs and mainframes to analyze software, maintenance, and personnel costs over time, enabling the organization to make the appropriate comparisons.[4]

5.2.3 Outsourcing in the banking industry

This section looks at some of the outsourcing trends in the banking industry; it is intended to give the reader a sense of the pros and cons involved in decision making.

"If cost reduction were all that there is to outsourcing, hardly a bank would not use it."[14] However, in spite of a handful of outsourcing deals in the early 1990s, full-scale IS outsourcing is found mostly in community banks and in small to medium bank holding companies ($1 billion in assets or less). The four large banks that had turned to outsourcing by press time, Chase Manhattan, First Fidelity Bancorporation, Continental Bank Corporation of Chicago, and NationsBank of Charlotte, all seemed to have elected outsourcing in order to find one-time solutions to specific organizational problems that may not be representative of the industry.[14] These organizational problems had spilled over to IT, requiring the bank to perform a total overhaul of the IS infrastructure in a very short period of time.

The speculation of the early 1990s that the decision by these four companies to outsource, given that the industry generally has a follow-the-leader attitude toward technology rather than being independently innovative, would create a ripple effect and generate a large turnover did not prove to be correct. The financial picture for banks changed substantially in the 1990s, with banks achieving good profitability because of low interest rates and, one hopes, more discipline in loan making (the infusion of half a trillion dollars of taxpayer money, revolving credit rates of 19.2 percent when the prime rate was 5 percent, and exorbitant user fees did not hurt the industry either). For years, banks were not well disposed toward outsourcing because they feared the loss of control over the IS function; as their profitability increased, the only pressure toward a change—that is, savings in the IS budget—became less important. Banks are sensitive to pricing changes, such as those based on change orders. They often require that outsourcing vendors provide costs for unusual events, such as buying out the contract.[14] For smaller banks, which are not able to support a large IS staff to develop new applications, the decision to outsource may be more defensible.

Chase Manhattan Bank.   This bank had a one-time problem which led, according to observers, to outsourcing. The FDIC gave the bank 120 days to work through the assets of two recent acquisitions and merge their operations. Chase's management concluded that the bank could not do that by itself, and therefore outsourced the task to ISSC.

First Fidelity.   In 1990 First Fidelity realized that because of the business climate, particularly the concern about being taken over, it only had 18 months to combine eight different banks and computer systems into one. EDS was selected based on its previous work on data center conversions and on its willingness to hire all of First Fidelity IT's employees. The consolidation enabled First Fidelity to reduce its annual IS cost from $390 million in 1990 to $350 million in 1992.

NationsBank.   The IS operations were outsourced to Perot Systems Group in 1991. The company had a large conversion task at hand. NCNB, NationsBank's progenitor, had been working for three years on converting three data centers. Perot Systems proposed taking over one of the bank's data centers and using it as a base for serving other customers and hence generating new revenues. That approach saved some costs and freed the bank to concentrate on the other two data centers.

Continental.   The bank outsourced its IS function completely. Savings in costs and developing new applications quickly were cited as the reasons for outsourcing.

5.2.4   Is client-server computing affecting outsourcing?

Many outsourcing deals in the late 1980s involved long-term solutions that were mainframe-based. At the time, when the promises of client-server computing still seemed distant, outsourcing vendors offered attractive savings to take over an organization's data center. Those contracts, however, did not include provisions for flexibility. IS planners did not anticipate how fast technology would change. Just five years later, the movement to smaller, less expensive platforms that run off-the-shelf software is allowing corporate planners to shift resources toward end users and away from centralized IS operations—including those that have been outsourced.[20]

An increasing number of companies are spending more on IT, but the distribution has changed: They are spending more directly and less with the outsourcer. Progressive organizations are leaving the legacy systems with the outsourcer but bringing the client-server systems in-house. According to client-server proponents, "outsourcers know how much leverage their customers have gained, but they still want your business—even at a diminished level."[20] The advice being given is not to outsource the things that are going to give the organization a competitive advantage; rather, pay the outsourcer to manage the client-server migration.

Traditionally, enterprisewide mainframe-based ISs have been restricted to large companies because of the expense of the system upkeep, maintenance, and staff training time. Outsourcing can be the answer to this challenge. However, because outsourcing can create its own set of problems, organizations must carefully choose a partner that understands the technology they want to adopt, their business goals, and the importance of working as an extension of their own business. For example, an organization using mainframe technology that is divested from a parent company may be left with a dilemma: (1) be without adequate computing support; (2) buy, install, and maintain its own mainframe; (3) outsource the mainframe operation; or (4) convert to a client-server system. Option 4 may not be appropriate at such a time (the shock of divestiture is large enough, without having to go through a conversion at the same time), and the other options carry their own burdens. Option 3 may be the only feasible approach given the situation. In fact, companies that have found themselves in this predicament have indeed taken such a course of action.[24]

A few examples of these new trends follow. Ultramar was in the fourth year of a five-year outsourcing contract with Power Computing when it decided it wanted to move to a client-server architecture. Under a renegotiated deal, Power Computing consulted on the design of the pilot project for Ultramar's client-server environment, but Ultramar took on the majority of the responsibility for strategic client-server applications. As another example, 4 years into its 10-year agreement with IBM's ISSC, Bank South has placed a Windows interface between its mainframe and most of its users and has assumed responsibility for the LANs in the corporate lending area, where servers linked to desktop computers run off-the-shelf software packages. As a third example, Revlon signed a outsourcing deal with Andersen Consulting whereby the outsourcer will manage Revlon's mainframe while also developing applications for the company's Hewlett-Packard platforms.

5.2.5 Outsourcing midrange systems

Most of the outsourcing of IS functions to date has involved mainframes; some outsourcing also supports client-server systems. However, even traditional midrange systems (e.g., IBM AS/400 departmental systems) are being outsourced. There is now a demand for midrange outsourcing in support of data communications, image processing, interconnectivity of dissimilar systems, software development, and other functions. Some attribute the trend to the fact that the AS/400 is easy to use but not so easy to optimize for performance tuning, increased response time, increased utilization, and proper allocation of resources as well as connectivity to non-IBM PCs and workstations.[2]

Some see things happening in the midrange arena that previously took place with mainframes: Midrange applications started simple but have become increasingly complex. At the same time, many companies that use midrange systems have determined that their main focus has to be on their business functions, not the processing of data. Some organizations have midrange systems that are at the end of their effectiveness.[2] A number of outsourcing vendors provide the functionality to keep an organization's business going while helping it figure out what to do next and then implement the change. This type of outsourcing has been called *transitional outsourcing*.

5.3   The Outsourcing Decision Process

Given the level of corporate investments in IT resources (from 2 to 12 percent of yearly revenue—5 percent on average), it makes sense to periodically reexamine the entire operation to determine if certain assumptions still hold (e.g., the transaction rate is still as high as the last time; users still require subsecond response time; certain needed equipment was not available last time, but is now entering the market; etc.), or if new, more efficient technologies for both data processing and communications are now available. This reexamination should be done at least once a year even if outsourcing is not being considered. Outsourcing may be a by-product of this reassessment; however, other solutions may also be identified.

As noted throughout this text, in general, the goals of an outsourcing arrangement are to reduce costs, increase the level of customer service and quality, and realize a better price/performance objective for IS functions. Outsourcing may not be the only option available to achieve these goals, as inefficiencies could be discovered and corrected by in-house staff and resources. The insight gained from such an evaluation makes it possible to improve the economics of the IS function without outsourcing, focusing instead on improving internal IS operations. Through internal consolidation, many companies have been able to achieve cost savings comparable to the 10 to 20 percent provided by outsourcing vendors and/or increase application development productivity by 50 percent.[1] Therefore, the value of a periodic reassessment of the computing infrastructure, whether with an eye to eventual outsourcing or not, is in affording a global view of the corporate strategic IS directions and, collaterally, identifying ways for improved IS performance.

An outsourcing evaluation can be undertaken in three phases:

1. Development of the current IS baseline model, the so-called present mode of operation (PMO), that is input to any financial evaluation that follows.

2. Determination of strategic objectives for the IS function based on current business requirements—since business needs change almost on a yearly basis (perhaps even sooner), last year's objectives may or may not be the ones that need to be pursued at present.

3. Evaluation of internal and external (outsourcing) alternatives. This evaluation involves a feature/requirements analysis, architecture development/design, and a financial evaluation. The future mode of operation (FMO), along with the PMO, is input into any financial decision support tool that will be used to make a rational assessment.

Such an evaluation seeks the optimal allocation of IT resources; as such, it is a complex undertaking that involves many, and perhaps all, functional areas within the organization. To accomplish the analysis, senior management must be prepared to support the individuals performing the evaluation as they develop performance models, conduct interviews and user surveys, perform industry comparative analyses, and attempt to quantify IS productivity. Such a fundamental assessment cannot be accomplished without the appropriate level of corporate commitment. In addition to the evaluation conclusions themselves, the organization can benefit from the evaluation in several respects. IS management can become better equipped to work in a more cost-conscious manner, realizing that technology is a means, not an end unto itself. This affords an improved business perspective on which to anchor decisions, which is especially valuable for managers who have come up through the technical ranks. IS management can develop a better understanding of the IS function's actual, rather than perceived, effectiveness, implying more knowledge about financial and performance metrics. Also, there will be greater insight into the role IS plays within the organization and how it can better support the various business functions and the organization's operation as a whole.

5.3.1 Step 1: Development of PMO

A baseline model of the existing IS function must be developed in order to identify and define organization IS functions, analyze the IS cost structure, and identify the embedded technology components that will have to be taken into account if a transition to a new technology platform is contemplated. One needs to develop an understanding of the organization's dynamics, its economics, and the functional and technological platforms. In view of the business process reengineering goals that an organization may have set for itself, this step should also include an analysis of the various existing processes that support the company's functions and the type of workflow interfaces that the organization currently has. This phase also includes establishing a framework for IS performance objectives and measurements (these will be used as normative parameters for either the new technology platform or the outsourcing arrangement). It should be a given that such analysis should be done objectively, that is, separating data and facts from perceptions. Figure 5.5 depicts some of the key steps required for preparation of a baseline model.[1]

As noted in the previous chapter, the IS manager should develop performance measures as part of an analytical assessment of outsourcing. Identifying the appropriate measures of productivity is by no means a trivial task, since philosophies and approaches for defining productivity differ from organization to organization. These measures should be developed with input from management, IS personnel, and users. Productivity measures are critical to the evaluation study for two reasons:

1. Implementation of these measures can identify processes and products that are subject to defects; once detected, these defects can often be corrected, with a resulting gain in productivity.

2. If the analysis supports a decision for outsourcing, these measures can be used as the basis for establishing acceptable levels of vendor performance.

5.3.2 Step 2: Setting strategic directions

This step of the evaluation process contemplates the global business posture of the organization and how this posture relates to IT: The IS function is evaluated as to whether it is (or should be) an important contributor to the organization's success. Questions such as the following are important points of departure:[1,2]

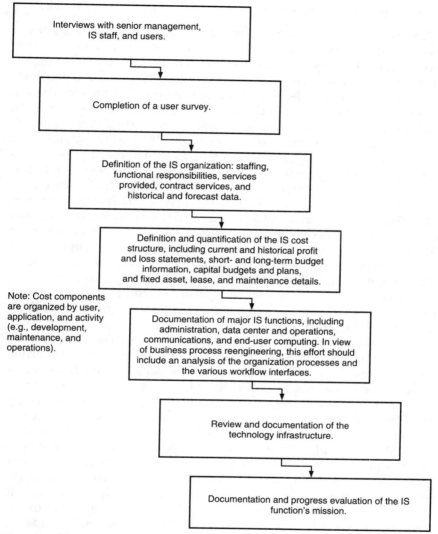

Figure 5.5 Construction of PMO.

- Who are the customers? How does one produce value? Is there a better structure? And how should goals and objectives be set?

- Does the organization's IS department provide a competitive or strategic advantage to the company?

- Can IS provide the organization with a component that differentiates the company in the marketplace?

■ Is IS simply a commodity service?

To answer these and similar questions, IS goals can be categorized into one of four groups: provides competitive advantages for the organization, enables the organization to be a low-cost provider, makes the organization a low-cost operator, and affords high flexibility for the organization. Competitive advantage implies that an organization plans to remain competitive through strategic investments in general, and implementation of strategic IS systems in particular, that directly increase market share or improve profit margins. A low-cost provider outlook takes the position that IS contributes to the organization's competitive posture by providing low-cost processes and operations through inexpensive transaction processing. The low-cost operator category assumes that IS will not play a role in differentiating the organization; therefore, the IS function is expected to provide adequate service while consuming a minimum amount of resources. High flexibility is a posture that enables IS to react quickly to support business contingencies, including the addition or divestiture of corporate divisions. It is likely that different departments of an actual organization may subscribe to different computing postures; the challenge of IS is to figure out how it can meet all or at least the majority of these requirements in an effective manner.

Perhaps outsourcing can help mediate some of these potential differences. Consider a large bureaucratic company (this is a real example) with ten departments. Nine of these departments have established procedures using mainframe legacy systems for customer records, inventory management, billing, etc., that work relatively well. However, the sales department, whose members are always on the road, needs a new flexible and highly effective order entry system that will enable salespeople to enter complex service orders (say, having 200 or 300 data fields) right at the customer site, rather than holding on to them for one or two days and then trying to enter the information off-line, where it is impossible to obtain (perhaps) a missing field in real time. Without such a system, it may take up to five days just to enter the service order, and filling the order takes an equally long or longer period. Clearly, the ability to use wireless technology for on-site entry is an excellent competitive advantage, improving the ability to deliver service ahead of the competition. If the IS organization is not able to design, deploy, and manage such a state-of-the-art network, this one function could be outsourced to a vendor that can do it. Hence, while the other nine departments may be low-cost operators, the sales department may be more in the competitive advantage category.

In some cases, outsourcing represents the contracting out of functions that have become too complex to handle in-house. Perhaps a better solution in this case would be to rethink the organization's business and reengineer IS and/or the function so that it becomes more manageable. But reengineering IS involves changing the organization's mindset, paradigm, and values. Organizations may find that in the short term is it simpler to unload complex jobs to an outsourcer than to reengineer the entire system, despite the fact that reengineering may have long-term benefits in increased organizational efficiency.[2]

5.3.3 Step 3: Evaluating alternatives

When the PMO has been constructed and the IS strategy and purpose clarified, the outsourcing evaluation process progresses to the third phase. The initial step of this phase is to establish how closely the PMO IS environment aligns with the strategic focus. If they are aligned, further evaluation is not needed; the evaluation effort is suspended for, say, twelve months, after which the process is redone. Often organizations find that the two purposes diverge. For example, the IS scenario analysis may demonstrate the need to be in the competitive advantage mode, but the PMO shows that the organization is actually geared to being a low-cost operator. In this case, IS restructuring may be (ultimately) cost-effective.

If restructuring (or reengineering) is needed, one should next evaluate the degree of restructuring that is required. After this, one needs to examine possible alternatives and determine the preferable approach. This is done using both technological considerations (Chap. 2) and cost considerations (Chaps. 3 and 4). As discussed in Chap. 4, two methods for restructuring exist: outsourcing and internal improvements (hybrid approaches are also possible). Finally, one needs to identify the steps necessary to implement the chosen alternative.

As discussed earlier, there are advantages and disadvantages to outsourcing. On the positive side, there can be significant gains from outsourcing IS functions, as noted earlier in the chapter. On the negative side, outsourcing implies having to establish an ongoing, long-term relationship with another vendor which has nontrivial complexity and business risk associated with it. Also, the impediments to withdrawing from this decision, once it has been made and implemented, are high. However, computing requirements may change radically over the life of the contract, and the future environment may bear little resemblance, if any, to the one in operation today. As a way to appreciate this, assume that today was Sept. 9, 1993. Now consider the computing environment in September 1983. First-generation 8-bit PCs were just appearing in the corporate environment. PCs used 3270 emulation to access the IS platform, which was, almost invariably, a mainframe. Applications were very different:

simpler and more basic. The business environment was much more stable. And in the communications arena, LANs were beginning to appear, and in the United States, divestiture of the Bell System still had to occur. That is radically different from the situation on Sept. 9, 1993. What will the environment be on Sept. 9, 2003? Is it likely that the radical changes that occurred in the past 10 years will be representative of the changes that will occur in the next 10 years? Perhaps even more marked changes will occur as corporations move to applications that use video, multimedia, and image. Distance learning, desktop videoconferencing, real-time video news feeds into PCs, and access to large "stores" of image-based information are just a few examples of how things could change.

Therefore the decision as to which alternative to choose, outsourcing or internal improvements, must be arrived at carefully, looking at both cost implications and organizational implications. There is no closed-form formula or computerized tool that tells the CIO when to outsource and when not to; the discussion included in this chapter (and in this text) aims at peeling the onion layers of this decision process by examining approaches, methods, techniques, aspects, issues, advantages, and disadvantages of outsourcing.

5.4   Selecting an Outsourcer

Some claim that almost all outsourcing deals are subject to failure if the IS user is primarily concerned with cost savings; in the view of these observers, the outsourcer's job is to help an organization become more competitive by getting people the information they need to make faster, better-educated decisions based on an understanding of the organization's market and business priorities.[5] Price and vendor reputation are the primary considerations reported by organizations when choosing an outsourcing provider.[19] The organization and the outsourcer should ideally function as partners, sharing information, strategies, and resources. This partnership is the difference between maintaining and losing control of the outsourcing process.[25] Some of the criteria that can be employed in making an outsourcing decision are as follows:[5]

- *Knowledge of your business.*   Has the outsourcing company worked with firms whose business is similar to yours? Does it have staff who know the details of information processing in your industry? Is it capable of bringing more than processing cycles to the planning of your information technology?
- *Flexibility.*   If your needs change in nature and volume throughout the year and over time, will the outsourcer negotiate an agreement that reflects that?

- *Technology leadership.* If you are relying on an outsourcer to help you make the transition from traditional host-centered computing to more modern technology, does the outsourcer have proven skills in distributed computing and client-server technology in particular?

- *Scope.* If your company is geographically dispersed, possibly around the world, can a vendor handle that? Does an outsourcer have the technical breadth needed to support legacy systems (possibly going back 15 years)?

A few years ago, facilities management experience was considered one of the major factors; now organizations tend to look for vendors that not only have this expertise but also have a business understanding of the industry to which the organization belongs. Figure 5.6 depicts an algorithm that can be used to initiate the vendor-selection process; the figure shows decision points in decreasing order of importance based on actual surveys of the industry (including Ref. 12). Also see Table 5.2.[2]

Some organizations want an outsourcer to take over the entire IS function; however, not all outsourcers buy real estate, do systems development, and then manage the day-to-day operation. The organization should clearly investigate what role a prospective outsourcer is willing to play. Some outsourcers are willing to pass back to the organization a portion of the savings (say the first year's worth) resulting from improvements that the outsourcer is able to make in handling customer information. At the other end of the spectrum, as already noted elsewhere, many companies do not wish to turn over *all* of their IS resources to an outsourcer. To serve these customers, a number of outsourcers now offer "modular outsourcing"; namely, they support specific tasks, such as help desks, asset management, and software license coordination. In terms of contractual arrangements, some outsourcers divide both the financial gains and losses of certain system integration projects with their clients.[7]

Flexibility is an important factor in making outsourcing a successful partnership. For example, outsourcing vendors have found that many customers are concerned with variations in data processing volumes that may occur during the life of a multiyear agreement. These changes may result from advances in computing technology (for example, applications may start to use embedded images or video clips, thereby generating more information that needs to be moved and processed) and/or changes in the organization's business posture, market, climate, etc. Volumes could also go down as an organization milks a sizable, mature market that is still profitable but on the down side of the product life cycle. The outsourcer must be able to accom-

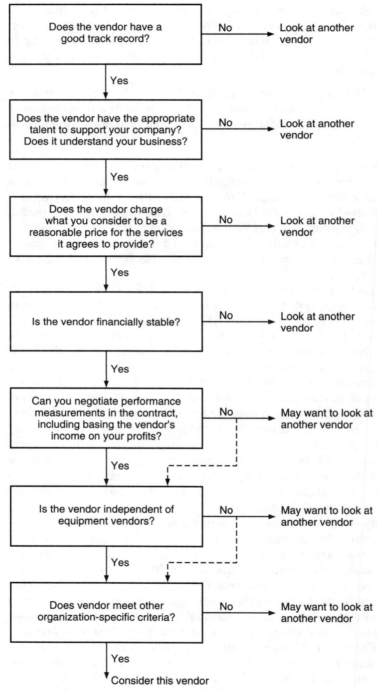

Figure 5.6 Some vendor selection decision points.

TABLE 5.2   Some Issues to Consider in Selecting an Outsourcer

Financial stability of the service provider

Importance of customer's business to the provider

Attitude and service orientation of the provider

Compatible cultures

Quality of service provider personnel

Turnover of service provider personnel

Staffing level of service provider vs. volume of business

Location of and communication with the service provider

Disaster-recovery plan of the service provider

Insurance carried by the service provider

Payment cycle of customer

Turnaround time for services

modate the growth in a seamless manner, and the charges must grow in a linear,* not a polynomial (or even exponential), manner. Similarly, if transaction rates are going down, the outsourcer is expected to be able to lower the cost accordingly over time.

Organizations are not static businesses, and they should not have to be locked in by a contract that requires the same disbursement even if their processing needs decrease or the technology affords processing efficiencies (e.g., improved cost of machine cycles) that should be passed back to the organization. Besides facilities management, some outsourcers concentrate on distributed network implementation, software development, and systems integration. The top ten outsourcing vendors employ thousands of people, enabling them to provide the appropriate talent for a client's need (for example, Integrated Systems Solution Corp. of Tarrytown, New York, is a wholly owned subsidiary of IBM with 8,000 employees providing worldwide IS services). Smaller outsourcing vendors derive their strength from specializing in a specific technology or computing platform.

The organization must make an effort to assess all the things that could change over the life of a contract, so that a new contract does not have to be renegotiated every time there is some business redirection (outsourcers may use change orders submitted by the organization as a way to increase their fees). Obviously such contingency analysis is not trivial, as discussed in Chap. 4, and it is not possible to anticipate all outcomes. Even a fairly simple outsourcing contract can be 200 pages long. The contract should be written in such a way that

---

*Actually it would be even better if the organization could receive bulk rates—namely, the higher the transaction rate, the lower the cost per transaction.

the organization knows ahead of time what a change would cost. For example, if there are acquisitions or the organization grows as a result of market forces, and the transaction rate increases, say, by 10 percent, 20 percent, 50 percent, or 100 percent, the contract should indicate the cost implications. Extra charges for change orders are common in service bureaus, where the processing is done at a remote site owned by the outsourcer, but should not be in facilities management, where the outsourcer assumes responsibility for an organization's data center.[14] In service bureaus, charges are typically based on the number of transactions and accounts; experience shows that cost variations from 5 to 10 percent more than the average base value are not uncommon. In facilities management, reasonably small workload variations may be absorbed by the on-site staff.

The issue of workload variations brings up the need for shared trust. It is difficult to form a workable organization-outsourcer partnership without trust. Organizations and outsourcers often find themselves having to go back to the table to either cover an unexpected situation or clarify some language that may be subject to different interpretations. A positive disposition based on mutual trust is key to making this aspect of the relationship work in a professional manner.

Some organizations have outsourced their IS operations not to a single vendor but to a few vendors, capitalizing on their individual strengths. For example, Eastman Kodak outsourced its computer operations to IBM, its applications development to Andersen Consulting, and its network management to Digital Equipment Corporation.

5.5 Managing the Outsourcers

Outsourcing agreements are complex contractual arrangements, and organizations that are in the process of moving to an outsourced mode need to be sure that they have a deal that is flexible enough to track the organization's changing needs for the late 1990s.

One must manage the outsourcer as one would manage one's own shop by setting priorities, making sure the right people are being brought in, and ensuring that the operation is being run efficiently.[5] To have a better chance of succeeding, an outsourcing arrangement needs to be viewed as more than just a service contract; it must be seen as a strategic alliance involving a long-term partnership and relationship between the organization and the outsourcing vendor. Outsourcing is "not a panacea—just because one turns something over to other people does not mean that you do not have to pay attention to it"; one still has the oversight responsibility of managing it properly.[14]

Business knowledge has become a point of differentiation and competition among outsourcing vendors. For example, EDS has set up 39 operating units, each of which concentrates on a specific type or family of businesses.[5] Some outsourcers have acquired industry expertise by hiring former employees from their customer base; once on the outsourcer's staff, these employees form the core of an industry group that can handle customers with similar IS needs. Large outsourcing companies may develop business expertise in several industries; smaller companies tend to focus on specific areas—for example, the defense industry, banking, telecommunication carriers, mortgage companies, the banking industry, etc.—maintaining a variety of operating systems on hardware from IBM, Unisys, Data General, and NCR.[26] For example, DEC usually emphasizes business process engineering and redesign and hopes to expand learning services to include multivendor product training. Three key elements in outsourcing are data center management, network management, and applications maintenance.[27]

Sometimes business knowledge is equated with familiarity with the basic hardware and software tools used in an industry. As noted, although facilities management experience is important, an examination of many of the recent outsourcing deals indicates that in a number of cases the decisive factor was the outsourcer's ability to provide integrated applications that communicate with one another to support many of the organization's data requirements.

Some organizations look for outsourcers that will hire and retain the organization's IS staff. Continuity (that is to say, the outsourcing vendor's taking over the organization's staff) is particularly important when many of the programs have been developed in-house and tailored to the company's business requirements. Many outsourcers ostensibly hire an organization's IS staff, but some may soon thereafter disperse the staff to other accounts or let them go. Sometimes well-known outsourcing vendors run the risk of losing an existing contract because of difficulties with the organization's managers over such issues as technical performance, cost, and the frequent replacement of key project managers (see Ref. 28, for example).

Outsourcing vendors may be responsible for compliance with software licenses on behalf of their client organizations. As a precedent, in 1993 an appellate court ruling gave Computer Associates International Inc. the right to sue National Car Rental Systems Inc. for breach of contract. National was being sued for allowing its service vendor to use software licensed to National by Computer Associates; Computer Associates is also taking action against National's outsourcing vendor, Electronic Data Systems. The outcome of the suit has important implications for companies that use outsourcing services. The case has caused analysts to warn companies to closely examine the terms of their software licenses and to take responsibility for compliance; other analysts suggest that businesses devise a contract with their outsourcing vendors that indemnifies them in the event of any illegal practices.[29]

5.6 Transformational Outsourcing/Strategic Planning

As noted, some high-end outsourcing vendors now emphasize strategic planning in conjunction with outsourcing. This enables the organization to look at the advantages of reengineering at the same time it reexamines the expenses associated with running and managing the IS function. Such an approach, called *transformational outsourcing,* is directed toward helping an organization place its IS strategy in the context of how to remain competitive in the market. Hence, as might be expected, this analysis goes beyond IS; it may entail examining whether the customer should be in certain businesses or not, and looking at user departments, policies, and procedures to decide if the company is organized properly.[5] Once this business analysis is completed, the IS implications emerge as a by-product of the more fundamental effort.

Although many organizations are just focusing on modernizing their IS infrastructure, some are also pursuing a global review of their business. Increasingly, service vendors are offering a combination of planning, design, and outsourcing services to meet these user needs. Therefore, in addition to traditional facilities management and assistance in modernizing traditional computer architectures, outsourcing vendors are moving into strategic planning. See Figure 5.7.

Outsourcing vendors are turning to reengineering services as a source of revenue. They are enticing reluctant customers by promising to uncover inefficiencies and to help implement changes. Some outsourcers are so confident of their skills that they guarantee that their reengineering services will produce savings.[21]

Outsourcing can free senior IS management from worrying about the detailed operational aspects, outage management, resource accounting and forecasting, short-term overloads, etc., and allow them to focus more on the organization line of business. In fact, in the past IS managers have been accused of being too absorbed in the technology to the exclusion of strategic business considerations.[3] Unfortunately, given the rapid rate of technological innovation and accompanying obsolescence, IT has properly demanded constant attention. By transferring some or all of the responsibility for tracking technology day by day, conference by conference, announcement by announcement to the outsourcing vendor, the IS managers can shift a major portion of their attention to business considerations.

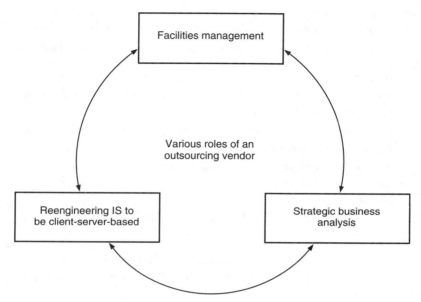

Figure 5.7   Expanding the role of outsourcing vendors.

For example, SHL Systemhouse Inc., Ottawa, Canada, positions itself as an outsourcer that can help its customers make the transition to client-server computing using a transformational outsourcing philosophy. Here the outsourcer takes over some or all mainframe applications while helping the customer migrate other functions to PC-based platforms, decentralized applications, and local area networks, at the same time enabling an organization to transform itself into a more effective business entity, at both the IS level and the core business level. Transformational outsourcing enables the organization to migrate to current and forward-looking technologies, with attendant functional and financial benefits. The crux of the transformational outsourcing philosophy is that by handing off mainframe processing to a third party, the customer frees up resources that can then be used to focus on core business strategies, on business process reengineering, on implementing a downsizing strategy, or on funding new business efforts, perhaps in pursuit of new markets. Chapter 8 covers transformational outsourcing in more detail.

5.7   Outsourcing Vendors

IS outsourcing vendors can be grouped as follows:

- A handful of large, broad-scope companies, including EDS,

Computer Sciences Corp., IBM ISSC,* Affiliated Computer Systems, Systematics Information Services, and SHL Systemhouse

- A number of medium-sized companies, including Digital Equipment Corporation,† First Financial Management Corp., Securities Industry Automations Corp. (SIAC), Shared Medical Systems Corp., Newfoundland and Labrador Computer Services (Canada), and Power Computing

- Startup or newly interested companies, including Genix Group, Perot Systems, and Litton Systems

- IS management consulting companies, including (beyond the ones listed above) Andersen Consulting, Nolan Norton & Co., Ernst & Young, and DMR

- Niche providers, including Marshall & Ilsley Corp and FIserv Corp.‡

This partial list does not include outsourcers that concentrate only on other functions, such as LAN and WAN maintenance—see the appropriate chapters.

5.8 Dealing with Outsourcing Vendors

Table 5.3 depicts some of the key steps required to implement an outsourcing decision.

Confidence that the outsourcer can meet the service levels and evidence that it has done so for other customers needs to be established as part of the vendor selection process. There are three important considerations, which if ignored will weaken the potential benefits of outsourcing and strengthen the potential disadvantages:[15]

1. An accurate cost analysis of the IS operation is required. Without cost metrics it will be impossible to assess the soundness of the outsourcing decision and the reasonableness of the charges proposed by the outsourcer. With such data, the organization will be able to determine which systems are to be outsourced and which should not be. Some of the required tools were discussed in Chap. 3.

---

*Sales of $4 billion were estimated for 1993.

†As of 1993 only about $100 million of DEC's $2 billion systems integration business was in outsourcing.

‡FIserv outsources for 1600 full-service clients, including banks, thrifts, and credit unions.

TABLE 5.3   Some Key Steps in Support of Outsourcing

Selecting the right vendor
Writing the right contract
Dealing with the transition
Bringing in the process
Dealing with dislocated people
Focusing on the bottom line

2. Effective communication is needed during contract negotiation and thereafter. Such communication is particularly important given the potential depth of the decision and its corporate and financial repercussions; a mistake can be costly. This topic was also covered in Chap. 4.

3. Audit rights. When dealing with outsourcers, the IS manager must be sure to acquire audit and access rights. These include[30]

   - The right to review the billing in detail
   - The right to formal responses to audit findings regarding internal control weaknesses
   - The right to have an outside party review controls

Because relinquishing responsibility for a major part of the organization's activities to a third party is such a profound move, it is vital to get the relationship established right the first time around. The contract must be carefully structured, and it must contain a clear statement of the responsibilities of both parties, juxtaposed with well-defined levels of service to be provided by the outsourcer. Service-level agreements (SLAs) allow the organization to monitor the outsourcer's performance. SLAs are generally connected with penalty clauses to cover degradations in service; however, penalty clauses should be a last resort. Organizations need to make sure that the performance criteria described in SLAs are described in user's terms, not in system jargon.

During negotiations, it is important that both sides be open in declaring what their future plans and strategies are, so that the outsourcer can accurately assess the service to be offered as part of the deal, and the organization can form realistic expectations of what can be achieved in terms of costs and service metrics.[31] Chapter 4 indicated that asymmetric information can affect the efficiency of the outsourcing transaction: Misinterpretations of what is expected and what can be delivered will lead to problems at a future point, whereas straightforward business dealing benefits both sides.

5.9   Some Specific Examples of Outsourcing

This section lists a few of the outsourcing contracts that were in the news at writing time, to give a sense of who the players are and what aspects of IS are being outsourced. This section is not intended to be exhaustive.

5.9.1   U.S. examples

McDonnell Douglas, an $18.4 billion leader in the aerospace industry, announced a $3 billion outsourcing deal with IBM's Integrated Systems Solutions Corp. McDonnell Douglas undertook a workforce reduction of 20,000; the outsourcing agreement will enable the company to release an additional 1450 IS employees.[32]

Armco Advanced Materials Co. has outsourced its DEC VAX-based payroll, financial, and trend analysis data processing operations to The Genix Group. Armco Materials also preferred being a larger Genix customer to being a very small ISSC customer, and felt a closer sense of kinship with Genix because it runs a data center in nearby Pittsburgh.[33]

Deere and Co. moved its mainframe-linked software development to India in an effort to save time. The tractor manufacturer outsourced part of its mainframe work to Satyam Computer Services Ltd. in Madras, India. Satyam uses fifty 80386- and 80486-based microcomputers linked by satellite to Deere's 3090 mainframes in Moline, Illinois, to convert programs from IBM database formats to DB2. The company uses KnowledgeWare's Application Development Workbench computer-aided software engineering (CASE) development tools. Communication between the microcomputers in India and Deere's mainframes in Illinois is faster than that between Deere's own development microcomputers and the mainframes because Satyam is 10.5 hours ahead of Moline. Satyam's daytime development crew accesses the mainframes in the middle of the night, when they are more accessible than they are during daytime hours. Deere considered both the time savings and India's lower labor costs when deciding to move development overseas.[34]

In March 1993 Armco Steel Co. announced a 10-year outsourcing contract with IBM's Integrated Systems Solutions Corp. Armco is seeking to focus on its central business of making steel. The company expects to save $100 million in information systems expenses, and indicated that one strong factor in its decision to outsource was high mainframe fees.[35]

Kaiser Permanente Health Plan has signed a $70 million outsourcing contract with IBM's Integrated Systems Solutions Corp. Industry observers say that this may be the start of growth in health care outsourcing contracts; growth in outsourcing may be fueled by the Clinton administration's interest in addressing the U.S. health care crisis.[36] Health care is technologically behind, and outsourcing expenditures from the industry may amount to an estimated $900 million annually by 1996. Blue Cross/Blue Shield of Massachusetts also has elected the outsourcing approach.

5.9.2   Canadian examples

SHL Systemhouse Inc.'s Northeast Data Centre recently signed a $100 million contract with the Department of Government Services of Nova Scotia. Two other major SHL customers are Maritime Tel and Tel and TransCanada Credit.[37] In 1993 SHL Systemhouse won a 10-year government outsourcing contract with the Canadian postal service for what may total $1 billion. SHL will migrate the postal service to a client-server computing environment that will include mainframe services as well as support for local area networks and wide area networks. SHL plans to offer about 250 Canadian postal service employees a job under the contract.[38] (See Chap. 8 for more examples.)

Datacor/ISM Atlantic Corp.'s major clients are NB Tel, NB Power, and Blue Cross of Atlantic Canada.[37]

Newfoundland and Labrador Computer Services (NLCS) performs mainframe computing operations for 15 government departments as well as private firms.[37]

Outsourcing is becoming the rule in Canada's oil industry.[39] In December 1992, Telus Corp. and ISM Information Systems Management Corp. launched a venture supporting outsourcing/systems integration activities. Contracts with Alberta Energy Company Ltd., Shell Canada Ltd., and AGT generated $45 million in revenues for the new venture. Minerva BP Canada signed a 5-year outsourcing agreement with Technology Inc. estimated to be worth $10 million. Another example is Amoco Canada. Chapter 8 discusses this case in more detail.

Oil and gas exploration and production firm Bow Valley Industries Inc. opted for off-the-shelf software packages in preference to in-house application development or outsourcing during its recent system conversion. Bow Valley converted its computer operations from an IBM mainframe computer and Wang minicomputer to DEC workstations running the Ultrix operating system. Although Ultrix is being phased out by DEC, Bow Valley used it as a stopgap until the applications it needs are available on the Open Software Foundation's OSF/1 operating system.[40]

5.9.3 British examples

British Home Stores PLC (BhS) has signed an 11-year contract with Computer Sciences Corp. to take control of its information and computer systems. BhS expects to save 30 percent on administration costs that now run at £10 million a year (that is, save £3 million).[41] The 11-year contract allocates management of BhS's data center in Luton and the 115 employees who work there. The head office, distribution base, and 136 stores with 500 microcomputers and 2000 point-of-sale terminals are linked to the data center by a digital services network. The center manages the company's marketing, finance, merchandise, and personnel systems. All systems such as warehousing, administration, and the executive information system are to be developed and maintained by CSC. The contract has left BhS with a comfortable measure of control over its operations, as it reserves the right to change the services that CSC provides.[41]

References

1. C. Benko, "Outsourcing Evaluation: A Profitable Process," *Information Systems Management,* 10(2):45ff, 1993.
2. M. J. Major, "Who's Minding the Store?" *Midrange Systems,* 6(4):23ff, 1993.
3. S. L. Huff, "Outsourcing of Information Services," *Business Quarterly,* pp. 62ff, Spring 1991.
4. J. P. McPartlin, "A More Selective Service," *Information Week,* November 16, 1992, p. 88.
5. D. Livingston, "Outsourcing: Look Beyond the Price Tag," *Datamation,* Nov. 15, 1992, pp. 15ff.
6. J. Cox, "The Essential Guide to Effective Outsourcing," *Computer Weekly,* June 10, 1993, p. 24.
7. W. B. Richmond, A. Seidmann, and A. B. Whinston, "Incomplete Contracting Issues in Information Systems Development Outsourcing," *Decision Support Systems,* 8(5):459–477, 1992.
8. L. Loh and N. Venkatraman, "Determinants of Information Technology Outsourcing: A Cross-Sectional Analysis," *Journal of Management Information Systems,* 9(1):7–24, 1992.
9. U. Apte, "Global Outsourcing of Information Systems and Processing Systems," *The Information Society,* 7:287–303, 1990.
10. G. G. Gable and J. A. Sharp, "Outsourcing Assistance with Computer System Selection: A Success Factors Model," *Proceedings of the 25th Hawaii International Conference on System Sciences,* IEEE, Piscataway, N.J., 1992.
11. U. Gupta and A. Gupta, "Outsourcing the IS Function," *Information Systems Management,* pp. 44ff, Summer 1992.
12. D. Thobe, "Who's Minding the Shop: BCR's Survey on Outsourcing," *Business Communications Review,* pp. 22ff, May 1992.
13. C. Wilder, "Analysis for Your Operations," *Corporate Computing,* February 1993, Vol. 2, No. 2, p. 23.
14. J. Radigan, "Outsourcing—A Complex Decision," *United States Banker,* pp. 39ff, December 1992.
15. J. L. Wagner, "Issues in Outsourcing," *1992 IRMA Conference Proceedings,* Idea Group Publishing, 1992, pp. 214ff.
16. D. Minoli, *Broadband Network Design and Analysis,* Artech House, Norwood, Mass., 1993.

17. J. Quinn, T. Doorley, and P. Paquette, "Beyond Products: Services-Based Strategy," *Harvard Business Review,* pp. 58ff, March–April 1990.
18. N. Ahituv and S. Neumann, *Principles of Information Systems for Management,* 3d ed., W. C. Brown Publishers, 1990.
19. S. Polilli, "Is Outsourcing a Bargain?" *Software Magazine,* 13(4):36ff, 1993.
20. T. Middleton, "It's Time to Duel for Dollars: Rethinking Outsourcing," *Corporate Computing,* 2(6):27ff, 1993.
21. L. Wilson, "Outsourcers Take an Inside View," *Information Week,* no. 408, p. 48, Jan. 18, 1993.
22. J. Kelly, "Outsourcing: Who Pulls the Strings?" *Datamation,* Sept. 15, 1990, pp. 103ff.
23. H. Mendelson, *The Economics of Information Systems Management,* Prentice-Hall, Englewood Cliffs, N.J., 1991.
24. B. Bass, "Outsourcing Decision Imperils $1.2B Bar Code Deal," *Federal Computer Week,* 7(13):6, (1993).
25. M. Robichaud, "Balancing Control with Partnership," *Computing Canada,* 19(4):38, 1993.
26. B. Caldwell, "FIserv: Buy and Excel," *Information Week,* no. 413, p. 37, Feb. 22, 1993.
27. M. McGee, "DEC's Outsourcing," *Information Week,* no. 428, p. 28, June 7, 1993.
28. T. C. Doyle, "DEC Retains Portion of Kodak Outsourcing Pact," *Computer Reseller News,* no. 529, p. 16, June 7, 1993.
29. M. Halper and T. Hoffman, "Ruling Hits Outsourcing," *Computerworld,* 27(16):1, 1993.
30. A. H. Friedberg and W. A. Yarberry, Jr., "Audit Rights in an Outsource Environment," *Internal Auditor,* pp. 53ff, August 1991.
31. P. Lloyd, "Outsourcing: Mutual Benefit or Mutual Risk," *Telecommunications,* pp. 37ff, February 1993.
32. M. Halper, "IBM/McDonnell Douglas Deal Questioned," *Computerworld,* 27(2):109, 1993.
33. M. Halper, "Armco Outsources to Genix; Flexibility, Proximity Cited as Reasons for Partnership," *Computerworld,* 27(17):58, 1993.
34. M. Halper, "Deere's Faraway IS Solution," *Computerworld,* 27(7):76, 1993.
35. M. Halper, "Big Iron Bills Drive Armco to Outsource," *Computerworld,* 27(9):55, 1993.
36. N. Margolis, "Outsourcing Can Cure Health Care IS Ills," *Computerworld,* 27(6):24, 1993.
37. A. Safer, "Outsourcing: Gentle Wave Sweeps Maritimes," *Computing Canada,* 19(8):16, 1993.
38. T. C. Doyle, "SHL Systemhouse's Outsourcing Coup; $1B Award: Tapped by Canadian Postal Unit," *Computer Reseller News,* no. 521, p. 210, April 12, 1993.
39. L. Nattalia, "How Outsourcing Rules the Oil Patch," *Computing Canada,* 19(2):1, 1993.
40. A. Eastwood, "Bow Valley Bucks Outsourcing Trend," *Computing Canada,* 19(6), 1993, pp. 5ff.
41. N. Edwards, "Store Saves by Giving IT Away, Which Computer?" 16(3):48,

Outsourcing of Telecommunication and LAN Functions

6.1 Overview

Corporation communication functions are now increasingly experiencing the trend noted in other chapters for data center operations, namely outsourcing. The demands of the economic environment of the 1990s are prompting organizations to reexamine the cost-effectiveness of their communication networks. Table 1.4 shows that communication represents about 18 percent of the typical IS budget; hence, senior management is interested in trying to reduce the relative as well as the absolute level of these expenditures. Yet, in spite of the outsourcing trend, the strategic value of information to an organization is becoming undeniably patent: There is a great demand to gather the information, give it promptly to the employees in the organization that need it, and provide it in a useful and understandable format.

Network outsourcing is an alternative which, through advanced technologies, standardization, and a close partnership between the client organization and the provider, facilitates an effective and economical means of meeting various present and future corporate communication requirements.[1] The continued emergence of relatively complex new digital transmission technologies such as frame relay, SMDS, and cell relay, as well as the pressing tasks of daily management of large networks based on these new communication systems and services (and also based on existing systems and services), is inducing many organizations to seek outside professional help. For example, corporations are becoming more involved in client-server systems and are now realizing how much human management the technology demands; however, because these companies often cannot afford to increase their own staffs, they are forced to look outside for support.[2] The outsourcing vendor can manage the network, or at least, a portion thereof, on behalf of the organization. According to studies, two-thirds of all large organizations currently outsource at least one communication function.[3] A 1993 Frost & Sullivan International report predicted that revenues from network outsourcing will triple by 1997, from $2.6 billion in 1992 to $8.5 billion in 1997.[4,5,*] Demand for networking outsourcing comes from medium and large national and multinational companies, such as finance, petrochemicals, transport, and distribution companies, and from government organizations. In particular, multinational organizations tend to be large users of telecommunication outsourcing. Saving money, making up for unavailable staff time and skills, and reducing routine management responsibilities are some of the key reasons for outsourcing data communication and telecommunication functions.[5]

End users, senior management, and customers are requesting integrated access to information stored in multiple distributed databases, placing greater demands on networks, systems, and support personnel; this is occurring during a period of increased pressure on the bottom line. Hence, improved utilization of existing information resources is viewed as key to surviving or, better yet, prospering in today's business climate.[1] With outsourcing, overall costs may be reduced or better service for the same price can be obtained.[6] Although there are tactical advantages to outsourcing communications, in the final analysis, unless outsourcing can be viewed as a strategically viable decision, it is generally not worth pursuing this approach. Besides data center operations, data storage management, help desks, and application development, companies have outsourced communication equipment, physical cabling, communication system integration, private switch management, site management, communication circuits, LAN management, LAN interconnection, disaster recovery, network design, wireless networks, entire subnetworks, and international networks. Global networks almost always involve outsourcing, since because of differing PTT (post, telephone, and telegraph) requirements, organizations have to plan and install these networks in cooperation with (1) the PTTs, (2) each country's system

---

*The combined network management and integration markets were worth some $1.45 billion worldwide in 1990, and various groups predict that by 1995 the figure will grow threefold, to somewhere between $4.2 and $5.6 billion. The portion of this figure coming from network management alone was about 20 percent in 1990 and should be around 33 percent in 1995.

distributor, and (3) the global carrier, and the organization may not have the resources to coordinate all that.

Because third-party communication service providers are continually improving the quality and extent of their service offerings, user organizations no longer need to assume that they must own and manage their own private network in order to ensure the best service.[3] Many organizations that in the past deployed a private communication network are now contemplating outsourcing not just the transmission facilities or the management of their private equipment, but also the design and operation of the entire network infrastructure, including equipment, connectivity, physical premises, and staff. On the other hand, some organizations are reluctant to outsource their entire network (or networks), but may consider giving up specific time-consuming or complex operations.[4] Also, organizations are not necessarily looking to a single vendor to manage an entire network but tend to allocate specific network responsibilities, such as a geographic area or a department, to a specific outsourcing vendor; this is also known as multisourcing. Specific vendors may be asked to handle a single task, such as help desks, disaster recovery, remote network management, or network inventory. For example, outsourcing the management of LANs is a growing opportunity for service providers who can maintain systems for organizations that are unable to expand their own staffs.[2] Many LAN integrators are sending out their technicians to be full-time, on-site network administrators for their customers (outsourcing services for LANs are expected to grow 15 to 20 percent annually).

At the other end of the spectrum, some organizations are making a renewed commitment to insourcing, based on recent technological trends. These trends include umbrella products that allow multiple networks to be managed from one remote location; wider acceptance of standards, which makes combining network products from several manufacturers cheaper and easier; and the recent availability of broadband transmission services along with the emergence of on-premises switching equipment and multiplexers to share the network capacity with lower-speed devices.[5] Network modernization, even when done in-house, can produce savings in the 5 to 15 percent range.

Handing over a network, particularly a global network, to an outsourcer can be a challenging task, even in light of the promise to streamline operations, reduce cost, and free management to focus on core business aspects. Individuals on both sides of the issue have described communication outsourcing in the best and worst lights possible: Proponents proclaim that outsourcing is an excellent approach for organizations that need to cut costs, add new systems and applications, and focus internal talent on mission-critical projects, while those on the other side claim that organizations that hand over part or all of their operation to an outside provider risk cost overruns, lose control, experience service degradation, and have to deal with vendor incompetence or indifference.[7] The realities of outsourcing generally fall somewhere between these two extremes.

It is almost universally true that today the communication network is a critical component of an organization; hence, outsourcing decisions must be undertaken with care and analytical credibility. This chapter examines issues associated with a potential decision to outsource communication functions. Outsourcing is being considered both at the WAN (telecommunication and/or data communication) and the LAN levels. The treatment that follows looks at both of these areas, since some of the decision points, considerations, cost/benefits, and approaches differ.

6.2   Telecommunication Outsourcing: Benefits and Risks

Initially, businesses saw computers as providing a service, not as office equipment that they had to learn to use and manage. The introduction of more cost-effective computing in the late 1960s and early 1970s, in the form of mainframes and minicomputers, shifted the emphasis toward in-house ownership and operation of this equipment. The microcomputers of the 1980s, in the form of desktop personal computers, reinforced that trend. As the processing units became smaller and more distributed around an organization, the communications links between the units became more important. That gave impetus to the growth of the private network. The trend now is to look, once again, at IT as a set of services; the main difference in the current situation, however, is that with the advent of distributed computing, the communications network is today's computing facility.[8]

Organizations need to look at where existing personnel create the most value and search for methods to deploy those talents to the greatest advantage of the corporation.[1] Communication functions that do not contribute to the core business, that can be clearly defined, and that can be provided by outside vendors at a lower cost or at a better service level, such as pulling cables, doing adds/moves/changes, and supporting desktop installations at remote sites, are among the best choices to consider for outsourcing.[6] Rather than spending time on these functions, in-house staff might better be involved in network design and duties that make full-time use of special skills. Since WAN links are still expensive, optimization of network design usually leads to worthwhile savings; freed-up personnel may be able to focus on such tasks. However, the assessment of whether to delegate responsibility for an application, a distributed computer system, or an entire network to an outsider is one of the most demanding decisions a network manager may be asked to make.[7] Some questions that are raised are:

- When should an organization outsource a network?
- Should the network be outsourced in total or in parts?
- How does an organization select the right vendor?

It is not possible to answer these questions unequivocally and with true analytical certainty. Service providers will always try to persuade customer organizations that outsourcing is in the customer's best interest. But as noted for data center outsourcing, there are both advantages and disadvantages associated with handing over responsibilities to a third party. It is generally accepted that, at the business level, outsourcing can play an important role in dealing with mergers and acquisitions, divestiture of units, restructuring, streamlining, technology modernization, and decentralization.[9] Running private networks has become fairly expensive; it has also become a complex task. The decision process is conceptually simple: Whether to outsource depends upon which alternative best meets the criteria that are determined to be critical to the organization. However, translating this conceptually simple principle into actual organization actions is more challenging. The criteria chosen may include the level of service provided to IS users, cost, flexibility and the management of risk. The decision, however, must be supported, to the extent possible, by appropriate data and analytical models.

6.2.1 Outsourcing approaches

The areas in which outsourcing is most effective continue to be technology applications development, network management, and computer operations.[10] In telecommunications, outsourcing takes two major forms:[11]

- The outsourcer can own or obtain the organization's network.
- The outsourcer performs overall network management for the organization.

The services provided by the outsourcer differentiate communication outsourcing from other communication services. In a network services or resale environment, the organization, not the network provider, is responsible for managing the telecommunications opera-

TABLE 6.1   A Taxonomy of Communication Options

	Organization responsibility	Outsourcer responsibility
Organization-owned	Private networks: equipment; national and international communication services: staff	Facilities management: basic service-level management
Outsourcer-owned	Network services: national and international virtual networks; managed private network services; global network services	Outsourcing in true sense: service-level management; network services; systems integration; consultancy

tion. Facilities management represents the reverse of the network services scenario, in that the provider manages the network but does not own it. At the other end of the spectrum from outsourcing, private networks are owned and internally managed by the organization. See Table 6.1. For some organizations, a modular approach to outsourcing works best, since it makes it easier for the organization to withdraw if the arrangement is found not to be appropriate, and if the arrangement works, its scope can be expanded. For instance, rather than hiring an outsourcer to manage its entire collection of remote LANs, an organization might target certain installations for outsourcing to evaluate its merits.[7] A modular approach to outsourcing can also be employed for quick implementation of specialized applications where there is no in-house expertise. For example, establishing the in-house capabilities to develop and implement a business image processing application can be expensive; for such a project, it may make more sense to utilize an outsourcer that is already familiar with the technology. There is also a growing trend for organizations to deal with multicompany outsourcing associations; these associations offer services to their constituents at a significant cost saving.[10]

When handled properly, outsourcing of telecommunication functions can be regarded as a strategic rather than a tactical decision.[3] Outsourcing eventually leads to a reduced workforce, enabling telecommunications managers to reexamine staffing and make effective use of human resources.[10] With more vendors entering the communication outsourcing field, price competition may drive potential savings for the organization somewhat higher than was possible in the past (by some small amount). Although each organization's reason for outsourcing is different, there are some motivations that recur; these fall into three categories: financial, technological, and human resources.[8] Outsourcing corporate telecommunications is most effectively managed if organizations choose noncore business functions, establish expectations of services and costs, and do not look for large instantaneous financial returns on their decision.* Experts suggest that outsourcing contracts should focus on the integration and management of systems and facilities; a goal of 15 percent savings per year is reasonable. Following these guidelines can result in increased attention to core business functions and the ability to have access to skilled technicians and network professionals. Unmanaged outsourcing can result in a lack of commitment from management or in domination of the corporate culture by the outsourcing vendor.[10]

Outside management of corporate telecommunications is now a well-established industry, accounting for more than half of all networking operations; data network management is the top activity being outsourced, with voice network management and system integration tied for a close second.[10] As noted in earlier chapters, organizations have long been using third-party contractors for services such as data processing and computer hardware maintenance. In the telecommunications area, outsourcing examples include third-party provision of the physical circuits supporting the (private) enterprise network and the use of the public telephone service for the corporate voice network. CIOs are looking at outsourcing as a source of expertise, since even the most technically proficient companies find data networks to be complex and costly; hence, communications has become a function that may be outsourced. Nonetheless, many companies have been reluctant to let go of such a critical operation, and outsourcing of communication has become popular only since the late 1980s.[12] Outsourcing of the data communication and telecommunication functions takes two forms:

1. Outsourcing of the design, deployment, and management of a private WAN[†] or LAN

2. Use of public switched services (such as cell relay, frame relay, SMDS, switched T1, etc.) in lieu of dedicated communication services that have to be managed by the organization

---

*Except when an outsourcer buys the network (particularly equipment) from the organization. Here the organization gets an upfront infusion of capital.

[†]A private network is a network that employs dedicated lines such as analog private lines or fractional T1, T1, or T3 private lines. It can also use private frame relay/cell relay switches interconnected with private lines. It carries exclusively the traffic of the organization. Such a network does not utilize public network services and/or switching. Such a network generally does not use transmission systems that have been directly deployed by the organization, such as a pair of user-owned microwave towers; we call such systems bypass systems. Generally, private networks use carrier-provided high-bandwidth low-functionality communication channels, over which the organization overlays its own valued-added.

As discussed previously, in the mid 1980s, large organizations often built their own enterprise communication network based on technical or cost justifications. First, private networks (e.g., based on T1 multiplexers and dedicated transmission facilities) afforded economies of scale unmatched by public switched networks.* Second, this approach was often the only way in which the required end-to-end response time could be guaranteed. Third, a private network could support value-added services that were not otherwise available. A private network, however, has drawbacks. These include the need for a substantial investment of funds, the difficulty of taking advantage of newer technologies, limitations in terms of expansion and scalability, and the uncertainty of whether the in-house service provider is really providing the best value for the money.[3] For applications that require support from many remote locations and/or locations with low volume, the installation of a dedicated network may not be justified. Such remote sites may be expensive to connect and to manage over a private network, and public switched services may be more cost-effective.

As discussed in Chap. 2, the 1990s are seeing the introduction of a plethora of new high-quality switched services which are beginning, in some cases, to rival the cost/performance metrics that customers have experienced with private networks. When a public communication service is used, the organization is letting the carrier design, engineer, manage, operate, test, optimize, grow, and migrate the network infrastructure—these are all functions that the organization would otherwise have to attend to. The possibility of this type of outsourcing leads to the question: If carriers and service providers are expending effort and funds on developing their network infrastructures and service capabilities, why should the user organization try to compete in this arena?[3] Just as with data center operations, it may be better to focus a company's attention, energy, and financial resources on the business applications, and leave the task of information delivery to a carrier.

An organization that does not make the appropriate investments in the analysis supporting the outsourcing decision and in the required ongoing monitoring can find itself with a network that does not meet

---

*It has been difficult to convince managers to employ public switched networks as long as the use of such networks for more than 30 minutes per day (1/16 of the 8-hour business horizon) turns out to be more expensive than using a private line for 1440 minutes per day. A common-sense example is offered by these managers: Nobody is going to use public transportation to go to work if after only 3 trips a month ($3/44 \approx 1/16$ of the commuting horizon) this approach is already more expensive than using a private car for the whole month. These managers reportedly feel that providers should spend less time on researching and developing unnecessarily complex technologies (usually in search of a problem for which this technology is an after-the-fact solution, as contrasted with a bona fide existing business problem in search of a solution) and more time in reducing the cost of moving a bit of information from point A to point B.

the end users' needs and potentially can lose revenue as a result of productivity impairments, blockage of business transactions (e.g., being unable to receive a client's order for goods if, for example, the 800 trunk bundle is not properly engineered), purchases of unneeded equipment and products, or recovery efforts to correct problems.

In some cases, the desire to outsource may be more of a political issue, rather than being based on justifiable technical or cost factors: Senior management may simply think that outsourcing is a "good thing."[3] The communication services provided by the in-house supplier may be (or be perceived to be) inadequate, but there may be no formal method of measuring the service actually received; this situation is similar to that described in previous chapters for data processing. One of the advantages of outsourcing is that it requires that the supplier-customer relationship be on a formal basis, with quantified service levels, audit trails, and a formal contract.* Telecom managers should conduct frequent ongoing analyses of department cost levels, service levels, and strategic directions. This analysis could, for example, be useful for convincing CFOs and CEOs that the department is already cost-effective. The analysis should aim at developing a service plan and preparing an outsourcing model that includes updatable counts of resources and costs; this allows the manager to update the plan (say) annually without having to redevelop the entire model.[6]

As stressed in this text, outsourcing decisions should be based on analytically demonstrable facts; just as for data processing, it is important that the reasons be specifically identifiable and readily quantifiable. An organization considering communication outsourcing must first examine its internal network operation. The *process of evaluating* whether or not to outsource is intrinsically beneficial, as discussed in Chap. 5. Current and future business requirements must be analyzed relative to the in-house options in order to get a sense of what improvements can be achieved, in both the short and the long term. In many cases, cost savings in the 20 to 40 percent range† may be possible by implementing improvements identified during the analysis process of the organization's network, without necessarily going to outsourcing (this is similar to the data processing results dis-

---

*Such service measures can also be introduced for the in-house service provider if deemed appropriate.

†Savings in the 5 to 15 percent range are more common, although occasionally the higher range is possible. If the network is well designed, it is likely that the higher additional efficiencies cannot be achieved. If the network is not well designed, e.g., if it has grown by incrementally adding nodes and facilities without an analytical design, then the higher efficiencies are possible. Usually replacing multiple lower-speed lines between two points with a single higher-speed line results in economies of scale and lower cost.

cussed in the previous chapter). Clients indicate that even if there are collateral benefits such as a better grade of service, they tend to outsource only if they can save money; additionally, those savings have to be substantial (of the order of 20 percent or more) for the company even to contemplate migrating from its private network to a third-party network.[3]

The analysis may show that only selected parts of the communications functions are candidates for outsourcing. As covered in Chap. 4 (Fig. 4.4), none, some, or all of the communication functions may turn out to be candidates for outsourcing. The following list represents some reasons for communication outsourcing:[9]

- Alter network loads or imbalances.

- Improve uptime, reliability, and performance.

- Facilitate network management.

- Obtain access to missing communication skills, while at the same time avoiding the need to permanently hire such talent.

- Respond to user dissatisfaction.

- Upgrade communication systems.

- Inject new technologies into the network.

- Move the organization's employees to strategic tasks and eliminate staff with redundant skills.

- Reduce communication costs through economies of scale, discounts, and shared expertise; the need for new capital investments may be reduced.

- Position the organization to respond more flexibly and rapidly to changes such as a business acquisition, a new application, or expansion to a new geographical area.[8]

- Realize fixed and predictable costs for budget planning; there also will be benefits from the infusion of cash under certain (but not all) outsourcing deals.

Outsourcing affects a range of networks, from networks supporting mainframes, to networks supporting midrange systems, to networks supporting PCs (typically LANs). For example, the increased use and power of the AS/400 departmental system has taken this type of computing to companies that could not afford it before; at press time, an increasing number of networks were being put in place to support AS/400 platforms. The nature of midrange computer operations also makes them prospects for network outsourcing. The AS/400 computers and the RS/6000 workstations are sold as stand-alone turnkey

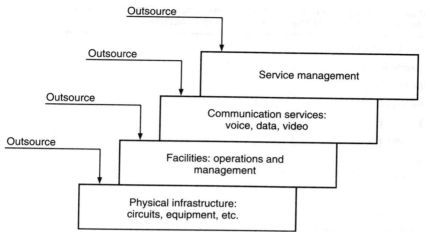

Figure 6.1   Tiers of communication outsourcing.

operations, systems that do not require large staffs to maintain and operate. Therefore organizations are looking for turnkey networks for those systems.[12]

Figure 6.1 depicts a four-tier model that can be used in discussing communication services delivery to give a sense of where outsourcing may fit in.[13] The first tier in this model supports physical transmission, value-added communication services, communication equipment, and communication software. This tier, which can account for as much as 60 percent of a network, has already experienced a trend in favor of outsourcing. The second tier represents network facilities for managing, operating, and administering the infrastructure upon which services rely. Many companies have also outsourced this tier. The third tier covers management and administration activities, including planning, monitoring, reporting, and end-user interface. Some companies have opted for the outsourcing approach. The fourth tier represents the overall communication posture of the organization: its policy, direction, and strategic goals (combined, these three management tiers account for as much as 45 percent of an organization's communication budget). This area is more difficult (and less desirable) to outsource. Of course, some organizations have outsourced the entire network.

Telecommunications companies have used outsourcing services over the years, but now it is possible for any company to outsource certain telecommunications operations.[6] Table 6.2 gives a partial list of U.S. companies and organizations that have outsourced some (major) portion of their communication requirements.

TABLE 6.2   Partial List of U.S. Companies and Organizations That Have Outsourced a Portion of Their Communication Functions

Aetna Life & Casualty

Airborne Express

Allied Corp.

American Airlines

American Express

Anheuser-Busch

Arco

Atlantic Richfield Co.

Avis

Boise Cascade

Bridgestone Firestone, Inc.

Cargill

Caterpillar

Chemical Bank

Chevron

Choice Hotels

Cigna Corp.

Citibank

Colonial Penn Group

Combustion Engineering

Computer Language Research

CSX Corp.

Defence Commercial Telecommunications Network

DuPont

Electronic Data Systems Corp.

Eli Lilly

EPSCS User Group

Federal Express

First Chicago Bank

Ford

General Dynamics

General Electric (Domestic)

General Electric (International)

Goldman Sachs

Hertz Corp.

TABLE 6.2   Partial List of U.S. Companies and Organizations That Have Outsourced a Portion of Their Communication Functions (*Continued*)

Hillenbrand Industries

Honeywell

Hospital Corp. of America

ITT

J.C. Penney

James River Corp.

John Hancock Financial Services

Kemper Financial Services

Litton Industries, Inc.

Marriott Corp.

MasterCard

McGraw-Hill

Metropolitan Life Insurance Co.

National Semiconductor Corp.

Nestlé Enterprises

Paine Webber

Primerica Corp.

Prudential

RJR Nabisco

Safeco Insurance

Security Pacific

Textron

Travelers Insurance

Unisys Corp.

US Air, Inc.

Xerox Corp.

6.2.2 Cost savings in communication outsourcing

As with data processing, relying on an outsourcer allows an organization's management to concentrate on the company's core business. Some of the benefits of outsourcing communication functions are shown in Fig. 6.2. Organizations that have made the decision to outsource have generally expected that it would deliver immediate (i.e., tactical) benefits. When outsourcing is the right course of action,

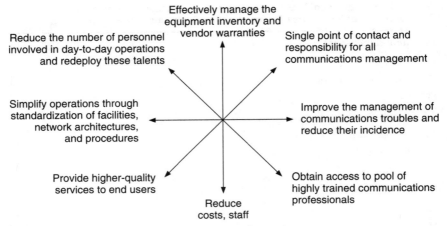

Figure 6.2 Some advantages of communication outsourcing.

which can be demonstrated only by valid financial, risk, and techno-logical analysis, it will indeed provide such short-term benefits (in addition to other long-term benefits). Cost savings can come about in a number of ways:

1. Using a public or third-party network service reduces the orga-nization's need for capital investment in the communications infra-structure for both initial deployment and further network expansion. In the United States, just after the breakup of the Bell System, some organizations thought that deploying a completely private bypass net-work (that is, raising their own microwave towers, purchasing their own satellite transponders, obtaining right of way for deploying pri-vate fiber in downtown areas, etc.) would save them money. Soon these organizations realized that the cost of managing and maintain-ing such bypass networks was prohibitive. Almost all of the bypass systems that were deployed by organizations have been scrapped (very small aperture terminal, or VSAT, systems and downtown fiber being perhaps two notable exceptions).

2. Savings in operational and maintenance costs are possible through the outsourcer's economies of scale (as discussed in Chap. 5), since the outsourcer is able to spread the cost of its network infra-structure, service management, and staffing across a number of accounts. Also, sometimes one can obtain a lower interest rate on a (much) larger loan. So, while an organization may be able to finance its communication infrastructure at, say, 6 percent, an outsourcer developing an infrastructure to support dozens of customers may be able to obtain the loan at, say, 5 percent. These savings may be passed back to the user organization. Also, an organization buying 20

bridges from a supplier may get a 20 percent discount, while an out-sourcer buying 200 bridges gets a 35 percent discount. Finally, there are a number of communication services that can be purchased at a lower per-unit cost when purchased in volume.

3. The organization's personnel costs can be reduced if a smaller in-house network staff is required, although some personnel must be retained to provide strategic control of the network and to manage the outsourcer. Some organizations view outsourcing as simply another form of restructuring: By outplacing selected functions, senior management is freed to focus on mission-critical issues, and scarce resources are released to focus on value-added activities.[1] Many telecommunication and data communications tasks neither require a permanent staff nor can be handled appropriately by the existing in-house staff. Consider, for example, the deployment of a large new corporate PBX supporting 5000 employees at a downtown corporate headquarters. Specialized skills are required only for the duration of the deployment of the PBX, say 12 months. If these specialized professionals are put on the payroll, what is the organization to do with them after the installation is complete? On the other hand, it is unlikely that the existing in-house staff can handle that (relatively) rare, yet demanding, deployment event in the most effective manner. The same could be said about installing an ATM-based LAN serving 2000 employees in a corporation utilizing dozens (perhaps hundreds) of ATM-based hubs; or the installation of a 500-site VSAT system; or the deployment of a workflow imaging system involving video juke-boxes, scanners, gateways, and desktop access for 500 employees. Hence, outsourcing of communication functions adds flexibility, since it is easier to expand and reduce an outsourcing contract than it is to hire and lay off personnel.[14]

4. Financial benefits may accrue from selling the organization's own network infrastructure to the outsourcer as part of some types of contracts (see, for example, Fig. 3.5). For the organization that has such a network, this type of contract implies an immediate cash injection that can be used to finance core business expansions, new ventures, etc., and removal of the network assets from the balance sheet.

5. Improved quality of communication services may result. In some instances, the improvement comes from the establishment of formal metrics included in the contract between the organization and the outsourcer. In other instances, improvements originate through the use of modern technology, particularly high-speed digital systems such as cell relay service. As was the case for data processing, the outsourcer typically deploys leading-edge technology on a regular basis in order to remain competitive (for the organization, it could be disruptive and expensive to regularly upgrade its private network).

Also related to cost savings, a cost/performance benchmark has been proposed that enables a telecom department to[6]

- Compare itself against other companies
- Compare itself against itself over time
- Benchmark what the department currently is doing against what it could be doing, considering possible alternatives

6. Hedging against technological obsolescence is possible. This is related to the previous point: By relying on the outsourcer to deploy evolving technologies, the organization is not forced to become expert in newly introduced communication systems, which is usually a fairly challenging task. Also, this provides a path for the introduction of technologies to support the more demanding applications that are likely to be introduced in the next few years: desktop video, multimedia, imaging, etc. The technological expertise and experience needed to make the transition from a traditional host-based environment to a cooperative processing environment (e.g., client-server) may not be available in-house; outsourcing can compensate for this gap in knowledge.

7. Expedited and more efficient deployment of networks, particularly for global connectivity that entails drops in foreign countries, is possible. Dealing with foreign PTTs can be a challenge. Nationally specific procedures may be required. It does not usually pay to make "specific investments"* to learn these procedures for one or two drops in a country; it is much more effective to rely on an outsourcer that is already familiar with these procedures because of the assistance it has provided to many customers over the years.

8. Communications-related billing can serve as a strategic tool that provides organizations with useful information about their business operations. From the organization's perspective, outsourcing simplifies billing in several ways. First, the organization can select a pricing structure to meet its individual needs and provide the most value—the pricing can be flat fee, on a per-transaction basis (per minute, per kbit, per packet, per frame, per cell, etc.), or on a fixed basis plus a per-unit cost. Second, costs can be measured and distributed on an as-incurred basis. This allows expenditures to be analyzed in order to understand structural IT costs, and also facilitates internal billing if costs are to be allocated to different profit and loss centers within the organization (it is generally more difficult to allocate the cost of a private network). Billing can be produced on a variety of media for additional automated analysis and management review.

---

*Refer to Chaps. 3 and 4.

9. The outsourcing vendor can typically be expected to bring advanced network and administrative management systems designed to optimize the performance of the networks, the service center personnel, and the field technicians. As discussed in the case of data center outsourcing, the vendor is motivated to use the most effective technology in order to improve its profitability.[1] For example, automated procedures can be used to ensure accurate and timely completion of work and trouble resolution; expert systems can assist the help desk personnel in diagnosing network troubles.[15]

10. Outsourcing frees the organization's network personnel from low-level tasks, such as network troubleshooting, and allows them and their management to concentrate on the development of new network applications. Outsourcing may also be the desirable long-term direction for an organization, in addition to being, perhaps, the optimal short-term solution. Ultimately, an organization must decide if it wants to be its own "mini phone company," or if there is an entity that can better handle such utility needs while the organization tries to devote all its resources to what it does best—namely, pursue its line of business. This point is even more profound in communication than in data processing because there is no such thing as a data processing utility upon which the organization could rely, whereas there are communication utilities (that is, carriers) that support a variety of communication needs: local, national, international, voice, data, video, mobile, etc. Therefore, the decision to shift responsibility to an outside agent is easier to implement.

6.2.3 Some disadvantages of communication outsourcing

A number of potential negative factors need to be taken into consideration as part of the analysis related to the outsourcing decision (also see Fig. 6.3).

1. Many network applications are mission-critical, implying the need for utmost reliability and availability. An in-house group has the needs of the organization at heart, and will normally be very responsive to outages. Sometimes service providers are perceived as being less responsive to a customer's individual needs, particularly if there is a backlog of outages that the carrier or the outsourcer is working on or if there is some major outage affecting multiple users.

2. An organization entering into an outsourcing contract must be prepared to take the communications functions back in-house if there is a need to do so at a future date. However, reversing an outsourcing decision and bringing the design and operation of a communication network back in-house after it has been relinquished can be a demanding and expensive task. Some refer to this as "entrapment."[13]

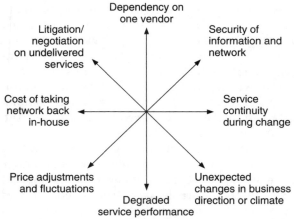

Figure 6.3 Some of the negative factors associated with communication outsourcing.

3. The information carried on the network is usually sufficiently sensitive that it must remain secure. At the practical level, sensitivities range from unimportant to vital. For example, a research firm might label everything that it produces, even a simple report based on the open literature, as "proprietary" and require E-mail, facsimile, and other methods of transmission to guard the data, although there actually may be no real sensitivity. On the other hand, data may involve mergers and acquisitions (for example, in an arbitrage room in a brokerage firm), competitive industrial plans, medical information, payroll information, legal proceedings, etc., where there is an obvious need for security. Sometimes a single piece of information coming off a protocol/network analyzer could help a technician on the staff of the outsourcer obtain inside information. In some of these cases, the user organization may be forced to build a private network in order to guarantee a level of security exceeding that provided by third-party operators.

4. In the United States there is the issue of interLATA versus intraLATA communication. The organization must assess the nature of its communications and determine if the potential outsourcer is able to handle the task effectively. A network that is mostly contained in a county, state, or region is different from a network that spans many states, as may be the case for the network for a financial services company. It is likely that different providers would be better suited to each of these cases.

5. Very few service providers today are able to support the requirements of global organizations for on-the-ground service. They may not, for example, have staff, technicians, troubleshooters, etc., in some secondary towns, or even in some countries, so that these

resources may have to be flown in overnight when needed. Some service providers have sought to become more global by signing up global customers, either using the contract to finance an extensive rollout of infrastructure or acquiring the organization's own global private network.[3] Even for national networks, carriers appear to have great innate difficulties understanding what an enterprise network is, as contrasted with just a set of links, and why users prefer the stability of private lines over the unpredictability and increased costs of switched service.

6. Corporate managers will have to work hard for outsourcing savings, since outsourcing requires a nontrivial level of managerial diligence; performance goals and guidelines must be clearly defined and codified, and vendor efforts must be continuously monitored.[7] It can take up to two years to negotiate a managed network outsourcing deal; even then, most organizations do not choose to hand over the complete running of their networks all at once.[8] Also, there is generally some finger-pointing in allocating responsibility for end-to-end delay between the computer system (people) and the network (people). Therefore, unless the data center is also being outsourced to the same vendor, it is important to put in place reliable monitoring capabilities to manage any disagreement that may arise.

7. A number of problems can arise if the telecom and IS departments do not control the process effectively. For example, there may be an inability to convert the corporate philosophy to the outsourcing concept, as discussed in Chap. 4, leading to a lack of attention to these critical issues on the part of senior management. There can be a shift of control over information networking from the organization to the third party; this leads to a situation in which the vendor's corporate culture begins to dominate the organization. A different culture-related problem can arise in merging the entrepreneurial spirit of the outsourcer with the corporate culture of the client organization.[10]

Outsourcing vendors and sophisticated organizations disagree as to whether networks can be outsourced in pieces or have to be outsourced as a whole.[9] For example, some organizations have outsourced their entire network; other organizations have outsourced voice or data but not both; yet other organizations have outsourced network management for the night shift but have retained control for the day shift, this being more critical.

A press-time survey of the top communication outsourcers indicated that about 95 percent support outsourcing of WANs, 70 percent support outsourcing of international data networks, 70 percent support LAN outsourcing, and 50 percent support voice outsourcing.[9] The same survey, however, indicated that organizational requirements may be somewhat different: the highest reported organizational need was LAN outsourcing, followed by voice outsourcing, international networks, and WANs. In particular, it should be noted that organizations generally spend more on voice than they do on data (by as much as 8 to 1); hence, it would appear that if cost considerations were the overwhelming driver, then the outsourcing focus should be on voice. However, the network management aspect of voice is usually a much smaller fraction of the total expenditure than that of data (in voice, transmission costs dominate expenditures). This arises from two factors: (1) A major portion of the voice network management is done by the carrier unless the organization has a private network of PBXs (private branch exchanges—that is, private voice switches); and (2) data communication networks are much more complex, particularly in terms of interworking equipment supporting dissimilar protocols.

6.3   Decision-Making Approach

Observers note that the "ideal profile" of the telecommunication manager of the 1990s is to be[13] (1) technically competent, (2) business-wise, (3) financially literate, (4) IT aware, and (5) a good presenter of a business case. These skills clearly come into play when considering whether to outsource some functions or not. In Chap. 5, a three-step analysis to assess the desirability of outsourcing in the data processing context was discussed. A similar analysis can be applied to the corporate communication function. This section refines that procedure and applies it to communication, as seen in Fig. 6.4. Usually, needs analysis is kept in-house, although in some cases the organization ends up "outsourcing the analysis to do outsourcing."[10]

Step 1: What communication problem is outsourcing supposed to fix?
The first step of the analysis involves a macro assessment as to what is the organizational problem that outsourcing of communication functions is supposed to fix. Outsourcing is a complex process, as noted in the previous sections; therefore, one needs to ascertain early on that it is indeed the effective thing to do. Perhaps outsourcing is not the best way to approach the challenge that the organization is facing. For example, suppose 200 customer service representatives in a customer service bureau were taking manual notes of customers' complaints. If management decided that it would be much more effective to automate the process with a computerized (communication-based client-server) system, but the 200 intended users were extremely reluctant to use it, then outsourcing will not solve the problem.

This part of the analysis can be initiated with a series of questions such as[7]

■ Why is communication outsourcing being considered in the first place?

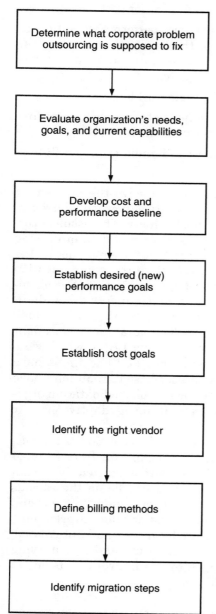

Figure 6.4 Multistep analysis in support of a communication outsourcing decision.

- Are tactical or strategic considerations at play, or both?
- Are network costs increasing and network performance suffering, either because of intrinsic growth of the business or because the existing staff is overwhelmed with IS/telecom tasks as a result of new technologies, new business climate, etc.?
- Are existing staffers overwhelmed by their workload?
- Does the organization wish to shift in-house talent away from fire-fighting chores so that they can tackle strategic projects?
- Does the organization have the ability to handle strategic IS/telecom projects?

Even if it has decided that outsourcing would solve the problem at hand, the organization must examine at this stage how well outsourcing fits into the way the organization does business. This issue of corporate culture was already discussed in the context of data processing in Chap. 4. However, it is possible that the IS culture may not be the same as the datacom/telecom culture; therefore the same question deserves to be answered in the context of communication. For example, IS may still be mainframe-based and may support a few disciplined subgroups over a long-established SNA network; hence, it may have a closed/stable/mechanistic* culture. The datacom group might have grown up from end users deploying PCs and LANs, which were then connected with bridges and routers; since PCs and LANs have become increasingly important, this end-user-based group may have grown to the point where it has become the established datacom organization. Such an organization may have an open/adaptive/organic culture.

The evaluation of the organization's needs, the selection of the outsourcing vendor, and the contract negotiation can take from 12 to 24 months or more. As soon as the analysis effort is started, organizations often realize that they have a less good handle on the various communication circuits, switches, multiplexers, modems, servers, applications carrier services, entire networks or subnetworks, etc., that are in place throughout the company than they had anticipated; this is due to the fact that either poor accounting and inventorying procedures are in place or the changes to the network in terms of add/drops/moves have come at a rapid rate.

Step 2: Corporate goals and needs.   On the assumption that the organization has decided at the macro level that outsourcing is the way to go, this step entails a thorough evaluation of an organization's com-

---

*Refer back to Chap. 4 for a discussion of these terms.

munications needs, goals, and current capabilities. Of course, the communication needs are related to the data processing needs; therefore, even if the datacom/telecom manager was looking at outsourcing only the communication functions, there must still be a very close interaction with the IS department. In many cases, even when total outsourcing cannot be justified, outsourcing only the international telecommunications function may still be desirable.

Step 3: Establishing the baseline. An inventory of applications, requirements, and supporting equipment must now be undertaken. This process can be daunting—existing network hardware, lease agreements, purchase/discount agreements, warranties, software versions, cable connectivity, and terminations must be inventoried. Few organizations have ready access to this information.[1] In the best of situations, the information will be stored in separate databases, some in the voice management system and some in various data or LAN management systems; more likely, the needed information exists only in manual records or does not exist at all. Corporate applications can be classified as critical, support, background, etc. For each application, the location and number of users, the traffic profile, and the response time requirements must be identified. Next, the communication systems and communication equipment supporting each application must be identified and inventoried. Finally, the cost of the communication equipment, either in absolute terms or in terms of cost per transaction, should be calculated. Costs that must be determined include the cost of maintenance and emergency repair service, as well as equipment replacement or upgrade costs; all owned and leased equipment as well as leased carrier communication lines must be valued accurately.[7]

At this point it may also be possible to look at other communication needs, such as voice, video, facsimile, etc., and determine if there are overlapping requirements (for example, a requirement that all of these services be delivered to the desktop or to specific remote locations) that can be met with an integrated network. Sometimes companies have dozens of overlapping but nonintersecting networks to support the various requirements; merging these networks can substantially reduce costs (from the points of view of operations, productivity, teletraffic economies of scale, and tariffing).

As a by-product of this step, the manager can establish minimum service requirements in terms of availability, reliability, response time, throughput, and other appropriate measures (e.g., responsiveness to a reported outage, etc.). The effort to establish a baseline for a given network or service starts with the question: What does the organization absolutely need from the network or service? These baseline parameters define the performance levels required by the organization for a given network or service; an outsourcer that agrees to take responsibility for that network or service must agree to meet these minimum goals.[7] In turn, the outsourcer's performance can be measured against this baseline: To what extent is the outsourcer exceeding or falling short of the baseline performance?

Step 4: Setting outsourcing goals.   There are situations in which the baseline parameters are only the absolute minimum required for a given function; in this case, the next step is to establish performance and service goals beyond this minimum. For example, the baseline may indicate that for equipment repair, the goal is 24 hours for a remote router. If network maintenance is being outsourced, the desired corporate goal could be to repair the router in 12 hours, in order to improve productivity. Beyond the obvious network performance and service goals (e.g., transaction response time, transaction loss rate, reliability, availability, etc.), an organization may include how quickly new services are installed, how quickly moves and changes are made, and how quickly a new site is added. Hence, SLAs for communication outsourcing should cover delivery, reliability, performance, and fault prioritization; they should also cover the hand-over procedures between the private and the managed network.[8]

Once defined, the objectives must be communicated to potential vendors. Many organizations state their managerial objectives and request potential vendors to structure a support program aimed at achieving these objectives. Other organizations delineate the functions to be outsourced and request specific bids. The first approach fosters creative ideas, whereas the second lays the basis for strict managerial control and easier comparison.

Step 5: Determining cost goals.   Since savings are one of the major reasons why organizations seek to outsource, it is important to establish financial goals. This is done using the cost baseline previously developed and applying the appropriate analytical machinery (e.g., as discussed in Chap. 3). Knowledge of both the baseline costs and the financial goals enables the organization to negotiate fair rates for services over the life of an outsourcing contract.[7] The overall goal is for services to be provided in a timely manner and for no unexpected charges to be levied. The benchmarking approach discussed earlier can also be employed.

Step 6: Identifying the right vendor.   Since an outsourcing decision means establishing a long-term relationship with an outside organization, it is important to identify the right vendor. This is usually done via an RFI/RFP approach. There are a number of possible vendors, as noted below, but each category of outsourcing vendor has strengths and weaknesses. The RFI/RFP should be written so that individual service elements can be compared across vendors; if the RFI/RFP is modular, the organization can derive the combined cost of selecting various combinations of outsourceable functions. In addition to the evaluation of the services and associated costs, the evaluation of potential outsourcing partners requires looking at a number of factors, such as:[1] What are the corporate qualifications? What is the vendor's primary business? What is the experience of the vendor's personnel, and what is their service orientation and their dedication? Who are the vendor's customers for similar services? How flexible are the contractual terms? Are there provisions for reevaluating terms based on changes in the corporate environment? How attractive is the employee-retention plan? Are there any hidden costs associated with it? How attractive are the financial arrangements? What are the terms for the purchase of existing assets? What is the vendor's ability to deliver better or equivalent functionality? What is the transition plan?

To accomplish some of this, the RFI/RFP should ask for a list of current clients and ex-clients; these references should be followed up in order to obtain additional insight into the service levels that will be provided by the outsourcer in question. Ex-clients should be asked why they decided to either terminate or not renew the contract. An outsourcer has the challenge of having to convince prospective clients of its experience in managing communications networks, its financial stability, and its commitment to the network management business. As was the case for data center outsourcing, it is advantageous for the network outsourcer to understand the client's business and its applications.[8] A middle manager or an interdepartmental committee can be given direct responsibility for managing the procurement process; responsibilities may include establishing the evaluation criteria, contract negotiations, transition planning, redefining key supplier relationships, and managing the relationships across vendors.[1]

Another option at this stage would be to determine whether there is a chance that insourcing might work. Usually, some form of senior-level management oversight is needed to ensure that management's objectives are met and to ensure that the internal proposal and the outsource vendors' proposals are evaluated in a consistent manner.[1]

The typical outsourcing evaluation process takes a year and a half or more; typically this involves six months to set objectives, two months to select a consultant to assist in the process, three months to prepare the RFP, and three months to select the vendor and negotiate a contract.

Given the declining profit margins and revenues from hardware operations, big systems vendors (computer manufacturers) are looking at outsourcing as a revenue source. Systems integrators that used to rely almost completely on federal government contracts are also looking for new sources of revenue. Because these systems integrators do not have their own equipment or services to sell, they may be more willing to support the heterogeneous networks that are typical of today's computing environments. A number of value-added resellers (VARs) that have grown out of the PC and LAN industries also provide outsourcing services. Some VARs offer nationwide services; others provide services on a regional basis. Outsourcing services are also offered by the traditional outsourcers of data processing functions. Manufacturers of telecommunications equipment have provided network management services like network design, remote diagnostics, and monitoring for a number of years. These vendors are now expanding into new product areas, such as LAN interworking. Carriers like the regional Bell operating companies, the long distance carriers, and the independent telephone companies have also entered the outsourcing business. It is to be expected that carriers that have managed their own networks for decades are well positioned to manage networks for commercial companies. Vertically integrated specialists focus on supporting outsourcing services for specific industries, such as the medical or educational field.

Step 7: Defining billing methods.   The organization and the vendor need to establish a suitable billing approach; the terms and conditions for payment are important details to be resolved in the negotiation process. Several generic approaches exist for constructing a billing plan, including the following:

■ In networks with stable traffic, the outsourcer may offer fixed monthly costs for each workstation in the network and fixed monthly transmission fees for traffic carried over public or private networks (in this arrangement, the outsourcer gambles that the organization will not exceed a certain baseline traffic level).

■ The outsourcer may charge for "time and materials" for all maintenance tasks and related support services. This arrangement can work well in cases where the outsourcer supplies a well-defined set of services.

■ The outsourcer may charge a fixed fee for a set of specified services to be delivered. An incentive is paid to the outsourcer if the outsourcer identifies a way to meet the organization's requirements at a lower cost. As implied in Chap. 4, an outsourcer may be more inclined to watch the bottom line if it shares in the cost-cutting rewards.

Both proposals and contracts tend to underestimate future outsourcing costs; while the base cost may be well specified, "residual," "overage," or "tilt" charges may be less conspicuously included in the fine print of the contract, or even omitted. These charges cover outsourcers' tasks such as sales/marketing, contract management, production control, and performance analysis. Some studies indicate that these ancillary expenses can almost double the official cost of the contract. Hence, the organization should seek to have all the pertinent costs clearly identified at project inception time.[9] Additionally, networking technologies and the economics of these technologies change at a fairly rapid pace; the contract and the associated billing should be flexible enough to allow future injection of new technologies and appropriate cost alterations (if needed).

Step 8: Undertaking the transition and identifying specific issues. After the basic issues concerning planning of the outsourcing decision, the proposal development, and the contract signing have been worked out, the implementation phase of the plan must start. Questions that come to play at this stage include the following:[1] How is the organization going to exercise control over the outsourced operation? What internal expertise is needed to ensure expected levels of service and performance?

There are a variety of issues to be worked out in this phase to successfully complete the outsourcing task, including the following:

- The migration of the organization's personnel to the outsourcer must be done in a smooth manner if the organization's operations are to proceed without complications, interruptions, or breaches. The internal organizations that are currently providing the services may view outsourcing as threatening or as a reflection on their performance. The staff should be informed that outsourcing is being considered or has been elected, rather than trying to keep it a secret for as long as possible, because if the staff finds out unofficially, the department could become paralyzed by worries about job change or loss.[6]

- A common fear among managers is that outsourcing may make their jobs redundant. Managers should be directed, instead, to effectively manage the outsourcer.

■ Internal procedures for PC or terminal purchases, telephone or data transmission services, LAN adds and moves, and so on, need to be documented clearly.

To discharge many of these duties, organizations often retain technical and managerial personnel to oversee the outsource operation; their ongoing responsibility may include contract management, performance evaluation, end-user satisfaction, and network planning.

6.4 Maintenance Contracts

A practice that has been in place for many years and that represents a low-level/low-risk type of outsourcing is to contract out maintenance of telecommunication equipment. In data processing, where the equipment in question is more or less centralized in a few locations (particularly in the case of mainframe operations), this may not be as important as it can be in communication. By the very nature of communication, the equipment tends to be spread out all over the map: from all over town, to all over the nation, to all over the world. Contracting with a third party to take over such maintenance can prove to be cost-effective when the true total cost of the organization's operation is taken into consideration. The other advantages are[8]

■ It ensures that the system or service is managed by specialists. The maintainer ensures the continued training of its staff.

■ Staffing levels are maintained through holidays, vacation, training, and sickness periods.

■ Through performance monitoring, the organization can identify where targets are not being achieved and remedial action needs to be taken.

6.5 Outsourcing Network Management

Outsourcing of network management functions is the implicit topic of this entire chapter. Table 6.3 provides a list of outsourceable telecom/datacom tasks from a functional perspective.[1] This type of outsourcing is equivalent to the top three tiers of Fig. 6.1. As noted earlier, outsourcing of network management represents about $1.2 to $1.5 billion; this is about 20 percent of the total network outsourcing market.

TABLE 6.3   Spectrum of Outsourceable Network Management Telecom/Datacom Functions

- Service center operations
    Help desk
    End-user consulting
    Problem analysis
    Problem management
    Billing inquiries
    Repair and installation dispatch
    Moves, adds, and changes
    Management reporting
- Network diagnostics
- Network operations
- Traffic analysis
- Capacity planning
- Performance management
- Network design
- Disaster planning (consulting)
- Disaster recovery
- Inventory management
- Warranty management
- Vendor liaison
- Technology assessment

Chapter 1 indicated that network management can represent as much as 40 percent of the cost of a network; therefore, the greatest potential savings can come about by outsourcing that function and transferring or eliminating the headcount. As a rule of thumb, outsourcing will save money when the internal staff is not too competent, is too highly paid, or is too large.[9] A clear definition of the objectives of going outside the organization is key to a successful outsourcing relationship for network management support. Unlike the purchase of other outside services, such as application development or consultation, outsourcing of network management functions entails management as well as human resource considerations. Therefore, the eight-step evaluation discussed above is of the utmost importance. Many organizations have found that just the evaluation of outsourcing may be beneficial in motivating the telecom/datacom department(s) to initiate new services and programs benefiting their clients.

6.6 Communication Outsourcing Vendors

Earlier, it was noted that a variety of outsourcing vendors are now available. The market for third-party network services is becoming more competitive as new players enter: systems houses (e.g., EDS) and computer manufacturers (e.g., IBM) are expanding into the networking arena, not only offering managed network services but also using their systems and computing expertise to offer packaged solutions; and specialist organizations, such as the airline reservations company SITA, are offering managed network services to other organizations outside their own industry.[3] Network outsourcing vendors offer a full range of services designed to improve operations while controlling costs; these include the services described in earlier sections, such as end-to-end responsibility for the design, implementation, management, and operation of all communications networks. Services range from commodity functions, such as moves, adds, and changes management, to strategic functions—enterprise network design, for example.[1] To support these services, an outsourcer typically needs a comprehensive management system that maintains a set of integrated databases including such things as cable management, billing, directory, order status, equipment inventory, user, warranty, and vendor information.

Of course, many traditional carriers, including interexchange carriers and local exchange carriers, offer communication outsourcing services. Carriers have made plans to deploy new switched networks based on evolving technologies such as cell relay service, frame relay service, SMDS, and so on, which support switched connectivity, and value-added services that approach, and even exceed, the functional capabilities of the private enterprise networks now in place. This itself is making organizations reassess their communication posture with regard to retaining a private network. At the very least, many are deploying a hybrid network, in which a certain core may be based on private transmission facilities, but the other tiers are based on public services. For example, a corporate network to support telecommuting may utilize a high-speed backbone of T1 lines connecting, say, three regional sites, with telecommuters utilizing ISDN to reach these regional nodes.

As part of provider differentiation, communication outsourcers are aiming at establishing themselves as regional and global service providers. Some international outsourcers are reportedly prepared to buy an existing organization's network simply as a means of entering the market.[3] The challenges for the network outsourcing vendors are to assess the current network operations, to assume control of this environment, to provide adequate security and network management, and to economically migrate to an environment that maximizes centralized control and accommodates user requirements.[1] Also, it is important for outsourcers to understand their clients' business needs, in addition to understanding their networking needs. For example, a soft-drink company wants to make sure that its network performs at its best when the sun shines, and wants the outsourcer to understand that; a bank wants to see its automatic teller machines have the best network response time during lunch breaks and in the early evenings, and wants the outsourcer to understand that; an airline reservation company wants to make sure that the network provides maximum availability during the high traveling season, and wants the outsourcer to understand that. Some shakeout is predicted, and it is possible that only the big players will survive beyond the late 1990s.

Communication outsourcing vendors can be grouped as follows:[7]

- Computer system manufacturers, such as Digital Equipment Corporation, Hewlett-Packard, IBM, Unisys, etc. Although vendors such as these may be able to handle a variety of computer systems, application development, and porting, they may lack experience in voice and data networking, particularly integration. Also, they are likely to prefer to sell the equipment they manufacture rather than developing or managing a heterogeneous network.

- System integrators that in the past worked on government contracts, such as Boeing Computer Services and Martin Marietta. Vendors such as these support a variety of computer systems and LANs, but they may lack experience in WANs and global networking; also, they may be more used to a government procurement cycle than to the commercial climate.

- LAN value-added resellers, such as Computerland, LAN Systems, and Valinor. These vendors tend to specialize in PCs, PC LANs, distributed off-the-shelf applications, and links to legacy mainframe systems. Usually they do not support WANs and/or voice and data integration.

- Traditional outsourcing specialists, such as Computer Sciences Corporation and EDS. These vendors have experience in many phases of outsourcing, particularly for data processing and system integration. However, they may not have experience in all WAN services and in network management, and they may rely on subcontracting to complete some jobs.

- Telecom equipment manufacturers, such as AT&T Paradyne, BBN, Codex, GDC, and Recal-Milgo, among others. Their forte is usually in the area of network management, but they may lack system integration experience; also, like the computer system manufacturers, they may prefer a homogeneous network over a heterogeneous one.

- Regional and other carriers. These vendors are strong in LATA-wide voice and data networks, including design and maintenance (interexchange carriers are nationwide). They are now also entering the LAN and PC markets. Their approach emphasizes switched network services. Global network coverage is generally not supported, although some interexchange carriers do provide global services.

- Vertical market outsourcers, such as Automation Partners, Shared Medical Services, and System Technology Corp. Vendors such as these usually have a strong understanding of the organizations' business needs and the specialized applications used. However, they have limited knowledge of other industries, and may not always be familiar with the latest WAN technologies.

- Value-added networks (VANs), such as Cylix Communications Corporation and others. Cylix manages the data communications networks of over 140 companies; it has provided equipment, data network services, and monitoring since 1970.[12]

6.7 Communication Outsourcing in Europe

Many European companies are entering an age of global competition, which offers not only new business opportunities but also considerable challenges. As in the United States, many corporations are undergoing restructuring and are subject to regulatory change. Additionally, these organizations also face technological changes, as do organizations all over the world. Yet these same organizations rely to an ever-increasing degree on information. Europe represents about one-sixth of the total communication outsourcing market (Japan represents about one-third and the United States represents about half); the United Kingdom represents about half of the European business, with the rest in France, Italy, Germany, and the Netherlands.[8] The outsourcing market in Japan is expected to double every year, that in Europe to grow at 50 percent a year, and that in the United States to grow at 30 percent a year.

The regulatory situation in various European countries plays an important role in what outsourcers can do. The European telecommunications industry is governed by both European Community law and the national laws of its member states. Outsourcers operate in most countries as VANs; therefore, a priority of most outsourcers with regard to regulation is to expand the definition of a VAN. VANs in many countries are restricted to carrying only data, although this situation is now beginning to change.[8]

Studies have shown that a typical United Kingdom–based 300-site private network, which would cost £5 million (NPV) to run over five years as an in-house system, could cost £3.5 million (NPV) as an externally managed network. This is a saving of 30 percent over the lifetime of the project. See Fig. 6.5.[8] Generally the same distribution of costs exists for U.S. networks.

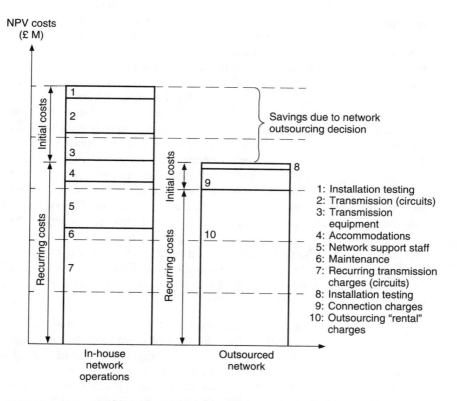

Network consists of 10 backbone links at 64 kbps and 290 drops at 9.6 kbps. Refer to Ref. 8 for other assumptions.

Figure 6.5 Distribution of pre- and postoutsourcing costs.

6.8 Outsourcing of Global Telecommunications

During the 1980s and early 1990s, multinational corporations built and managed increasingly complex private international networks, while facing uneven service levels and network performance from country to country, a patchwork of regulatory environments, and a growing need to support an infrastructure that required an increasing level of technical skills in many new areas, including frame relay, cell relay, client-server systems, and new applications. In the current environment, it is not easy to obtain adequate or flexible bandwidth across an international network, nor are there efficient and timely processes for identifying and managing network problems. In many cases, telecommunications managers cannot even ascertain how much they are spending on international communications, since, unlike U.S. carriers, non-U.S.-based international carriers do not routinely provide detailed usage data or cost allocations. The concept of outsourcing international communications is relatively new.[11]

Typically, up to 90 percent of a company's telecommunications needs are domestic, and most multinational organizations have deployed domestic networks and put in place in-house telecommunications experts to support these networks. Keeping abreast of technological, regulatory, and marketplace conditions in the domestic arena is already a challenge for a telecommunications manager. Doing the same at the international level is much more difficult; therefore, it is often cost-effective to outsource international communications needs. As in domestic environments (described earlier in the chapter), outsourcing allows the multinational organization to determine its service requirements, then let the outsourcer meet them. International outsourcing permits the organization to share risk in a partnership arrangement.

In addition to these technical reasons, outsourcing of global telecommunications has emerged because of at least three significant market factors (these factors affect not only multinational companies, but all companies to some extent):[11]

1. There has been a major increase in international investment as companies start to recognize that the face of commerce has changed permanently. Over the past 10 years, foreign investment in the United States has grown nearly fivefold, to $400 billion. At the same time, U.S. companies have increased their international investments from $125 billion to more than $420 billion. Similarly, multinational companies are investing in European, Asian, and Pacific markets, which make up larger shares of their worldwide sales revenues. This growth in investment presents a global communications demand that

must be satisfied. For example, one entrepreneurial manufacturer reduced its time to market significantly by setting up design teams around the world: at the end of the working day in the United Kingdom, the design in its current state was transmitted to the United States; when that working day was over, it was sent to Singapore, and then returned to the United Kingdom. This illustrates that information technology is playing an ever more important role in the way companies do business.

2. Organizations must now function with the streamlined infrastructure that has resulted from the widespread corporate downsizing of the last five years. Gone are the days when some companies could put three people on a project that only needed one person, using this sledgehammer coverage to make sure that the unempowered employees could pull off the project. One empowered employee can certainly do a task more efficiently than three employees who are fighting for turf and wasting time trying to convince their management that each is better than the other two. These reorganizations have affected company processes at all levels. At the management level, the typical company has reduced its layers of management from eleven to seven through massive corporate restructuring; the most streamlined companies now have only three or four layers of management. The flattening of the pyramid structure, with nearly one of every four middle management positions having been eliminated since 1980, has required corporations to widen the span of control. At the nonmanagement level, many corporations are reluctant to hire permanent employees when their anticipated needs are uncertain in a volatile economy. The new infrastructure has compelled companies to demand more from IT to replace the previous middle management functions lost to downsizing, all the while doing this with reduced technical and managerial support.

3. Information is a clearly recognized strategic capability of the organization. Companies now need information at a faster rate, in a wider variety, and in more remote geographical locations than was the case in the late 1980s or even the early 1990s. This trend is common to most if not all industries and affects the front office as well as the back office. For example, customer service representatives need instantaneous access to up-to-date customer information, records, correspondence, image material, account information, and so on; retailers need delivery systems that enable them to manage their inventories and make effective purchasing decisions from the point of sale; the financial services industry depends on information technology to support global round-the-clock trading, where immediate trading decisions need to be made without human intervention. In fact, in the service industries, information itself is often the product, or is funda-

mental to delivery of the service. At the same time that the communications needs of multinational organizations have increased, frustration with the current state of international telecommunications has set in: Less than 5 percent of surveyed telecommunications executives reported few or no problems with their international networks. The most demanding issues are in the areas of service provisioning, problem management, and quality.

One example of a newly conceived global outsourcing company is Syncordia. Syncordia* was launched by British Telecom (BT) in September 1991, with a key mission of providing international outsourced network solutions to the world's largest multinational corporations. Although Syncordia uses network services as building blocks for solutions it develops for customers, it is not a network services company, it is an outsourcing company. As such, it manages and operates all or part of a customer's communications services, and it can draw on services provided by BT elsewhere. As an outsourcing company, it can replace the customer's internal business functions, such as procurement, planning and design, operations and customer support, internal marketing, and administration.

At the heart of Syncordia's solution is an integrated approach to service-level management. This approach allows the customer to monitor and control its international telecommunications service from a single platform: Concert, which is BT's network management system. Concert facilitates the integration of network management, customer support, and billing capability. As an outsourcing partner, Syncordia acts in a consultancy role, working with the customer to improve the overall performance of the business.

Network services are managed through network control centers located in Atlanta and London. Syncordia's network interconnects the 70 major manufacturing, industrial, and financial centers of the world through numerous diverse-routed high-capacity digital links between locations. Customer support centers are located in Atlanta and Paris, offering service in five languages. These centers provide a single point of contact for all customer needs, including ordering, fault reporting and resolution, service status, performance reporting, and customer assistance. Syncordia has created a service-level management approach that integrates all of its management functions, including customer support, network management, system integration, and consultancy, under a common scheme, which allows BT to

---

*The material that follows is based directly on Ref. 11; it is included here to illustrate some of the features and services that a sophisticated outsourcer may offer.

provide multinational customers with solutions that are consistently managed end to end. Syncordia's service-level management includes

- Integrated network management systems
  - At the network control centers to manage the physical network
  - At the customer support centers to manage the customer interaction
  - On the customer's premises to manage the network services and related systems and equipment that combine to form the network
- Single-source support centers around the world offering personal help in five languages, seven days a week, 24 hours a day
- Integrated customized bills in any language, currency, or format the customer requires

Integrated billing eliminates the need for the organization to execute complex algorithms to measure usage, reduces inaccuracy and risk, and provides a decision support mechanism for management. As discussed earlier, billing issues can be important.

6.9   Tariff 12

As a defensive move against customized price/service packages offered by its competitors, AT&T has instituted custom price/service agreements under special tariffs. In 1989 AT&T filed a tariff—Tariff 12, Custom-Designed Integrated Services (CDIS)—offering custom-designed service packages for telecommunication capabilities. This type of mechanism represents one possible way in which a carrier can provide outsourcing services. AT&T's Tariff 12 provides customized contracts for a mixture of voice and data services to large telecommunications users at rates that are lower than regular tariffs for services.[16] AT&T has more than 120 customers generating over $4 billion in services for the duration of their contracts.

Tariff 12 is discussed here only for illustrative purposes and to highlight how one carrier has approached the market, not to sanction or recommend the approach, the carrier, or the tariff. It should be noted that Tariff 12 has been mired in numerous regulatory proceedings, particularly with regard to including 800 services as part of the package. AT&T has been active in signing customers for Tariff 12, despite the fact that the customized service has been under review by the FCC and has faced several court challenges. So far, the courts and the FCC have reaffirmed the validity of AT&T's Tariff 12 offering.[16]

The custom-designed integrated services are described below in terms of virtual telecommunications network services (VTNS).

VTNS* is a general offering of custom-designed voice and data telecommunication capabilities to meet specific customer requirements. VTNS is designed by AT&T based on customer-specific information, such as calling patterns and traffic volumes, jointly developed by AT&T and the customer. Consistent with customer-specific information and objectives, AT&T retains the right to use either shared or dedicated facilities to provide VTNS. AT&T provides the customer with a network provisioning plan for VTNS. VTNS is available only for multiyear service periods, and there is a minimum charge. VTNS is arranged into service "Options," some of which are discussed below for illustrative purposes. Rates for VTNS are stabilized and can be distance-sensitive or postalized, sensitive to time of day, or otherwise developed to suit customer needs as specified in the Options covering various custom designs. VTNS is furnished among locations on the mainland except as may be specified in the particular Option.

In response to the FCC's April 18, 1989, ruling on the legality of Tariff 12, AT&T revised the VTNS Options that had been challenged; these revisions were approved by the FCC's Common Carrier Bureau on June 30, 1989. In addition to changes to particular provisions, AT&T removed the geographic limitations for each Option. Thus each VTNS Option is "generally available to customers under conditions not substantially different from those specified" in the Option. In August 1991, the FCC barred AT&T from bundling 800 services in Tariff 12 and other business contracts until 800 services became more portable in 1993 (portability of 800 numbers across carriers is an important issue for many organizations). An FCC decision on April 17, 1992, reversed the August 1991 decision. Now AT&T can offer inbound services in future Tariff 12s if customers are willing to change their 800 number.[16]

As can been seen from the descriptions set out below, VTNS is an evolving service, and AT&T has revised earlier Options as agreements with new customers have yielded new service features and terms. For example, at the time it introduced Option 14, AT&T modified earlier Options to provide for a phaseout of services upon termination of VTNS, including price stability for three months and a restoration of the customer's premises to the original condition. AT&T has also lowered the rates on many Options as this very competitive market has evolved. It has incorporated into the general regulations provisions originally applicable to only a few customers, including full and partial discontinuance, rate schedules for international calling, and a number of other features, such as Automatic Number

---

*The material that follows is abstracted from a noncopyrighted memorandum of unknown origin entitled "Inside AT&T's Tariff 12 Deals." Implicit credit to the unknown author(s) is given by way of this footnote.

Identification. More recent additions include rates for international satellite, data, and voice transmission capabilities (approved by the FCC's Common Carrier Bureau on June 8, 1990) and an "Expanded Discount Plan" that permits customers to aggregate their usage under VTNS with intrastate usage for certain other AT&T services for the purpose of calculating their VTNS discounts. Tariff 12 customers make commitments for a fixed, minimum annual usage. A Tariff 12 contract has two parts. One part, which contains rates, terms, and conditions, is filed with the FCC; the other part is a private contract with the organization in question.

A few of the Options are described here to illustrate how Tariff 12 works.

6.9.1 Introduction

Defense Commercial Telecommunications Network. AT&T's *first* Tariff 12 offering was the Defense Commercial Telecommunications Network (DCTN), the product of a process begun in 1982 when the Defense Communications Agency solicited bids. AT&T's bid was submitted in November 1983, prior to the FCC's elimination of the requirement that regulated and nonregulated activities be conducted by separate corporate entities. To conform to this requirement, AT&T submitted a two-part bid. One part was submitted by AT&T Communications and covered the provision of regulated communication services; the second was submitted by AT&T Technologies and covered the provision of customer premises equipment (CPE). Only the former portion of the successful bid was filed in Tariff 12 because the Commission had deregulated the provision of CPE.

The DCTN package included channels for network entry, nodes (switches), satellite and terrestrial internodal channels, and a network management center to integrate a variety of services ranging from voice grade to video. There was a minimum monthly charge of $3,049,043 and a termination charge of $7,265,400, which was to be reduced by 1/120 for each month of service over the 10-year term. The tariff also included a new billing mechanism called "subscriber rate," which combined numerous elements in the DCTN network into a pricing by service application concept. The subscriber rate is the sum of local channel, interoffice channel, and internodal network charges, a scheme used by AT&T in its private-line tariffs.

In September 1989, AT&T reduced the per-mile rates for local high-capacity data channels by nearly 58 percent; those rates produce 26 percent of the revenue for this service. AT&T told the FCC that the rates continued to recover AT&T's access costs and that the rate reduction would encourage the customer to use the DCTN service rather than turn to a competitor. The FCC's Common Carrier Bureau upheld the revision on November 22, 1989. AT&T subsequently added 14 additional locations at which 1.5-Mbit/s internodal channels are available.

General Electric Telecommunications Network. AT&T filed its *second* Tariff 12 offering in 1987. Developed in response to a bid solicitation from the General Electric Company, the offering was called the General Electric Telecommunications Network (GETN) service. AT&T entered into a five-year agreement in March 1987, with service scheduled to begin within one year. The 1987 filing required GE to purchase a minimum of 4400 voice terminations spread among no more than eight central offices, and specified an installation charge of $270,000 and a fixed monthly charge of $176,000 for service in each of eight nodes. AT&T estimated the total value of the five-year package at $300 million.

The tariff also gave the customer the right to terminate without liability if (1) there was an increase in any rate-stabilized offering used by GETN or (2) AT&T did not comply with any of the material terms and conditions under which GETN was ordered. GE also had the right to cancel services found to be "excessive" in a review conducted three months after the start of service.

GETN combined a variety of tariffed services, including AT&T's Software Defined Network, Megacom, and private lines, with a set of unique switching, testing, and administrative functions. The offering included a new switching service to route traffic based on the customer's instructions.

AT&T sought a waiver of Section 61.74 of the Commission's rules in order to reference the GE contract in its Tariff 12 filing, which triggered a wave of protests from competitors claiming that the service was not a tariffed offering but an individually negotiated contract available only to a single customer. Several parties also argued that if the GE contract was referenced in the tariff, it must be filed (publicly) with the Commission to allow the agency to judge the reasonableness of the tariffed service.

In an effort to make GETN a more generalized offering and avoid disclosure of the contract, AT&T modified its proposal by withdrawing cross-references to the GE contract, renaming the service Digital Tandem Switched Network Service, and deleting all tariff references to GE. In Transmittal No. 961, AT&T also unbundled the switching arrangement from the backbone network, renamed it the Digital Tandem Switching Arrangement, and specified that it could be purchased on a stand-alone basis.

6.9.2   Options

VTNS Option 1: DuPont.   AT&T's *third* Tariff 12 offering, VTNS Option 1, was originally developed through negotiations with DuPont. It has become the foundation for a series of VTNS Options that share general terms and regulations but differ as to the specific service arrangements. VTNS Option 1 combines voice and data communications with switching and management functions to form a complete network service offered at stabilized rates over a five-year period.

Option 1 includes an installation charge of $1,337,200 and a combination of fixed and usage-sensitive charges, with a total minimum monthly charge of $1,237,000 (less applicable outage credits). It also contains termination liability provisions. AT&T estimated total revenues for VTNS Option 1 at $90 to $100 million over the five-year term.

Option 1 was originally intended to incorporate a multiplexer manufactured by Network Equipment Technologies that was compatible with DuPont's existing CPE. AT&T sought a waiver of the FCC's network disclosure requirements to permit it to use the NET multiplexer as network equipment without disclosing the interface specification to competing CPE vendors. In response to opposition from other parties, AT&T withdrew the waiver request and revised VTNS Option 1 to exclude the multiplexer from the tariffed offering. It is instead treated as CPE owned (or leased) by DuPont and collocated at AT&T central offices under a licensed space agreement.

VTNS Option 2: Ford.   On February 29, 1988, AT&T introduced Option 2, an integrated voice and data network designed for the Ford Motor Company.

The rate structure is similar to that established for Option 1. The monthly basic charge of $588,091 was set to recover approximately 27 percent of AT&T's annual revenue requirement for the service, with the remainder to be recovered through usage-sensitive measured charges. Option 2 has an installation charge of $1,778,150 and a minimum annual charge of $20,590,944 to accommodate variations in Ford's usage. AT&T projected annual revenues from VTNS Option 2 of $25,728,848 by 1990.

Option 2 has incentives for early completion of the initial installation and penalties for delay. The customer must pay $100,000 for each 30 days AT&T is early; AT&T pays a like amount for each 30-day delay.

VTNS Option 2 allows the customer to discontinue portions of the service experiencing chronic outages, which are defined as three or more interruptions lasting four or more hours within three consecutive calendar months. However, the customer must give 90 days notice, and AT&T has a right to cure the problem by means of extraordinary repair efforts or reprovisioning. Two additional service features not found in the previous custom offerings are (1) authorization codes, to which any call can be billed from any phone, and (2) Port Access Telephone Numbers, a feature which assigns numbers to specific ports, thereby allowing calls from any location inside or outside the system to be billed to that port.

Two years later, AT&T amended Option 2 to add capabilities, revise rates, and establish volume discount plans.

VTNS Option 3: American Express. AT&T introduced VTNS Option 3 on September 1, 1988. This Option, which has been amended numerous times, provided a custom network for American Express.

Like previously filed Options, Option 3 has a fixed basic charge, which was set to recover all the fixed costs and a portion of the installation charges during the three-year service period. If the customer continues service beyond the initial three years, the basic monthly charge is reduced. Measured charges consist of rate schedules applicable to calls from or to Measured Ports, Measured Remote Ports, or non-Port locations. New features with this option include the use of customer-specified rate periods, volume discounts for preselected points on the network, 1.544-Mbit/s data transmission service, network prompters, and Automatic Number Identification.

Option 3 allows for discontinuance of service elements suffering chronic problems. As in later Options, AT&T will pay installation charges incurred for AT&T or other services used to replace the discontinued portion of VTNS.

Option 3 introduced a system of outage credits reflecting the proportional cost of providing each element of the service. The credits were designed as an incentive for AT&T to provide uninterrupted service.

AT&T later revised Option 3 to unbundle dedicated local access, thereby permitting the customer to obtain access itself from the local exchange carrier or an alternative provider. In addition, it revised the Option's volume discounts. The threshold for application of the basic discount was reduced from $30,000 to $25,000 per month, and the discount itself was reduced from 10 percent to 5 percent. AT&T added an additional 1 percent discount where annual measured charges exceed $55 million; the aim is to favor those users whose heavy demands are largely responsible for the efficiencies achieved by Option 3. In addition, the customer can commit to one of two monthly charge levels; the customer will pay the committed amount (discounted by 5 percent or 10 percent) regardless of whether it falls short of, reaches, or exceeds the target. These revisions were approved by the FCC on June 30, 1989.

A subsequent modification increased the minimum annual charge from $45 million to $47 million for the first year, $53 million for the second year, and $53.4 million for the third year. This revision was approved by the FCC on August 26, 1989. Later still, AT&T reduced the minimums to $45.34 million, $51.04 million, and $51.14 million for the first three years, respectively.

VTNS Option 47: Unnamed customer.

Option 47 provides for domestic and international service for a three-year term. The minimum annual charge is $7.37 million, and anticipated revenues are $9.21 million per year.

The rate structure is comparable to that of earlier Options. The domestic volume discount is small: 2.5 percent on monthly measured charges that exceed $400,000. In addition, a usage credit of $0.0006 per call is applied to inbound 800 calls at locations where the monthly average length of such calls is less than 18 seconds. Installation charges are waived (up to a maximum of $7.5 million) for service elements added within 45 days of the initial service date. A volume pricing plan offers discounts that depend on the customer's commitments.

VTNS Option 48: Xerox Corp.

This option is a five-year domestic and international service package. The minimum annual charge is $20.8 million, and the anticipated annual revenues are $25.22 million.

The rate structure is similar to that of earlier Options, except that the only volume pricing taper is for international service. The customer may, at any time, increase its minimum annual charge in exchange for additional discounts on measured charges. For example, raising the minimum slightly to $21 million would produce a 0.2 percent discount; a minimum of $31 million would entitle the customer to a 1.2 percent discount. Installation charges for additional service elements up to a maximum of $15,000 are waived for 45 days after the initial service date. The domestic volume pricing plan entitles the customer to discounts on charges in exchange for commitments on combined data transmission capabilities (DTCs) and voice transmission capabilities (VTCs) network component charges. Discounts on aggregate monthly charges for international DTCs and VTCs range from 32 percent to 38 percent. Option 48 was approved on June 22, 1990.

VTNS Option 49: Goldman Sachs.

Option 49 is a domestic and international service package available for a three-year term, with an optional one-year extension (if AT&T and the customer agree). The early termination charge is a percentage of the minimum charge for the remainder of the term; the percentage declines from 60 percent during the first year to 40 percent in the second year and 30 percent in the third year. The minimum annual charge is $4.91 million, and anticipated annual revenues are $6.1 million. The customer may, in the case of force majeure conditions, defer 15 percent of the first year's minimum charge to the second year, 30 percent of the second year's minimum charge to the third year, and up to $300,000 of the third year's minimum charge to a month-to-month arrangement. Usage in excess of up to 15 percent of any year's minimum charge may be rolled forward to the subsequent year.

For 1.5-Mbit/s DTCs, the customer may receive above-run-rate interruption credits ranging from 5 to 50 percent of the monthly value of the DTC for each incident; the total credits earned in any month may not exceed the DTC's monthly value. This parallels AT&T's Service Assurance Warranty for ACCUNET T1.5 service. The partial discontinuance provisions give AT&T greater leeway to correct chronic problems in domestic access components and somewhat greater leeway for ports and domestic DTC network components. The rate structure is comparable to that of recent Options, including a volume pricing plan for international measured charges and discounts based on commitments for aggregate domestic and international usage.

6.10   Example of an Outsourcing Contract for Communication Services

This section provides the skeleton of one type of outsourcing contract for communication services. This skeleton is modeled on Tariff 12 and identifies some of the issues that would normally be included in such a contract. Naturally, there are many possible contracts that can be written.

The outsourcing contract must allow for future changes in requirements and flexibility in how services are to be provided. This is often best realized in the form of a collaborative approach in which both parties share the benefits (as discussed in Chap. 4) and the risks. The organization can protect itself by ascertaining that the contract includes safeguards against escalating costs (such as a percentage price cap or indexing against public tariffs or the Consumer Price Index) and the right to withdraw from the contract under specified conditions. The outline that follows indicates a possible form of the contract. Appropriate text would be included under each subsection (the contract may be 50 to 200 pages or more).

1. Services to be provided
   1.1 Responsibilities of the outsourcer
       1.1.1 Locations to be interconnected
       1.1.2 Topology of the network
       1.1.3 Service levels (SLAs), e.g., connectivity, bandwidth, end-to-end delay, bit/block/frame/cell error rates and losses, maintenance, testing, modifications, etc.

16. Extension of contract beyond normal expiration
17. Glossary of terms

6.11   Outsourcing of LAN Functions

Interest in outsourcing remote LAN management has been growing recently because many corporations are recognizing the expense of supporting LANs: A survey of *Fortune* 1000 companies indicated that annual LAN support costs average $1,270 per user.[17] Many companies have a need for remote LANs; for example, over 47 percent of companies with annual revenues in the $25 million range and over 64 percent of the companies with revenues in the $500 million range have remote LANs.[18]

An outsourcing firm specializing in LAN management can eliminate the need for an organization to hire a LAN administrator, a staff function that many of the 700,000 U.S. firms with LANs may be unable to afford.[14] Small LANs located at remote branch offices are subject to the same technical and user-caused problems as the more reachable LANs located at an organization's headquarters. However, it usually costs too much to maintain a trained LAN manager at each remote site—a typical *Fortune* 1000 company has several hundred field sites.[17] The most important aspect of outsourcing is to use it strategically by choosing functions that do not contribute to the core business. These functions may include pulling wire and cable or supporting desktop installations.[6]

This section looks briefly at two LAN functions that can be outsourced: LAN backup and LAN management.

6.11.1   Outsourcing of LAN backup

Many LAN administrators realize that they have what appears to be a new priority: developing a disaster-recovery plan (DRP) for LAN-based applications. Events such as the World Trade Center explosion and hurricane Andrew illustrate how dependent businesses are on LANs and the value of being prepared. Developing the DRP internally can be a demanding and detailed project: Every aspect of the system must be reviewed, documented, and organized, as must all the vendor relationships (see Table 6.4).[19] Observers suggest that LAN administrators can develop a disaster-recovery plan through outsourcing: with a partner, an organization can control the costs and enjoy full participation and the benefit of someone else's expertise.

LAN backup is a new area in which outsourcing may make major inroads in the future. As an example, in 1993 California's state Health and Welfare Agency Data Center (HWDC) started to offer a central LAN backup service to the 15 state agencies it serves (sys-

TABLE 6.4   LAN Disaster-Recovery Planning Where an Outsourcer Can Be of Assistance [19]

Diagram the LAN. Organize data by floor of the building and categorize the diagrams by the backbone (bridges, routers, communication lines, etc.), the distribution system (writing hubs, organization, etc.), and the user systems (PCs, printers, etc.).

For each diagram, create a narrative listing the quantity and configuration of each component; where possible, attach configuration sheets that detail the equipment configuration.

Develop full profiles of all bridges and routers, communications servers, etc.; include software and firmware revisions and site-defined parameters.

Document file servers. In addition to the technical settings, include information about the user community served, disk capacities, and network operating system (name and revision). Include information about installed peripherals (such as network interface cards), jumper settings, boot information, NLMs, and value-added processes. A pictorial file-structure diagram, such as those generated by the DOS "Tree" program, should be included in this documentation. Also document other servers.

Make a listing of communication services and their structure. Lines used for modem pooling, fax servers, remote access, etc., should be listed by function and phone number. Note whether the line is inbound, outbound, direct (central office) service, or PBX-based.

If leased lines are used for wide area network services, list all circuit identification information. Some services will have multiple identifications, each of which may be necessary in order to relocate or restore your service.

Make copies of backup schedules and step-by-step restoration procedures.

Compile a list of key vendors, telephone names, contacts, contract numbers.

---

tems administration services for its customers' PCs were also being planned). In this arrangement, backing up files is done within what is called an efficient, fast, reliable, and secure environment of mainframe archiving.[20] Just one of the agency's user organizations, the Department of Health Services (DHS), has 18 different LANs, and the 18 LAN administrators who run them do not use a standard method to back up data at the file server—and many workstation users do not back up at all.

Figure 6.6 depicts an example of network-based (outsourcer-provided) on-demand file storage and backup. In this example, the user initiates communication with the network-based file backup facility as needed. The length of the storage interval can be specified. Security is guaranteed by the network. The user has access to a catalogue (directory) of stored files for information and/or selection purposes. The backup copy can be retrieved or erased by the user at any time. Charges can be based on access activities and on storage (file size and temporal length).

Figure 6.7 depicts an example of a network-based (outsourcer-provided) automatic file storage and backup service. This service pro-

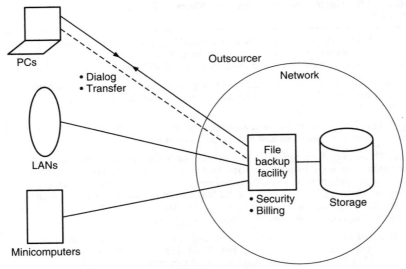

Figure 6.6 On-demand file storage and backup by outsourcer.

vides periodic backup, where the time and frequency may be set by the user. The network backup file server initiates the process and copies only files that have been modified or newly created. Security is guaranteed by the network. The user has access to a catalogue (directory) of stored files for information and/or selection purposes. The

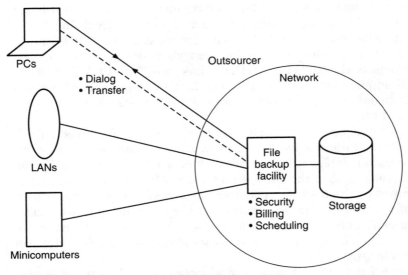

Figure 6.7 Automatic file storage and backup by outsourcer.

backup copy can be retrieved or erased by the user at any time. The user can set the length of storage on a per-file, per-directory, or per-pack basis; this can be done via a prespecified configuration file (a mechanism to update this file is also available).

Moving to outsourcer-supported LAN backup can be a two-step transition. The first step might be establishing in-house mainframe-based archiving. At some future time, the mainframe function can be made remote and/or outsourced.

Mainframe archiving of LAN data is being considered by organizations that are seeking to ensure data integrity and want to leverage their existing investment in mainframe storage management. For example, some organizations have found that they would have to assign upwards of 100 people to perform client-server backup/restore activities, as opposed to one or a few at a central mainframe site.[20] Mainframe archiving also allows faster restoration of data than is possible with server-based backup systems; for example, 8-millimeter tape drives, which are read sequentially, can take as long as five hours for a restore operation; in contrast, file pointers in a mainframe backup product enable a file to be restored within a few minutes. Companies such as McDonalds Corp., Blue Cross of Idaho, and GPU Services Corp., among others, have chosen to use mainframe-based backup. At press time there were nearly 40 vendors offering backup products. Users who seek products in this category should search diligently for features that match their needs. Many backup products use the incremental storage approach, which reduces file backups by initially backing up all files on all LAN nodes, then storing only changes in files. One needs high throughput to handle the task in an effective manner (e.g., 22 Mbits/s would deliver about 12 gigabytes per hour, enough to fit the nightly window that usually is allocated for backup). Remotely located outsourcers need both high-throughput software and high-capacity communication (possibly ATM-based networks) to make the service viable.

6.11.2   LAN management

Until recently, there have been two basic options for supporting remote LANs:[17]

1. Local staff can contract with value-added resellers or systems integrators in the area.

2. Central IS can provide some remote diagnostics and management of the LAN and send IS staff to the site whenever hands-on repairs are necessary.

A local-site contract removes the onus of day-to-day management, but it leads to a proliferation of contracts with service vendors; the issues of cost-effectiveness and vendor reliability surface immediately. Monitoring of remote LANs by the central IS staff helps in identification of problems and allows users at the remote sites to be guided by a central help desk, but when repairs are required at the remote site, central staff still must visit the site or call in local VARs, systems integrators, computer dealers, or consultants. A third option is now available: Vendors such as Digital Equipment Corp., IBM's Integrated Systems Solutions Corp., Unisys Corp., SHL Systemhouse Inc., and Syncordia, to list a few, support outsourcing of the management of remote LANs (see Table 6.5). One effective way to provide support for remote LANs is to automate the function and perform it over a network (often the public network) that functions as a diagnostic network. This requires installing a central control center and amortizing the cost of management over many sites to achieve economies of scale. This is the approach followed by the outsourcing vendors. Assigning an employee to a customer site, as some of the outsourcers do, cost about $60,000 to $80,000; however, this is considered worth the cost, as the employees often gain important insight into and influence with the client company.[2]

Outsourcing, however, is not always the appropriate solution to LAN management. The decision may be contingent on the following factors,

TABLE 6.5   Partial List of Outsourcing Vendors for LAN Management at Press Time

Advantis Inc.

AT&T

Bell Atlantic Corp.

BT North America

Bull HN Information Systems Inc.

Computerland Corp.

Digital Equipment Corporation

Evernet Systems Inc.

Integrated Systems Solutions Corp.

Memorex Telex Corp.

SHL Systemhouse

Sprint Corp.

Syncordia

The Asset Group

Unisys Corp.

among others: Has central IS invested in remote service and support tools? Does IS have the well-trained staff to respond quickly? Can remote users do a lot for themselves? Are the "remote" LANs relatively near the central site? If the answers to these questions are yes, it is likely to be more economical for a corporation to manage its remote LANs itself than to outsource.[17] Not all outsourcing firms support all LAN technologies, nor can they get to sites equally rapidly (in some remote areas some outsourcers even subcontract their on-site maintenance).

When considering outsourcing, in some cases, local managers may find that locally supported services cost less than a national outsourcing vendor. In other cases, national outsourcing vendors may be less expensive in the aggregate when a good contract is secured (outsourcing vendors often promise to save as much as 10 to 40 percent of the cost of unmanaged LAN configurations[17]). Additionally, they may provide such technical and organizational advantages as monitoring the LAN; taking responsibility for the quality of the service on all remote LANs; and providing centralized billing, accounting, and reporting. At press time the national outsourcers were not yet a significant factor in the remote LAN management market because they can do only part of the job, namely, the remote automated management; if they need to visit the organization's site, they have the expense of travel, which can be similar to the expense incurred by the organization (except, perhaps, that the outsourcer can obtain negotiated discounts on car rentals, hotels, tickets, etc.). Some major U.S. long distance telephone carriers (AT&T and Sprint) are also getting into outsourcing through router management services. These vendors tend to have an existing presence in the top business locations (over 500 points of presence), enabling them to have easy access to remote user locations.

Table 6.6 (p. 238) depicts key factors to take into consideration when looking at an outsourcer, and some of the parametric ranges.

References

1. R. G. House and L. A. DeLozier, "Network Services—Outsourcing," *International Journal of Network Management,* pp. 39ff, September 1991.
2. T. C. Doyle, "Outsourcing: A Smart Plan for Service Providers," *Computer Reseller News,* no. 510, p. 2, Jan. 25, 1993.
3. P. Lloyd, "Outsourcing: Mutual Benefit or Mutual Risk," *Telecommunications,* pp. 37ff, February 1993.
4. "Network Outsourcing Market Could Triple by 1997," *CommunicationsWeek,* no. 435, p. 32, Jan. 4, 1993.
5. M. J. Major, "Who's Minding the Store?" *Midrange Systems,* 6(4):23ff, 1993.
6. C. Morken, "Outsourcing: Worst Nightmare or Useful Idea?" *Communications News,* 30(2):38, 1993.
7. A. Llana, "The Ups and Downs of Outsourcing," *Data Communications,* pp. 69ff, Jan. 21, 1993.
8. P. Morley, "The Advantages to Outsourcing," *Networking Management Europe,* pp. 24ff, January–February 1993.

TABLE 6.6   Issues to Consider in Selecting a LAN Outsourcer

Issue	Typical ranges
Geographic availability	Continental U.S., national (50 states and Puerto Rico), international
Speed of on-site appearance: large city	2–6 hours
Speed of on-site appearance: remote city	2 hours–2 days
Routers supported	Key ones (e.g., Cisco, Wellfleet) or nearly all
LAN systems supported	Key ones (e.g., Novell NetWare, Banyan VINES, IBM LAN Server) or nearly all
LAN protocols supported	Key ones (e.g., TCP/IP, IPX, AppleTalk, Decnet) or nearly all
Remotely manage desktop hardware	Yes, no
Remotely manage server hardware	Yes, no
Remotely manage server software	Yes, no
Remotely manage adds/moves/changes	Yes, no
On-site desktop hardware	Yes, no
On-site server hardware	Yes, no
On-site cabling support	Yes, no
On-site server software capabilities	Yes, no
On-site moves/adds/changes	Yes, no
On-site staff	Yes, no

9. D. Powell, "To Outsource or Not to Outsource," *Networking Management,* pp. 56ff, February 1993.
10. A. Stewart, "How to Get the Most Out of Outsourcing," *Communications News,* 30(2):39, 1993.
11. G. W. Thames, "Outsourcing Global Telecommunications," *British Telecommunications Engineering,* 11, 153ff, 1992.
12. J. E. McKendrick, "Long Distance Dedication," *Midrange Systems,* 6(4):15, 1993.
13. G. W. Marriner, "Outsourcing Telecommunication Services," *The 4th IEE Conference on Telecommunications.*
14. H. Landa, "Outsourcing Network Management—Pros, Cons," *LAN Times,* 10(9):49ff, 1993.
15. D. Minoli et al., *Expert Systems Applications in Integrated Network Management,* Artech House, Norwood, Mass., 1989.
16. Datapro Report 4020, "AT&T Tariff FCC No. 12, Custom-Designed Integrated Services: Overview," Delran, N.J., July 1992.
17. A. Radding, "Now You Can Outsource Remote LANs," *Datamation,* July 15, 1993, pp. 36ff.
18. "A Need for Remote LAN Access," *Datamation,* June 15, 1993, p. S-13.
19. P. Merenbloom, "Plan Ahead to Protect Yourself and Your LAN from Disaster," *Infoworld,* 15(13):50, 1993.
20. T. McCusker, "Big-LAN Backup without Backaches," *Datamation,* Apr. 15, 1993, pp. 48ff.

7

Outsourcing of Other Corporate Functions and Related Issues

Data processing departments and their systems are a legacy of an era when computers were viewed as instruments to accelerate back-office operations. Companies have invested significant amounts of effort and capital in developing and maintaining these systems and their support structure. Retiring the data processing department and starting from scratch is impractical and unrealistic; therefore, rather than abandoning the embedded base, organizations have looked to an interim solution: outsourcing—the entire IS group (the people, the systems, and the operations) becomes the outsourcer's responsibility.[1] The previous chapters described the main IS and communication functions that are being outsourced by many corporations. This chapter examines a number of other areas that are being outsourced to various degrees, as well as some related issues. Areas of interest include

1. Software

2. Document processing and archival functions

3. Disaster-recovery functions

7.1 Software Development Outsourcing

7.1.1 Overview

As organizations and decision making have become more dependent on computer technology, the need for rapid systems development has increasingly become an issue; however, the traditional organization and structure of IS groups do not lend themselves well to this need.[1]

Applications development refers to creating computer systems (hardware and software) to address specific organizational needs; maintenance of an application refers to the ongoing upkeep of an existing application, once it has been installed and is in regular use.

When an organization decides to buy packaged software rather than developing its own, it is already embarked on a form of outsourcing: The organization depends on the vendor for updates, maintenance, training, and a number of other services.[2] At press time, 36 percent of large (surveyed) organizations relied on packaged software, 53 percent used an inside staff, and 11 percent utilized outside services.[3] Organizations that outsource are inclined to seek already developed software packages that can be installed "as is," rather than having systems custom-built; however, in most cases, some customization of existing software is required.[1] The question of outsourcing applications typically affects large companies: These companies have well-established information systems and data processing organizations and have developed most of their existing applications in-house. Small companies, unable to sustain the overhead of a permanent systems group, of necessity already contract the services of third parties for applications development, or purchase ready-made software. Software programming can and has been outsourced to third-world countries for a mere fraction of the cost of doing development in the United States.

Outsourcing is a reasonably good solution to the problem of quickly developing new systems using advanced technologies. Outsourcing applications projects may be totally developed outside of the company (referred to as pure outsourcing) or developed partially by outsiders and partially by company employees (referred to as hybrid outsourcing). How does one decide which computer applications to outsource? While part of the answer depends on the company culture, there are some general characteristics that managers can use to determine whether to outsource application development or not.

The software application projects which fall into the pure outsourcing category have these characteristics (although there are always exceptions to any type of generalization):[1]

- The applications require expertise which exceeds that found in the company—knowledge of either the hardware or the software application, or the combined hardware and software, is not found within the company.

- The applications are end-user-driven—the people who initiate the project are users of computers and often are not technology-driven. Usually someone champions the project, gets approval from management, and guides the project within the company so that interfaces with other groups and systems are smooth.

- The applications are relatively isolated, having little or no effect on day-to-day production systems. They are mostly independent of mission-critical systems that affect customer balances and major transaction systems that are run routinely in the company.

- Applications imply little or no liability for the outside company (projects which make the developer liable financially if the system errs or fails are often refused by outsourcers and have to be developed in-house—outsourcers normally accept limited liability or no contingent liability past the value of the contract).

- Projects are short in duration; they generally take less than a year, with modules completed in a short time and delivered incrementally. This often entails small project teams, although as noted in Sec. 2.1.5, some software development projects can involve millions of dollars.

Characteristics of hybrid outsourcing projects are similar to those of pure outsourcing, but with some differences:[1]

- They significantly affect customers' balances and transaction systems in the company.

- They involve a large amount of liability: if the system fails, the developer must pay to fix the mistake.

Although development of applications is slow even when they are targeted to traditional mainframes, departmental systems, and PCs, applications meant for fully integrated, cross-platform heterogeneous networked environments are even more complicated. Yet these applications are the key to client-server computing. End users now "demand" client-server applications, as such applications are much easier to use than terminal-to-host applications; additionally, putting data access closer to where the users are located generally increases the efficiency of the organization.[4] But developing networked applications takes more than cabling desks for LAN access or providing a WAN transport capability, such as a digital channel at 64 kbits/s or even a cell stream at 353,207 cells per second (135.63 Mbits/s throughput on a 155.52-Mbit/s ATM access channel). Some are discovering that they have underestimated (perhaps greatly) what it takes to make network computing a reality: getting the network right is only part of what it takes to achieve network computing.[4] Making code run under one operating system in one machine is not the same as making the code run across a network with hundreds or even thousands of computers, possibly with different operating systems or different versions of the same operating system.

Given the complexity, one must face the decision to develop the needed applications in-house, outsource them, or utilize "shrink-wrapped" software. Shrink-wrapped applications are relatively inexpensive and generally work right. They can be brought in-house simply by generating a purchase order and properly installing them on the server. The decision-to-fruition delay is negligible compared with the delay of developing the applications in-house (which is at least 6 to 12 months for a relatively simple application[4]). If these applications support at least a workable subset of the original "laundry list" of features, they represent the least expensive way to meet the organization's software requirements.

Alternatively, the organization needs to go through the traditional cycle for in-house development (requirements, system design, coding, testing, documenting, training, etc.) or go through the steps of lining up an outsourcer. A typical custom application is 50,000 lines of code; a full-time C programmer can generate 100 lines of useful code a day when working alone,* so the application will require approximately two staff years to complete.[4] At $125,000 of loaded salary, that is an investment of $250,000. Assuming that a typical purchased application costs $799 and that no multiple-licenses discounts are available, as long as less than 312 users need access, it would be cheaper to purchase copies of the application. Contracted development, often done by system integrators, can be a good compromise between off-the-shelf software, which can be too general, and full custom applications, which can be too expensive and time-consuming to bring on-line.

As discussed elsewhere, companies are planning to implement downsizing strategies with their computing environments. In particular, there is a trend away from mainframe legacy systems and to Unix and open communication. A growing number of software manufacturers are offering communications and migration tools, known as application generation environments (AGEs), that facilitate the move away from proprietary systems. However, there is a danger that organizations may attempt too much using AGEs technologies, particularly for distributed Unix and personal computer-based networking environments, which present AGEs with a considerable challenge. It is best to attempt most downsizing using computer-aided software engineering (CASE) tools to partition the project as necessary; AGEs can then be applied with discretion on and off during the migration move (refer to Ref. 5 for a discussion of these tools).

7.1.2 International information processing

Unlike material goods, information can be transported quickly and cheaply. Thus, tasks that involve information can be relocated to

---

*Some believe that a programmer working in a team of 10 people produces only about 50 lines of code per day.[4]

another country anywhere within the footprint of an INTELSAT satellite, including, for example, a remote outpost in the South Atlantic or South Pacific, as long as doing so makes economic sense and is technologically feasible. In fact, clerical and back-office service jobs such as data entry, transaction processing, database creation and/or update, and programming, among others, are beginning to migrate to countries such as Barbados, the Philippines, India, and Ireland. These countries enjoy the advantages of offering low wages, an educated and talented English-speaking workforce, and a telecommunication infrastructure that can easily connect a remote outpost to a mainframe on the U.S. mainland.

The trend toward global outsourcing of information services can be traced primarily to two factors: cost reduction pressure and advances in information technology. Faced with increasing pressure to reduce costs, a growing number of U.S. companies are finding global outsourcing a cost-effective option, since wages in many underdeveloped and emerging countries are significantly lower than those in the United States. For example, wages of data entry clerks in the Philippines can be as low as one-tenth those in the United States; those in India, one-sixth; and those in Singapore, one-half. This also holds true for other industrialized countries such as Canada, France, Germany, Japan, and Korea. Some well-known companies, such as Digital Equipment Corporation, Hewlett-Packard, IBM, and Texas Instruments, have set up operations in the cities of Bangalore and Bombay, India, and have linked these sites with the United States, using satellite links.

In 1991 R. B. Reich proposed three categories of jobs in an information-based society: routine production services, in-person services, and symbolic-analytic services.[6] Routine production services involve the performance of simple repetitive tasks for material transformation or information processing and account for about 25 percent of the total U.S. jobs. These jobs, which include data processing, are likely candidates for outsourcing in general, and global outsourcing in particular. The second category, in-person services, accounts for 30 percent of the total U.S. jobs; these jobs entail a person-to-person interaction and are not good candidates for outsourcing. The third category includes all problem-identifying, problem-solving, strategic decision-making, and brokering activities; information system professionals, software developers, research scientists, bankers, lawyers, and so forth, belong to this category. These jobs account for about 20 percent of U.S. jobs. Since the analyst rarely needs to come in direct contact with the recipient of the work (if it is needed, this can be done through an initial meeting with follow-up electronic communication), many of these jobs are candidates for eventual global outsourcing.[6]

7.2 Document Imaging Outsourcing

Outsourcing of office services is becoming increasingly popular: Many companies are outsourcing their support services, including copying, mailing, filing, food services, security, and payroll processing. Office outsourcing firms provide all the equipment, supplies, and personnel necessary to perform a variety of tasks. This frees the client organization from many human resource management duties and the added pressure of purchasing and maintaining equipment.[7] Related to this trend is the outsourcing of business imaging for the purpose of replacing file cabinets of forms and documents with optical disks that contain digitized versions of the documents. Often imaging systems (scanning stations, optical servers, and supporting LANs and WANs) are designed on behalf of the organization by system integrators. Also, rather than undertaking the document conversion task in-house, organizations usually ship documents to professional companies that scan, verify, and store them on optical media; the organization can then load these optical disks into its server(s).[8]

Imaging is defined as the combination of capture, compression, storage, transmission, and display functions. Issues pertaining to the compression of information, such as algorithms and related efficiencies, play an important role. At the hardware level, an imaging system typically consists of (1) scanning station(s) for the capture of information, (2) the computer-based imaging system itself, and (3) local or remote output devices (e.g., a display station or printer). Imaging is the process of (1) obtaining or creating digital image data from a paper document, graphic, or video source, (2) performing optional compression of the data, and (3) storing the information in electronic or optical memory. The stored data can be accessed by a computer and directed to an output device for visualization. Image communication (transfer) is rapidly emerging as an important business application for the 1990s in the insurance, banking, medical, publishing, and scientific communities, to list just a few areas. Initially, communication capabilities have been targeted to a building or campus; requirements for wide area communication are now emerging.[8]

Businesses and governments are turning to imaging to improve the productivity and effectiveness of office workers. Document imaging is seen as a way to reduce the paper load in the office, as well as increasing the efficiency of the corporation. At the application level, imaging includes document management, engineering document management systems, desktop publishing, medical applications, scientific visualization, and geographic information systems, among others. The financial services industry and the government are the largest markets for business imaging at press time; other industries—notably legal, healthcare, and manufacturing—are in the process of introducing the technology. According to proponents, office productivity is expected to soar as the capture, storage, manipulation, and retrieval of document images are computerized. Workflow can be streamlined, resulting in reductions in paper and storage costs. In practical business terms, most systems in use today are on small LANs and are yet to be used for true workgroup applications; also, these systems are used principally for archival and retrieval functions rather than workflow functions.[8]

Optical storage media can store large amounts of information. CD-ROMs (compact disk read-only memory) stores 0.6 Gbyte (about 16,000 40-kbyte business documents); 12-inch WORM (write once, read many) disks can store 6 Gbytes (about 160,000 40-kbyte business documents). One way of appreciating this is that 16,000 documents are the equivalent of four file cabinets (160,000 documents equate to 40 file cabinets). A typical CD-ROM jukebox stores 25 disks (400,000 documents or 100 file cabinets) and needs less space than a single file cabinet. A jukebox with 50 12-inch disks can store the equivalent of 8 million documents, or about 2000 file cabinets. Jukeboxes storing as many as 250 disks are appearing on the market. At the document level, scanning a document for storage on a WORM disk typically costs $0.10 to $0.30 per page, including quality checking and verification.[8]

The interested reader is referred to Ref. 8 or other books for an extensive treatment of this topic.

7.3 Technical Support/Help Desk

Both software vendors and user organizations are increasingly turning to third-party contractors for technical support of complex products. Analysts say that the high costs of supporting multivendor distributed environments have accelerated the trend. Borland International Inc., WordPerfect Corp., and Corel Corp. have all announced plans to hand over portions of their technical support to outside specialists: Borland and WordPerfect are offloading support of older products in order to focus better on new products, while Corel is outsourcing support for new products as well.[9] Observers say that independent support companies can provide support more efficiently because they have higher volumes and more expertise than the vendor's own support department. Large corporate users are also contracting with third-party firms such as Corporate Software to provide help desk services, freeing their information systems departments to focus on solving business problems.[9]

Chapter 5 discussed the key advantage of this type of outsourcing: the economies of scale in the number of employees required to support the function. Also, where 24-hour-a-day coverage is needed—for example, for multinational networks—this affords coverage in a more cost-efficient manner. The centralized help desk may also be able to afford automated tools that could not be afforded by a smaller group.

7.4 Disaster Recovery*

An unforeseen disaster can strike at any time; such disasters include fires, floods, earthquakes, hurricanes, and even sabotage. The industry defines *disaster* as a "sudden, unplanned calamitous event that brings about great damage or loss. Any event that creates an inability on the company's part to provide critical business functions for some undetermined period of time." *Disaster-recovery planning* is defined as "the advance planning and preparations which are necessary to minimize loss and ensure continuity of the critical business functions of an organization in the event of disaster." Generally, disaster recovery deals with problems associated with an organization's own failure (for example, a fire in the data center); the term *service continuity* is used to describe a carrier's internal network survivability and self-healing aspects, as well as service availability (for example, utilizing route diversity). On its face, outsourcing seems to help the disaster-recovery situation, because the organization has (potentially) removed the data center from its premises; however, often the responsibility has simply been shifted to the outsourcer: What happens if the outsourcer has a data center fire?

This section looks briefly at the issue of disaster recovery (some aspects of which were already discussed in the previous chapter). It does not address the issue of how an outsourcer can design its own disaster-recovery plan to ensure uninterrupted service in view of some kind of disaster—that is disaster recovery pure and simple. Rather, the section looks briefly at organizations outsourcing (only) their disaster-recovery plans, rather than developing them in-house.

Many organizations now depend on the continual availability of computing and communications for their income and long-term viability; they can be critically affected and suffer business losses if they cannot quickly reestablish operations. Companies are beginning to recognize the business implications of such a possibility and build backup systems; more companies need to do so. Disaster-recovery planning in a large corporation typically involves the following four tasks:

---

*This material is based loosely on Ref. 10, where one can find additional supporting references.

1. Provision of a physical alternative data center, including computers, disk drives, and communication equipment. This could be an
   alternative center owned and maintained by the user's organization, or it could be a rented shared environment provided by a
   company specializing in supporting these types of computing
   requirements.

2. Storage, movement, and installation of the major computer operating systems and the organization's key applications.

3. Predisaster and postdisaster storage, movement, and installation
   of the databases required to support the applications selected.
   Backup sites can be *hot,* i.e., requiring a real-time copy of the data
   and hence requiring an on-line transmission path, or *cold,* i.e.,
   only receiving data from tape and thus not requiring an on-line
   transmission path. Since hot sites are expensive (also requiring
   spare computers and staff), the majority of backup systems are
   cold.

4. Provision of a mechanism to transfer all communications to the
   alternative site following a disaster. This transfer must be consistent and compatible with the predisaster communication architecture employed by the user. The transfer is usually undertaken
   within 24 to 72 hours, except for the hot backup environment,
   where the transfer must be accomplished in minutes.

   Products and services related to disaster recovery include (1) fault-
tolerant computers, (2) power control systems, (3) computer locking
systems, (4) on-site backup storage, (5) off-site backup storage, and
(6) disaster-recovery services (there are over 100 disaster-recovery
vendors, and the industry is growing at 40 percent a year). The total
market has been forecast to grow to $4.4 billion by 1997 (of this, $600
million is for on-site backup, $350 million for off-site backup, and
$350 million for disaster-recovery services; the balance is for physical
security, backup power, and fault-tolerant computing). On-site backup storage protects against loss of or damage to primary storage
media. Off-site backup is done only partially by most large computer
sites.

   Practitioners divide the issues related to an organization's computer and network security into two categories: management issues and
technical issues. The management issues are the responsibility of
senior management, since these are business-related. The technical
issues are clearly the responsibility of IS and network management
staff.

   IS and network security managers must take action to ensure that
contingency planning is performed in a manner that adequately pro-

tects the business from excessive loss and insulates them from liability. They should conduct a legal audit to determine the ramifications of inadequate disaster control and recovery. One should consider specific legal liability questions. The manager must determine who to hold responsible and whether contingency planning is sufficient to establish such responsibility. The manager in charge of contingency planning should focus on information and corporate data as a strategic organizational resource. Since information crosses many departmental lines, this manager should have enough authority to handle these boundaries. The issues that concern management fall into five categories:

1. *A defined and documented computer security policy.*   This specifies the scope and direction of the company's involvement in computer security. Aspects of disaster-recovery planning and operation under contingency conditions must be included in this policy.

2. *Standards and procedures.*   These are the detailed, day-to-day guidelines that should be followed during any type of data processing operation or activity. They are designed to help protect the firm's computing assets from most security threats. The guidelines should also include disaster recovery; for example, if a new communications line is added or removed, a procedure to update the contingency plan must exist.

3. *An outline of responsibility for computer security.*   This involves division of responsibility among the computer security function, the data processing department, the personnel department, and top management. In case of crisis, it must be known who will attend to each preestablished activity. Many companies want to restore operations within 24 to 48 hours; the first few hours are critical, and one should not have to waste time trying to determine who should be in charge of various activities.

4. *A personnel security program.*   This program should also address such areas as preemployment screening, conditions of employment, security training, employee morale, and employee termination procedures.

5. *A complete asset-threat inventory.*   This provides a set of safeguards designed to protect a firm's computing assets against a group of predetermined potential threats. The inventory includes identification and valuation of the assets, identification of the potential threats, a risk assessment process, identification of the potential safeguards, selection of safeguards, adoption of contingency plans, testing of contingency plans, auditing of the computer systems, and ongoing computer security evaluation. This is the most critical factor in communications disaster-recovery planning.

Organizations may find that they cannot develop an effective disaster-recovery plan internally, covering the issues discussed above, because of resource constraints or lack of skills, and that outsourcers, such as large consulting firms or disaster-recovery firms (see Ref. 10 for a partial list), can help the organization establish a reliable disaster-recovery system. There are certain nuances related to establishing a viable disaster-recovery plan, and professionals who have developed several of these are better at it than the staff on the organization's payroll, who may be involved with only one plan (actually, as discussed under the software section, a hybrid approach involving both the organization and the outsourcer may be best).

7.5   Writing the Right Contract

Contract issues were covered in Chaps. 3, 4, 5, and 6 (Sec. 6.10 in particular). Some aspects of contracting are revisited here. Organizations considering outsourcing need to be aware that outsourcing contractors are not friends and that in any disputes, an organization must place its own needs first; it is critical for a firm to ensure that an outsourcer is legally bound to meet the organization's needs before it signs any contract.[11] To affect an outsourcing agreement, the terms of the contract must be enforceable; in turn, this means that they must be verifiable. A contract condition is *verifiable* if a third party, frequently the courts, can determine whether it has been met. A weaker condition is observability: A condition is *observable* if the contracting parties can decide, but cannot prove, that the condition has been met.[12] When the terms of the contract are based on output, the output must be measurable if the contract is to be verifiable. However, many IS outputs are not easily measurable. Examples of characteristics that are difficult to measure include quality of system design, ease of system maintainability, and user-friendliness.

As alluded to in Chap. 3, contracts can be comprehensive (complete) or incomplete. A complete contract specifies every possible situation or outcome. Such a contract, if it could be written, would not need to be revised until it expired or was completely fulfilled. Some simple transactions, however, could be written as complete contracts. For example, the purchase of a batch of 500 blank diskettes could be written as a complete contract, since there are a few specifiable outcomes, such as

1. Diskettes are delivered on time or are not delivered on time.

2. The diskettes are consigned to the right party or they are not.

3. The diskettes are delivered at the right corporate location or they are not.

4. The diskettes are of the right density or they are not.

5. The diskettes are of the right size or they are not.

6. No more than 1 percent of the diskettes are defective or more than 1 percent are defective.

Most contracts are incomplete because one cannot anticipate all possible outcomes (or the process would be too laborious). In particular, most outsourcing contracts are incomplete. For example, an outsourcer may be required to maintain a state-of-the-art computing platform in support of a certain organization. However, the contract would not normally specify the exact technology and equipment that the outsourcer is expected to install.

As companies negotiate outsourcing contracts, they should concentrate on flexibility, provisions for early termination, unforeseen conditions, and recovery following a disaster.[13] When a conflict arises, the parties must bargain to resolve the conflict. These contracts should provide for (1) arbitration, (2) renegotiation, and (3) early termination. Although complete contracts affecting intracompany entities or intercompany entities could be written differently, at the execution level such a distinction would not be necessary, since the action would be prespecified regardless of the situation. However, whether incomplete contracts are intracompany or intercompany needs to be taken into account because the ultimate disposition may be different. Assume, for example, that an outside company has been contracted to develop an IS application. If at some point during the development cycle a new prepackaged application that meets the requirements becomes available, the organization may find it too costly to renegotiate the contract. However, if the software was being developed internally, senior management might force the cancellation of the development project.[12]

Outsourcing contracts can last from 5 to 10 years and cost millions (or even billions) of dollars. It is important that IS managers be able to adjust their outsourcing contracts to match their real needs. Many IS managers are negotiating outsourcing contracts that provide an escape clause, also called an extraordinary event clause, in the event of a significant change in their company's location, product lines, or financial status.[13] While outsourcing companies may not like this new negotiation strategy, most of them are accommodating it in order to remain competitive.

Regardless of the function being outsourced, the following points will improve the posture of the manager contemplating such a decision:[11,14]

- Get senior management to agree on outsourcing objectives. This will help discourage lobbying and disputes between internal business units over turf as outsourcing progresses.

- Specify, in both RFPs and contracts, who will be the single internal contact for all supplies. This helps diminish vendor attempts to do an end run through a good-buddy corporate executive or professional.

- Get to know potential outsourcing vendors. Find out why some outsourcers set up a new legal entity for each outsourcing contract they sign. Keep in mind that it is difficult to obtain any compensation from a suit against a shell company.[15]

- Set up an internal group or individual to monitor the outsourcer's performance and contract compliance, and to recommend needed changes.

- Insist on receiving price decreases when carriers, system providers, or outsourcers decrease their own costs. One way to do this is to contractually set the outsourcer's profit at a fixed percentage above its real costs.

- Specify contract renegotiation points, such as corporate acquisitions, changes in network staffing needs, or technology changes.

- Specify that if schedules are missed, any staff hours or system resources that the outsourcer adds to catch up are its expenses, not the organization's.

- Provide contractual disengagement procedures for both vendors and clients. Regardless of the desire for a positive relationship, the organization must also specify how and when to disentangle the partners' systems resources and personnel, if necessary.

- Never undertake negotiations without involving a skilled outsourcing lawyer.

7.6 Some Human Factors

Research shows that the success of outsourcing is more likely to be hindered by human problems than by technological problems; however, if both the outsourcing vendor and the organization address employee concerns, outsourcing has a good chance of yielding positive results.[16] As it might be expected, outsourcing is not always viewed favorably by the people in the IS department. It can be difficult for them to acknowledge that change should occur, or to accept that change is going to happen. IS personnel fear the possibility that their operations will be outsourced. Some individuals may not agree with the process, the analysis, or the conclusions, especially if their job security is at stake; some individuals may go out of their way to make the analysis even more difficult to complete.[17] Executive management should clearly support the decision, and this message must be communicated and periodically reinforced.

When an IS department receives the news that it will be audited, and that the object of the audit is to determine whether the department should be outsourced, some on the staff may believe that the announcement is only a tactic aimed at improving their performance. This is particularly true when some degree of mistrust exists between employees and management, and this belief is heightened when the audit extends over many months. An illustrative example is the relative apathy demonstrated by employees in Canada's Post's Computing & Communications utility when the outsourcing vendor (SHL Systemhouse) was awarded the right to negotiate an outsourcing contract. This came after studies and negotiations with another vendor had been under way for two years. During that period of time, Canada Post employees had gradually come to believe that outsourcing would never be implemented. This indifference continued through the early phases of the new negotiations, and did not significantly change until employment offers were made by the outsourcing vendor.

At whatever point the IS employees recognize that outsourcing will indeed take place, numerous concerns surface. A key observation is that employees are thrown into a period of uncertainty and feel that they lack control over their future. Job security and career progression, once a function of known criteria, are up in the air. Employees must face the fact that their professional futures may be decided by outside consultants.[18] IS professionals indicate that it can be very challenging to change over from internally managed IS to IS operations managed by an external organization. Chief among the concerns is the reputation of the outsourcing vendor as an employer:

- Does the vendor routinely hire all or a significant number of employees from the outsourcing organization?
- Following the initial hires, does the outsourcing vendor retain these employees, or does it reduce headcount after the critical six- to eighteen-month transition period?
- How do the vendor's compensation program and compensation levels compare to the current program?
- Will the benefit program decline in value? Will employee premiums, copayments, and deductibles increase? Will there still be a pension plan? Will seniority be valued in any way, especially for vacation entitlement?
- Are there differences in working conditions, such as increased work hours, longer shift schedules, reduced overtime premiums or hours, etc.?
- What are the career opportunities with the outsourcing vendor? Are there other operations in the same geographic region, or is a

relocation in the cards? Is there a commitment to training and development (especially retraining for newer technology, systems, and application)?

- What happens to the perks of belonging to the current organization, such as office size, secretarial support, social events, employee discounts, free parking, subsidized lunches, unlimited travel, flexible work hours, short workdays, etc.?

- What has happened to employees involved in previous outsourcings by this vendor? Were all promises kept?

As one can see, the concerns are many, and the specifics and degree of concern are related both to the organization and its employee relations and to the outsourcing vendor and its reputation. Where there is a disconnect, the cost may not be limited to contract service levels. For example, Eastman Kodak Co. employees filed a court case because they felt they did not receive promised job security benefits when Kodak implemented an outsourcing contract (the case was still pending at press time.)[16] Programmers in the IS department may be nervous about the results of an audit because if outsourcing is selected as the path to follow, it can mean the elimination of jobs; the experience can be even more frustrating if the results of the audit are delayed. The audit may suggest hiring some new personnel, while laying off other people.[19]

In a number of cases, internal resources are used for the study. Personnel assigned to evaluate the viability of outsourcing should be dedicated; their daily responsibilities should be temporarily reassigned. Ideally, the team should be made up of respected individuals from IS, finance, purchasing and contracts, human resources, and the user community, all of whom must have well-honed analytical skills. The following steps can be utilized:[15]

- Establish a strategy for proper balance of management, contracting, and consulting. Investigate the possibility of turning some IS employees into internal or external contractors or consultants.

- Establish a strategy to deal with burned-out or redundant staff. Consider how the situation happened and how to prevent it from happening again. Retraining or career counseling may be one solution.

- Keep the staff informed. Let IS members participate in setting the outsourcing strategy. Treat employees fairly. Do not blame them if the business climate has changed such that the organization is forced to reduce its ranks. Also, move early to retain quality people; these people have the best prospects on the open market, and they may have already built up an external reputation. Either they must have an important part to play in the outsourcing decision and implementation, and be given assurances about future job security, or they must be retained through other measures, such as a stay or retention bonus.

Which professionals are likely to suffer the most in case of outsourcing? We believe at least three categories:

1. Professionals who put little emphasis on keeping up their skills—purchasing a book, taking a course, going to an industry conference, routinely reading a magazine, reading a report, or subscribing to an information service (e.g., Datapro). They focus only on what they are doing that day or that week. A decade ago, what was important (at the time of an interview) was what *one knew.* This is excellent when the discipline is highly stable, say, changing every 50 years (e.g., teaching calculus, actuarial techniques for life contingencies, or medieval poetry). Today, what is more important, in our view, is *how quickly one can learn something new,* say, by reading a technical book on the topic. Since the technology is changing every 1 to 3 years, what one knew four or five years ago may be of little use. A college graduate who left school 6 years ago may be in the same predicament, in terms of being out of date, as someone who left college 20 years ago, but has kept up through reading and education.

2. Ultra-specialists—professionals who refuse to broaden their knowledge base, assuming that information at the bit, nibble, byte, cell, or frame level that they learned a decade earlier will automatically assure them a job, although they have done (and can do) nothing but that one thing. Being a specialist gives them a tactical advantage, but a great strategic disadvantage. Because they know a technology (say, bridges) down at the quantum physics level, they tend to get short-term attention—when a corporation has a need, for example, to install 100 bridges. However, as soon as the 100 bridges are installed, the corporation is no longer interested in an employee's ability to describe the bridge at the chip and algorithm level—now it may be interested in video compression equipment. Generalists, who have a more comprehensive understanding of the entire field, may be at a short-term disadvantage when their colleagues make a show of their apparent erudition by taking something simple and making it sound artificially complex and by always looking for the four-sigma exception to some generic rule. However, generalists have a much better opportunity to adapt to a new facet of this fast-moving field when needed. Also, because they do not "own" any technology, they are more objective about the relative merits of one technology over another. In the end, they earn the trust of senior management as objective, flexible, adaptable, and versatile professionals.

3. People who are not attentive to the corporate environment and are oblivious to all culture and business-cycle changes. These individuals rarely attend area meetings and may not even listen to corporate video broadcasts of CEO presentations to the organization. They focus only on what they are doing that day or that week. They are never able to anticipate corporate changes and often appear to be in a self-complacent limbo. Nor do they read any of the business press, such as *The Wall Street Journal, Business Week*, etc., to see where the rest of the world is going.

In trying to deal with redundant staff, some ways are better than others. The best way is to declare an entire group surplus and the jobs gone, then allow members of that group to bid for other openings in the organization, if any. For example, if the company is pulling out of an X.25 network in favor of an outsourced frame relay network and if there is a need to reduce staff (in some cases it may be desirable to retrain the staff and retain it), then the entire X.25 group could be declared surplus. The same could be done for a legacy mainframe, departmental minicomputer, or LAN. This approach has also been tested and upheld in the courts. However, if the company has a liberal severance policy, declaring all jobs surplus may trigger a significant termination cost that might be avoided by treating the employee transitions as transfers. The outsourcing vendor of course would be concerned about any termination cost liabilities, and this would probably be a case for negotiation.

The worst way to downsize is to start telling employees that they are not good enough and that they are being laid off because of performance considerations, when in fact negative performance ratings are forced by management as a way to deal with downsizing. These employees may come from the best colleges and may be the top of their graduating class. It is not productive to attack them personally because, for example, some business venture undertaken by senior management a few years earlier (e.g., lending billions of dollars to a bankrupt third-world country) has failed. Antagonizing these employees could have future repercussions in terms of bad publicity, lawsuits, and even loss of business. Mention some well-known IS shops in large companies to a colleague and you will get an instantaneous reaction, "That's a meat shop/meat grinder/sweat shop." In one example known to this author, a certain communications manager was mistreated while working with carrier X. When the manager got a senior CIO position in a top-ten international bank, the manager systematically proceeded to move the bank completely away from carrier X, resulting in a loss of revenue for carrier X in the millions of dollars per year.

When a significant number of employees are hired by the outsourcing vendor, both the company and the vendor have a vested interest in ensuring that employees will maintain prior service levels, without any drop during the transition period. To make this happen, a solid foundation for the new employee-vendor relationship must be built. This can only be done by communicating in a forthright and timely manner, treating people equitably and with respect and dignity, addressing the primary employee concerns about differences between the two employers, and demonstrating flexibility and willingness to deal with the employees' concerns. While this sounds like a generic prescription for good employee relations, given the circumstances of an outsourcing contract, these steps are all vital to the success of the partnership between the vendor and its client.

References

1. M. Buck-Lew, "To Outsource or Not?" *International Journal of Information Management,* 12:3–20, 1992.
2. M. J. Major, "Who's Minding the Store?" *Midrange Systems,* 6(4):23ff, 1993.
3. *Datamation,* June 15, 1993, p. S-3.
4. A. Wittmann, "Network-Based Applications: To Build or to Buy," *Network Computing,* pp. 86ff, July 1993.
5. J. Costello, "The Generation Game," *Computer Weekly,* Feb. 25, 1993, p. 36.
6. U. Apte, "Global Outsourcing of Information Systems and Processing Services," *The Information Society,* 7:287ff, 1990.
7. M. Kaufman, "Outsourcing: A Concept with Renewed Meaning," *Office,* 117(1):50, 1993.
8. D. Minoli, *Imaging in Corporate Environments: Technology and Communication,* McGraw-Hill, New York, 1994.
9. S. Willett, "Vendors, Users Turning to Outside Help for Technical Support," *InfoWorld,* 15(18):12, 1993.
10. D. Minoli, *Enterprise Networking, Fractional T1 to SONET, Frame Relay to BISDN,* Artech House, Norwood, Mass., 1993.
11. L. Fried, "Outsourcing Confessions: Revealing Talk about Why Partnerships Sour," *Computerworld,* 27(6):67, 1993.
12. W. B. Richmond, A. Seidmann, and A. B. Whinston, "Incomplete Contracting Issues in Information Systems Development Outsourcing," *Decision Support Systems,* 8(5):459–477, 1992.
13. Willie Schatz, "Get Ready for Bail Outsourcing," *Computerworld,* 27(4):57, 1993.
14. D. Powell, "To Outsource or Not to Outsource," *Networking Management,* pp. 56ff, February 1993.
15. R. T. Due, "The Real Costs of Outsourcing," *Information Systems Management,* pp. 78ff, Winter 1992.
16. E. Horwitt, "Outsourcing Hits Human Snag: Contractual Pitfalls," *Computerworld,* 27(6):15, 1993.
17. C. Benko, "Outsourcing Evaluation: A Profitable Process," *Information Systems Management,* 10(2):45ff, 1993.
18. D. Crenshaw, "Outsourcing: To Be? Or Not to Be?" *Computerworld,* 27(10):120, 1993.
19. D. Crenshaw, "The Escape from Outsourcing," *Computerworld,* 27(11):114, 1993.

8

Transformational Outsourcing*

8.1 Introduction

Transformational outsourcing can best be defined as the operation of a client's mainframe applications, migration to a lower-cost and flexible client-server platform, and the operation of that distributed environment, on either a transitional or a long-term basis.

8.1.1 Transformational outsourcing overview

Transformational outsourcing, first discussed in Chap. 5, provides a unique approach to outsourcing that enables companies to quickly and cost-effectively transform their information technology operations to more current technologies, including the client-server technologies discussed in Chap. 2. Extending the benefits of traditional outsourcing in which a vendor assumes responsibility for a company's IT functions, transformational outsourcing provides a new technology platform which yields even greater value. It paves the way for companies to downsize mission-critical systems to client-server networks of smaller, more flexible, and less expensive computers. The entire process can be self-funding, and it should be possible to achieve an immediate reduction in IT expenditures. Figure 8.1 depicts graphically the concept of transformational outsourcing.

---

*This chapter was provided in its entirety by Tony Gaffney of SHL Systemhouse. The chapter affords the reader the point of view of one of the major providers of outsourcing services. It contains a discussion of transformational outsourcing and a number of study cases that put into practice many of the principles discussed elsewhere in this text.
   TRANSFORMATIONAL OUTSOURCING is a registered trademark of SHL Systemhouse.

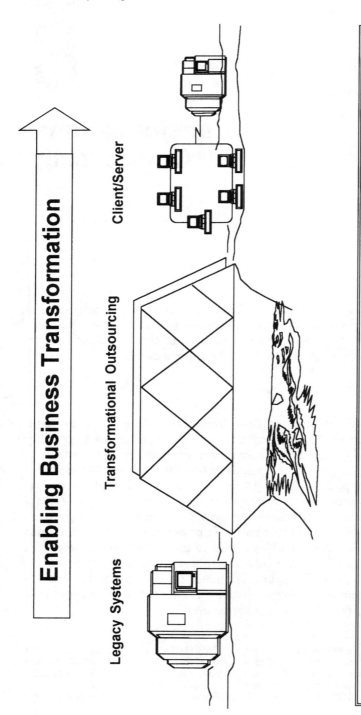

Enabling Business Transformation

Legacy Systems   Transformational Outsourcing   Client/Server

- Legacy Application Management
- Legacy System Operation

- Systems Integration Services

- C/S Application Management
- C/S System Operation

Figure 8.1 Transformational outsourcing. (*Source: SHL Systemhouse.*)

The transformational outsourcing process has three primary phases. Initially the vendor assumes responsibility for some or all IT functions; as covered in previous chapters, this typically includes data center, telecommunications, and PC/LAN operations, with application management and development nowadays also commonly included. IT strategy development and other CIO functions are usually retained by the client organization. The vendor frequently acquires the IT assets and often employs many of the client's IT staff. Second, low-risk, low-disruption applications are migrated from the expensive mainframe to the more cost-effective client-server platform. Finally, sophisticated resource management products and services are implemented. This means that the client-server platform can be engineered to provide the same degree of reliability as the mainframe, thereby harnessing this heretofore underutilized asset for the downsizing of other more critical applications.

Many companies are choosing transformational outsourcing as an interim strategy because it allows both downsizing and reengineering objectives to be achieved, while still allowing the IT organization to operate on its own after a certain period of time. Contracts are frequently of short duration (five years or less) and are designed with the flexibility to migrate IT functions back in-house when the transition is complete.

Transformational outsourcing can be an attractive strategy for accelerating and financing downsizing. The savings usually achieved by migrating the low-risk, low-disruption applications off the mainframe can fund the establishment of an integrated client-server platform. This reduces the incremental cost of migrating other more critical applications off the mainframe because the client-server platform

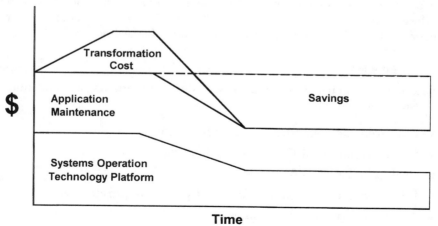

Figure 8.2 Financial time line for transformational outsourcing. (*Source: SHL Systemhouse.*)

and supporting infrastructure are already in place. Figure 8.2 shows a prototypical financial model for transformational outsourcing.

The flexibility to change technology is an important advantage of transformational outsourcing. It assumes that companies will reduce their reliance on the mainframe, whereas traditional outsourcing arrangements usually assume the opposite. Traditional outsourcing agreements usually include a "technology lock" which keeps the company's outsourced operations on the mainframe for the full duration of the contract. Cost savings are usually provided in the early years of the contract, but the vendor typically builds in large profits towards the end of the contract. If the company wants to change technology during the contract, cancellation may be its only option, and high cancellation fees are usually incurred. Transformational outsourcing vendors, on the other hand, are willing to provide the flexibility to decrease mainframe usage because they see these revenues being replaced over time by revenues from transformational services, technology deployment, and client-server systems management. Transformational outsourcing is therefore a more attractive relationship because it provides companies with the flexibility to take full advantage of new and evolving technology.

An increasing number of companies are choosing transformational outsourcing as an alternative to traditional outsourcing. One such company is Canada Post Corporation (CPC). SHL Systemhouse Inc.'s $1 billion contract to shift CPC from a mainframe to a client-server system is the largest transformational outsourcing deal to date. Canada Post selected transformational outsourcing after careful evaluation of several outsourcing alternatives. Reasons include the fact that "it offered a unique solution which was consistent with CPC's business and financial goals and objectives for improved efficiency and cost reduction"* and "it offered a unique strategy to achieve the transformation to client-server computing, which matched our future strategy for technology."*

8.1.2 Benefits

Transformational outsourcing provides all the benefits of traditional outsourcing, including

- Improved earnings through cost reductions
- Conversion of fixed IT costs to variable costs
- Cash infusion from fixed assets
- Elimination of current and future IT capital requirements
- Ability to focus on core business

---

*Hank Klassen, Vice President of Information Technology, Canada Post Corporation.

Additionally, transformational outsourcing provides benefits that are unique to this approach:

- Improved earnings through even greater cost reduction
- Utility pricing of IT services
- Continuous technology refreshment
- Flexibility to "crumble" legacy systems and downsize to client-server
- Ability to accelerate the implementation of current technology
- Funding of downsizing from future savings
- Deployment of a reliable and secure client-server environment
- Achievement of anticipated benefits of downsizing

In summary, transformational outsourcing provides a complete business solution to organizations that intend to downsize their legacy systems. It provides a high degree of flexibility and addresses the multitude of issues associated with crumbling the legacy environment, transforming to client-server, and efficiently operating and maintaining the new systems.

8.2 The Business Needs

8.2.1 Driving factors

Outsourcing is anticipated to grow significantly through the 1990s. The consensus among industry watchers is that the majority of *Fortune* 500 companies will choose to outsource, either partially or fully, their IT functions over the next three to five years. Frost & Sullivan estimates that companies will spend $104 billion annually on outsourcing services by 1999. There are several factors underlying this growth in outsourcing and the now emerging trend towards transformational outsourcing.

As covered elsewhere in this text, the industrial world is changing rapidly. Traditional blue-chip giants are faltering, and many specialty, service, and offshore companies are experiencing major growth. This is not incremental change but a transformation driven by three powerful change agents: the emergence of the global economy, rapid technological advances, and the rise of the empowered knowledge worker.

Global economy. Information, communications, and transportation technology are shrinking the globe. Consumers, supported by the elimination of trade restrictions, have become an international power. The global economy is driving the need for more responsive processes, competitive costs, and higher quality. All businesses must meet this challenge.

Technological advances.   Technology continues to evolve at an ever-increasing rate, and this is having a profound impact on business operations. The economics of technology now dictate maximizing the use of desktop computers. An organization performing a function on a workstation will have a lower cost structure than a mainframe-based competitor.

Empowered workforce.   Today's workforce is better educated and demands greater responsibility and decision-making power. Not that many years ago, decision-making authority was concentrated among a few individuals. Information was funneled up the hierarchy for decision making, and work was handed back down. As technology enables vast amounts of information to be rapidly synthesized at the fingertips of the knowledge worker, decision-making power moves like a wave down to the lowest levels in the organization. This will have dramatic effects on today's and tomorrow's organizations. Organizations are becoming flatter, and layers of redundant management are being eliminated. Workforce productivity is expected to increase.

Organizations must become more efficient in order to survive in the global marketplace. A key factor in their success will be a better educated, more independent workforce—supported by technology that can provide complete customer service at the point of contact. Organizations will be forced to reengineer their business processes in order to create empowered knowledge workers. Transformational outsourcing can play a key role in this process. It can assist organizations in streamlining business processes, creating faster information flows, satisfying more customers, delivering higher margins, and, thereby, maintaining a competitive advantage.

8.2.2 Downsizing challenges

Transformational outsourcing can provide a solution to the many challenges companies face in downsizing their IT functions.

While an increasing number of organizations are moving or planning to move toward client-server computing (see Fig. 8.3), the reality is that many organizations are burdened by significant investments in legacy systems and do not have the financial resources, people, or skill to make the transition. The challenge is to transform an organization to client-server computing, and one such solution is provided by transformational outsourcing. Transformational outsourcing addresses the following challenges.

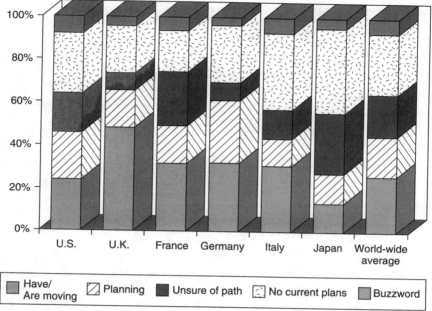

Figure 8.3 Deployment in 1993 of client-server technology in key industrial countries. Numbers of respondents: U.S., 858; U.K., 617; France, 957; Germany, 750; Italy, 807; Japan, 897. *Note:* Italy is not included in worldwide average. (*Source: International Data Corp.*)

How to fund the initiative. Securing the necessary funds to finance a significant downsizing initiative can be a major challenge. Downsizing usually requires significant up-front operating and capital expenditures, whereas most IT departments are under pressure to reduce costs now rather than later. New capital is scarce, and IT must compete with other areas of the organization for whatever funds are available. IT frequently loses in this competition for capital, which tends to be directed to higher-profile initiatives with more immediately perceived benefits.

Transformational outsourcing can be self-funding, and current costs can often be reduced to achieve immediate savings. IT services can also be purchased on a fee-for-service basis. The need for capital is thereby eliminated, and the cost of transformation can be funded from future savings. See Fig. 8.4; also see Sec. 8.2.4.

How to "crumble" the legacy systems and infrastructure. Many organizations have significant investments in legacy applications and infrastructure. Technology assets are frequently depreciated over long periods of time, resulting in asset book values that are often much greater than fair market value. Disposal or resale can result

Transformational Outsourcing

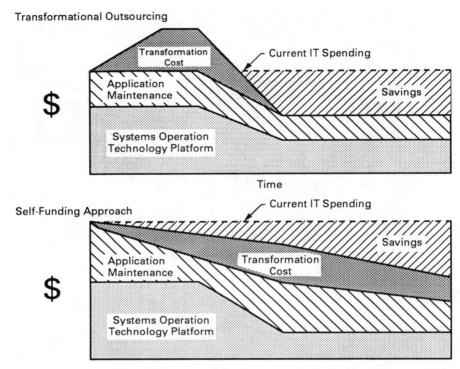

Figure 8.4 Financial performance of transformational outsourcing. (*Source: SHL Systemhouse.*)

in a net book loss. In addition, legacy infrastructure is a fixed cost, so that IT costs do not decrease as usage decreases during the transformation. The transition of support personnel is also an issue. Fewer people with different skills will be required to support a client-server environment, and personnel need to be either retrained or redeployed.

In a transformational outsourcing arrangement, the vendor assumes the responsibility for this challenge by acquiring the legacy infrastructure. What was previously a fixed cost structure now becomes variable, and the cost of legacy systems can be reduced as usage decreases. The vendor usually buys the assets at a price equal to or greater than NBV (net book value), thus solving the disposal problem. The vendor must also deal with the issue of legacy support personnel. Many of these people are hired, retrained, or redeployed. The vendor is often able to make use of the assets to support other clients' legacy systems and utilizes the staff to do so, or redeploys them to new client-server-related activities.

How to provide the necessary resources. Freeing up the resources required to plan and implement a downsizing initiative can be a real challenge. In many organizations, the majority of management and staff are focused on the maintenance and enhancement of legacy systems—it is not unusual to find between 50 and 80 percent of IT resources dedicated to this function. Legacy systems tend to become more complex and expensive to maintain over time, which exacerbates the situation. This fact, along with users' increased demands for system improvements as they become more sophisticated in the use of technology, frequently leads to a significant backlog of work. One- to five-year backlogs are not unusual. Companies rarely have sufficient resources to simultaneously maintain legacy systems, engineer business processes, and build new applications.

Transformational outsourcing provides full access to the personnel required to plan and implement the downsizing initiative. These personnel are provided by the vendor.

How to acquire client-server skills. Acquiring the skills to successfully undertake a downsizing initiative is another major challenge. Client-server computing demands a set of skills far different from that required for the more traditional mainframe and midrange environments. The client-server environment is more complex, and a greater number of components need to be selected, integrated, and supported. The learning curve to achieve proficiency in these technologies is also significant. Table 8.1 identifies some of the key skills needed in client-server application development.

Few organizations can afford the learning curve associated with client-server deployment, since competitive and time pressures are intense when it comes to the deployment of new products and services. Technology must become an enabler, not an inhibitor, to such progress. It is no longer acceptable for a systems project to span one or more years, particularly in industries such as telecommunications, where a new product or service may be a differentiator for only several months.

Transformational outsourcing provides organizations with access to the vendor's client-server expertise, methodologies, and experience, derived from the successful completion of many other client-server projects. This expertise can be transferred to in-house personnel during the transformation period, if so desired.

In summary, transformational outsourcing helps companies overcome the many challenges involved in successfully downsizing the IT function.

TABLE 8.1 Skills Needed in Client-Server Application Development

	Customer	Project manager	Architect	Business/ systems analyst	Designer/ developer	Quality assurance manager	Implementation/ training/support
Business skills and experience	Group dynamics BPE	Group dynamics BPE Timeboxing Contract management	Group dynamics BPE	Group dynamics BPE	Group dynamics BPE	Group dynamics	Group dynamics
Technology/product skills and experience		Process management tools	Numerous products: servers, workstations, middleware, connectivity, network management, databases, CASE, development tools Systems development environment design Network design System management environment design Technical prototyping	Business and application modeling tools Reverse engineering tools Prototyping tools	Modeling tools Numerous products and development tools System management environment design	Automated testing	Mulitmedia training design Performance support environments Procurement Network and system deployment Remote system management
Methodology skills and experience	Organizational change management ISO 9000	Organizational change management ISO 9000	Enterprise-wide architectural planning Benchmarking and capacity planning Process and data allocation	RAD workshops Iterative prototyping GUI design OO modeling Process and data allocation	RAD workshops Iterative prototyping GUI design Process and data allocation OO design OO programming	Continuous process improvement Statistical analysis Quality function deployment ISO 9000	Organizational change management

Source: SHL Transform

8.2.3 Client-server implementation issues

Transformational outsourcing can provide a solution to the many problems associated with the implementation of client-server systems. As client-server becomes the technology of choice for many organizations, skepticism as to the true benefits that can be achieved is rising. An article published in Canada's *Globe and Mail* stated, "Downsizing, as the industry calls the shift to networks from mainframes, almost invariably takes longer to implement, costs more and is riskier than most people think." It went on to quote several failed downsizing initiatives. An analysis of such failures usually points to the following critical success factors, which need to be adequately addressed:

1. The transformation needs to occur in a well-managed, timely, and quality manner. The use of client-server skills and methodologies is essential.

2. The client-server environment must be cost-effectively operated and maintained.

3. The client-server environment must provide "mainframe-like" levels of availability, performance, and security.

The reality is that downsizing to a client-server environment is a complex and potentially risky process for any organization to embark upon. A well-executed strategy will therefore deliver significant benefits. The strategy, however, must address several important issues related to this new technology, including (1) the lack of stability in today's PC/LAN environment, (2) the true cost of supporting client-server computing, (3) the underlying complexity of client-server, and (4) the radically changed role of the network.

A well-executed transformational outsourcing strategy fully addresses all of these factors.

Achieving platform stability. The downsizing strategy will need to ensure that a stable environment is provided and the necessary levels of availability, performance, and security are delivered. The fact today is that in most organizations, management practices for client-server environments are not as mature as those for mainframe complexes. The managerial effectiveness in these environments currently averages 35 percent, whereas in mainframe environments it is 85 to 95 percent.

A reliable and secure client-server environment is provided as part of a transformational outsourcing arrangement. The levels of availability, performance, and security are similar to those historically provided in the mainframe environment.

Reducing the true cost of end-user computing (EUC). The downsizing strategy will need to deliver the required infrastructure and management services at a cost that is significantly lower than today's industry norms, thus enabling the targeted economic benefits of distributed computing to be achieved. The cost of providing PC/LAN technologies and support on an in-house basis is higher than most organizations realize, according to a number of recently conducted industry studies, exemplified by the following quotations:

> The visible cost of end user computing is in the range of $2k to $6.5k per user per year. The "hidden" cost is at least double ranging from $6.5k to as much as $15k per user per year.—Nolan, Norton & Co.*
> A ratio of 1:50 support resources to users is required in a networked end user computing environment.—Forrester Research[†]

Transformational outsourcing provides the required infrastructure and management services at a cost which can be significantly less than industry norms and which enables the expected economic benefits of downsizing to be realized.

Sheltering the user from platform complexity. The downsizing strategy will need to ensure that users are able to operate applications seamlessly, regardless of the underlying technologies and complexities. It is critical that they be free to simply use the technology, rather than spending time understanding and managing it. Client-server environments are complex, with many more devices, applications, and points of failure to be managed than in the mainframe environment. Faults are therefore a common occurrence, and users can waste a lot of time determining the nature of the problems and attempting to correct them. Many elements within transformational outsourcing shelter users from this complexity and allow them to simply use the technology. One such element is the Super Help Desk (see Sec. 8.3.2), which provides a single contact and coordination point for the resolution of all end-user problems.

Recognizing the new role of the network. The downsizing strategy will need to recognize the role and value of the network and integrate its management into an overall management approach. Client-server computing involves a high degree of hardware and software integration (LANs, servers, hubs, routers), as well as use of new telecommunications methods like ISDN, frame relay, and ATM, discussed in

---

*"Managing End-User Computing", multiclient research study, 1992.

[†]Janet L. Hyland, "Holistic Systems Management," *The Network Strategy Report*, October 1993.

Chap. 2. The network is adding more value and therefore more complexity.

Transformational outsourcing recognizes the role and value of the network and integrates its management into an overall end-to-end client-server management approach.

In summary, transformational outsourcing helps companies to address the many issues which need to be dealt with as they implement client-server systems.

8.3 Transformational Outsourcing Components

8.3.1 Overview

Transformational outsourcing provides a fully integrated suite of services to assist companies in making the transition to client-server computing and efficiently operating and maintaining the new systems. Many companies will choose to include all these services within a transformational outsourcing arrangement, whereas others will select whatever subset best complements their own internal skills and resources.

The key components of transformational outsourcing are

- The Super Help Desk
- Networked systems management
- Telecommunication services
- Mainframe processing services
- Transformational services
- Application systems management

These are discussed in the sections that follow.

8.3.2 The Super Help Desk

The Super Help Desk is an important component of transformational outsourcing. It gives system users a single point of contact with the multitude of support services which are drawn upon at each stage of the transformation to client-server computing. Whenever users encounter a problem, they simply call an 800 telephone number for access to, and assistance from, the appropriate support service. This shelters them from the ongoing changes and increasing complexities in the underlying technology as the transformation to client-server occurs. An overview of a Super Help Desk service is provided below. Figure 8.5 depicts the functions of the Super Help Desk in a graphical manner.

What are the service elements of the Super Help Desk?

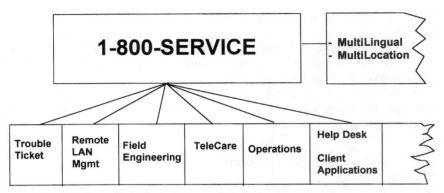

Figure 8.5   The Super Help Desk. (*Source: SHL Systemhouse.*)

Tier 1.   This is the initial point of contact for the user. Access is usually provided through an 800 number. Users are greeted by an automated attendant that guides them through a sequence of interactive voice response (IVR) prompts. The user's call is logged by an automated problem management system, and the problem remains active until it has been completely resolved. Many problems are corrected automatically at this stage; for example, 50 percent of mainframe processing support calls received at the SHL Super Help Desk are resolved without any operator intervention.

At any point the user can request to speak directly with an operator. Calls will also be forwarded to an operator automatically if it is determined that this is necessary given the information provided during the IVR sequence.

The nature of the problem is determined primarily at Tier 1. If the problem cannot be resolved at this level, it is dispatched to the appropriate support agency (a network analyst, the application support group, or field services). Automated tools such as automated call distribution (ACD), paging technology, etc., are used to hand over the call.

The problem management system in Tier 1 continues to track the call until the problem has been resolved. The user can inquire at any point in time as to the state of the call. The Super Help Desk also enables accurate and comprehensive service performance reporting to be provided.

Tiers 2–N.   These are the various support agencies, such as specialized technical support, application support, product support, and field services. The call is handed over to increasingly specialized agencies until it is fully resolved. Call status is continually monitored at Tier 1.

This service provides a number of benefits to the user, who is

- No longer required to determine the nature of the problem and contact the appropriate support agency directly

- Sheltered from the complexity of the underlying technology

- Provided with a simple method of access to the wide variety of support services

- Less likely to draw upon his or her professional colleagues for support, significantly reducing the level of hidden peer-to-peer support costs

8.3.3 Networked systems management

In many organizations, the financial and performance advantages of client-server computing are dissipated by failure to implement the management infrastructure, processes, and technology needed to efficiently and cost-effectively control the new environment. An effective client-server management strategy is therefore critical to the success of any downsizing initiative. A modified management approach, different technical skills, and a new infrastructure are required to support a client-server environment. The majority of critical business applications today are supported in reliable and secure host environments. The client-server environment must provide levels of reliability and security that meet or exceed those of traditional mainframe environments if the anticipated benefits of downsizing are to be fully realized.

Many organizations are addressing the challenge of transforming their distributed PC/LAN environment to one capable of supporting client-server systems by totally outsourcing their distributed systems environment, an approach described as networked systems management (NSM). Under this arrangement, the vendor assumes total responsibility for management and transformation of the current environment. Assets and support personnel are usually transferred to the vendor as part of the transaction. Through implementation of a support infrastructure and services, in combination with a commitment to service-level achievement, the vendor can provide companies with cost savings and end-user service-level improvements. Additionally, the current PC/LAN environment is stabilized and upgraded to the levels of availability, performance, and security required to support client-server systems.

NSM provides a fully integrated suite of support services focused on the end user, as illustrated in Fig. 8.6. What are the service elements of NSM? They are as follows:

Service-level commitments.   Service levels are defined and contractually committed to as part of the outsourcing arrangement.

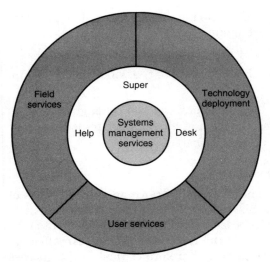

Figure 8.6 Networked systems management services. (*Source: SHL Systemhouse.*)

Systems management services. These are the cornerstone of efficient management of the entire networked system. Services are provided from a centralized network operating center (NOC), staffed by network and communications specialists equipped with the tools that enable them to manage many of the technical services from a remote location. The services provided are fault management, performance management, configuration management, software asset management, security management, data integrity, and accounting management.

Field services. Field service technicians are deployed regionally to provide on-site technical services as required.

Technology deployment. Services can include the acquisition, financing, and disposition of hardware and third-party software assets.

User services. These provide a tailored approach to increasing end-user effectiveness, including training, coaching, and help desk support to improve productivity and increase self-sufficiency.

What architectural components does NSM support? Support is provided for all critical system elements, from the WAN interconnect to the end-user device. These include

Hardware devices. Hubs, routers, bridges, concentrators, servers, workstations, and other end-user devices (including mobile computing devices)

System software.   Novell, Unix, OS/2, LAN Manager, Lotus Notes, etc.

Software products.   Lotus 1-2-3, WordPerfect, CCMail, etc.

What are the service features of NSM? They are as follows:

Industrial-strength operations.   Achievement of the high levels of system availability, performance, security, and integrity which are a prerequisite for the deployment of mission-critical systems in client-server environments

Cost-effective end-user computing.   Delivery of the required infrastructure and management services at a cost that is significantly less than today's industry norms and that enables the projected economic benefits of client-server computing to be achieved

World-class expertise.   Access to world-class expertise in the wide range of specialized technical areas which are required to efficiently support complex client-server environments

Comprehensive and integrated support services.   The seamless provisioning of all required end-user support services, sheltering users from the inherent complexity of client-server environments

End-to-end support.   Support for all critical hardware and software system elements down to the end-user device, enabling the achievement of enterprisewide (vs. device or LAN) service levels

Heterogeneous environment support.   An integrated management infrastructure that enables the support of a diverse set of technologies, providing support resources with single window/GUI-based access to the various tools they require to perform their function

Continuous technology refreshment.   Refreshment that ensures that both the enterprise architecture and the support infrastructure remain technically current, allowing the organization to achieve the benefits of rapidly evolving technology and support tools

Utility pricing.   The ability to benefit from a wide range of pricing and financing options, including an all-inclusive fee-per-workstation approach which enables usage-based pricing in the end-user computing environment

What range of end-user service levels can NSM provide? Three levels of service are provided (as shown in Fig. 8.7):

Level 1.   Stand-alone devices which are not attached to the LAN, including nonintelligent devices (e.g., IBM 3270)

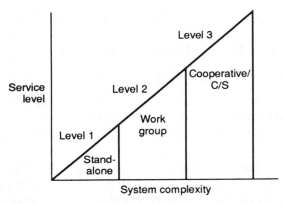

Figure 8.7 Service-level options. (*Source: SHL Systemhouse.*)

Level 2. Workgroup devices which are connected to the network but do not require advanced support for client-server applications (e.g., shared devices such as printers)

Level 3. Advanced support to enable the deployment of mission-critical applications in client-server environments

What are the benefits of NSM? They include

- Comprehensive and fully integrated end-to-end support
- System availability, performance, integrity, and security
- Cost-effective end-user computing
- Single point of contact and coordination for problem resolution
- Access to world-class technical expertise
- Continuous technology refreshment
- Utility pricing in the EUC environment

In summary, networked systems management is an important component of transformational outsourcing. It enables end-to-end management, combined with mainframe-like reliability and security in the client-server environment. These capabilities and characteristics are essential components of any downsizing strategy.

8.3.4 Telecommunication services

Many organizations are taking advantage of the rapid improvements in telecommunication technologies and services by outsourcing their telecommunication infrastructure, assets, and personnel, as discussed in Chap. 6. Outsourcing telecommunications within a transformational outsourcing arrangement provides the flexibility to shed investments in legacy private networks and take full advantage of new and improved services.

Telecommunications has always been a key enabler for most data processing systems. Mainframe computing typically involves a proprietary, hierarchical network based on low-speed lines (9.6 kbits/s or less) connecting dumb terminals via concentrators. An example is IBM's traditional SNA. The network adds minimal value.

The role of the network is different in a distributed computing environment. Here the network will usually provide peer-to-peer communications, allowing routing in a matrix. Line speeds are higher (56 kbits/s or higher), and network elements are intelligent. The network can add significant value. In fact, the demarcation between computing and communications blurs to the point that the network becomes the computer.

The traditional data communications network has been private. This means that dedicated lines leased from the telephone companies are combined with customer-owned premises equipment to create a network used exclusively by that company. An emerging trend is to migrate from private dedicated networks to virtual private networks (VPNs). Expensive private lines are replaced by the public switched network at a lower cost. Software programs in the telephone company's central offices emulate the features of a private network.

Private networks were built for two reasons: (1) dedicated private lines were cheaper than switched services, and (2) the switched network was not capable of providing the required services. Competition and network modernization have undermined both reasons. Virtual networks provide an alternative to multinode private-line networks. Costs are lower because the carriers are able to achieve better network efficiencies. Private networks require capital and create ongoing expenses. Engineering and maintenance staffing alone can be considerable. Expensive equipment becomes obsolete in ever-shorter intervals.

A typical private-line network now carries only half of a company's traffic; the rest is switched. With virtual networks, public switched calls are drawn into the corporate network through dial-up access. Virtual networks function like private networks. There are on-net and off-net points. On-net generally involves point-to-point calling via dedicated facilities. Calls travel off-net when they terminate at a site not linked to the dedicated backbone network. A virtual private network is ideal for companies in which people work out of their homes or on the road and which have small offices that are widely dispersed. Outlying or small locations dial access the network.

Virtual private networks use the new capabilities of the public switched network to provide features previously available only via a private network. Dedicated high-speed lines can be replaced with bandwidth on-demand services like switched 56, ISDN, and frame relay. Asynchronous transfer mode platforms will soon provide a single switching fabric for video, voice, and high-speed data communications. This will lead to a migration from shared access technologies (LANs) to high-speed switched connectivity.

An important aspect of virtual networks is special pricing for users who can aggregate their traffic to a carrier's point of presence (POP) for subsequent delivery to multiple destinations. Virtual services are targeted at companies with long distance spending of more than $1 million per year and 20 or more locations. The range of traffic needed is between 150,000 and 600,000 minutes of traffic per month.

Carriers will design a pricing solution, or tariff, for a customer's particular environment (as discussed in Chap. 6). A virtual private network agreement can encompass a variety of services, including switched and dedicated access for voice and data, 800 service, private lines, and travel cards. Global VPNs are starting to emerge.

Telephone companies are moving along a path of modernization, driven by user requirements and competitive pressures and supported by high technology. In the first wave, electromechanical central offices were replaced by stored program controlled switches. Next, multiplexing technologies and fiber optic transmission systems improved a telephone company's outside plant capabilities. Now comes the Advanced Intelligent Network (AIN), wherein general-purpose computers and overlay signaling networks enable new offerings like the virtual corporate network, ISDN, and flow-through provisioning.

With the advent of frame relay and ATM, the network is becoming the computer. The downfall of the mainframe and the rise of client-server computing requires the network to add value beyond traditional private-line services. Customers are migrating from hierarchical networks (e.g., SNA) to peer-to-peer networks (routable internets). The network adds more value, and the lines between computing and communications blur.

The telephone companies in the United States, Canada, and the United Kingdom have invested billions in their switching and transport systems. Competition and rapidly advancing technology have combined to significantly upgrade the public switched network. The degree of investment and the pace of change are expected to continue.

An emerging telecommunications strategy is to operate a hybrid network composed of dedicated and virtual services. Virtual voice and data services incorporate the most sophisticated offerings of the telephone companies. Ultimately, the virtual enterprise computer will utilize a virtual enterprise network.

A telecommunications utility is complex to plan, implement, and operate. Technical cost issues dominate managers' attention. This often leads to an unpleasant surprise when competitors arrive who use telecommunications as part of an ambitious business strategy. Telecommunications managed as a utility responds to business needs, but does not initiate business strategy.

When managed as a utility, telecommunications is viewed as a technical function, and the focus is on providing facilities as needed and controlling costs. Some degree of central planning and oversight is provided in an environment of highly decentralized operations. Typically this is done by setting up a new bureaucracy that coordinates planning through budgeting and corporate accounting. Costs are controlled by tracking them and charging them back.

Another approach is to outsource the network to a company that can leverage the costs of managing and administering a complex network. Networks can be transformed through outsourcing in the same manner as mainframes. In fact, given that the mainframe network will need to change along with the computing platform, outsourcing provides the best strategy to coordinate this process.

What are the elements of telecommunication services?

Service-level commitments.   Service levels that are clearly defined and contractually committed to as part of the outsourcing arrangement

Design.   Network design, ongoing modification, and optimization

Provisioning.   Procurement and commissioning of network circuits and services

Operations.   Management and operation of the network

Support.   Second-tier support to the Super Help Desk, responding to problems associated with the network component of the architecture

Administration.   Security, contingency planning, disaster recovery, change management, billing, and general network administration

What are the benefits of outsourcing telecommunications services?

- Cost savings
- Enhanced telecommunications services
- Single point of contact for end-to-end systems management
- Transition to virtual private network
- Ability to benefit and choose from evolving telecommunication services

In summary, transformational outsourcing provides organizations with a means to transform legacy private networks and take full advantage of new and improved telecommunication services.

8.3.5   Mainframe processing services

As discussed in previous chapters, many organizations are choosing to outsource their mainframe operations as a first step in the transformation to client-server computing.

What are the elements of processing services?

Data center operations.   The vendor typically assumes responsibility for some or all data center functions. These include host and midrange computing services.

- *Service-level commitments.*   Service levels are clearly defined and contractually committed to as a part of the outsourcing arrangement.

- *Client services.*   Tier 2 support is provided to the Super Help Desk; assisting users in the resolution of any problems related to the systems supported by the data center.

- *Operations services.*   Data entry and preparation; mainframe and minicomputer operations, including backup and library services; and production services, including forms design, production, dispatch, and delivery.

- *Network support services.*   Management of telecommunications from a data center perspective.

- *Technical services.*   Technical support to the operations and client services groups.

- *Administration services.*   Data access control, physical security, contingency planning, disaster recovery, and general data center administration.

National Education Corporation (NEC) is an educational provider with schools and learning centers throughout the United States. NEC chose to outsource its mainframe processing as a first step towards client-server computing. The arrangement provided NEC with access to a state-of-the-art mainframe processing platform combined with the flexibility to reduce mainframe processing costs as mainframe usage decreases over time.

Sale of assets.   IT assets are usually purchased by the vendor. The attractiveness of this option will depend upon whether assets are owned or leased, their residual value, and the potential for the vendor to leverage the assets. Cash payments for the purchase of assets are common, and the cash infusion may be an attractive proposition for many organizations.

Canada Post Corporation sold its information technology assets as part of its transformational outsourcing deal with SHL. These include a variety of mainframe and distributed computers: two IBM 3090s, an IBM 4381, 40 DEC VAXs, 2 IBM AS/400s, and several Tandems; CPC's network, which includes Postpac (X.25), Postcct (frame relay), and Posttel (voice); and various PC/LAN assets.

Personnel transfer. IT personnel usually become employees of the vendor. Some or all of the employees will transfer, depending upon circumstances. This helps to ensure that knowledge and expertise in the client's operational processes are available. From an employee perspective, a move to the outsourcing vendor can open up many new career opportunities.

Providing rewarding career paths was an important element of Amoco Canada's outsourcing arrangement with SHL. Prior to outsourcing, Amoco was quoted as saying, "We had to wrestle our G&A budget down, but we didn't want this to be at the expense of the employee." Many of the former Amoco employees now working with SHL have received promotions, retraining, and reassignment in new technology areas such as Super Help Desk and networked systems management operations and support. Those who were keen to travel have been engaged on projects such as data center consolidations in Mexico, system migrations in Los Angeles, and the commissioning of new data centers in Korea.

The reality is that information technology professionals are often motivated by personal development, including training and the opportunity to work on good projects. Remuneration and security are important, but not always the prime factors. A career with the outsourcing vendor frequently offers such benefits.

Transition planning. Continuity of service through the period of transition from in-house operations to full outsourcing is key. The development of a well-considered transition plan is essential.

Processing services in the client-server environment. The mainframe will continue to play a key role in many corporations. It provides a reliable, secure, and well-managed environment for the provision of many services and will continue to be used for support of critical applications either indefinitely or until the distributed environment can provide comparable levels of reliability and security. Some industry observers suggest that the mainframe cost curve will outperform expectations.

The mainframe is also likely to become the central server in many client-server architectures. In this scenario, the mainframe would be the server, providing a repository for critical corporate data. It provides the benefit of a mature and secure environment supported by strong systems management practices. It also enables connectivity between diverse architectures. The workstation environment would work in combination with the mainframe, providing the client component of the client-server architecture. This approach provides an optimum combination of mainframe and desktop computing.

Mainframe processing services are therefore likely to continue to be a key element in client-server management and operations. Integrated with telecommunication services and networked systems management, they provide end-to-end processing in a client-server environment.

In summary, transformational outsourcing provides for outsourcing of existing data center operations and provides the flexibility for these to be either partially or totally downsized.

8.3.6 Transformational services

These services enable applications to be downsized from legacy to client-server environments. The transformation usually consists of a series of systems integration projects where the target environment is a new technology platform.

Many organizations initially focus on downsizing noncritical applications, such as office automation and development. This provides early results with tangible savings and has minimal impact on and disruption of operations. The resulting savings are frequently deployed within transformational outsourcing to finance the cost of upgrading the existing PC/LAN environment and implementing a more robust distributed environment.

Life-cycle approach and client-server methodologies. The downsizing of critical applications is typically undertaken utilizing a life-cycle methodology adopted for the client-server environment. The complete process usually entails business process engineering, architecture and design, application development, and change management.

SHL Transform™ is an example of a client-server generation methodology, designed and engineered specifically for the client-server environment. It provides a complete and integrated environment to support the transformation to client-server computing. Its major components include

- An integrated management workbench that provides access to estimating and project management tools, CASE tools, software development environments, computer-based training, and productivity support tools

- Multimedia presentation, with audio, video, and hypergraphics
- State-of-the-art navigational and search capabilities
- A repository of process experience, derived from successful completion of many client-server projects
- An educational environment, developed by client-server experts, employing hypermedia technology
- An ongoing service providing continual refinement of the content and technology, with access to client-server development and methodology experts

Transformational outsourcing provides companies with access to the client-server methodologies and implementation skills required for a successful transition to client-server computing.

Alternative downsizing strategies.   Figure 8.8 depicts a number of downsizing strategies that an organization can implement. The methods used to migrate applications off the mainframe range from automated methods such as rehosting to rewriting of the software. It is worth noting that although rewriting can entail higher risk and often requires significant time and investment, it also usually presents the greatest opportunity for business process reengineering and allows users to more fully benefit from the advantages of new technologies.

Tools and techniques that are intended to automate downsizing and rehosting of operations on new technology platforms are rapidly emerging. Many are at the early stages of development, and proof-of-concept is a prerequisite prior to selection and implementation.

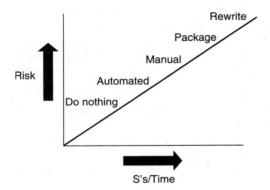

Figure 8.8 Possible downsizing strategies.

Planning the transformation: enterprise-wide architecture strategy.
Planning, an important first step within transformational outsourcing, is usually done through the development of an enterprise-wide architecture strategy (EWAS). The EWAS defines the benefits that can be gained from a client-server environment, quantifies the costs of the transformation, and defines a plan for its implementation. EWAS combines, in a time-compressed manner, the best of business process engineering and architectural approaches to maximize advantage from enabling technologies as the business is transformed over the period of the contract.

EWAS consists of three primary steps: business modeling, architecture strategy, and transformation planning.

Business modeling. The objective of the first step is to understand what business processes need to be reshaped for the organization to gain competitive advantage over the period of the transformation. This often requires intensive workshops with key executives and users to determine the enterprise's key opportunities for business process change. High-level visioning and analysis techniques are used. Enterprise-wide models of the current and planned business processes, applications portfolios, technology platforms, and organizational infrastructures are built, in order to determine the shortfall of the current environment in meeting business needs.

Architecture strategy. The objective of the second step is to discern what enabling technologies and architectures can best be deployed to support the evolving business. The technology architectures include systems development environments and systems management environments, as well as architectures for client, server, and connectivity. The architecture strategy is an important method of managing rapid changes in the business environment: it needs to be based on open systems concepts, standards, maximum interoperability, and maximum independence between layers of the architecture, and should leverage reusable components. These attributes permit an organization to be responsive to changing business requirements and technology improvements by facilitating the plug and play of newer, more-powerful products without compromising the overall architectural framework and strategy. The strategy should be designed to accommodate continuous change throughout the term of the outsourcing agreement.

Transformational planning. The final step determines the sequence in which applications should be migrated in order to generate the greatest payback over the term of the agreement. First-phase projects may range from business process engineering (BPE) with client-server implementations of new business processes, to offloading development work from mainframes to LANs, to consolidating parts of the technology infrastructure to gain economies and take advantage of new operating and communications technologies. Second-phase projects may involve the migration of data to relational environments on local servers, reducing mainframe-based database processing, and placing data closer to users. Third-phase projects may be based on migration of application functionality to a fully cooperative processing environment.

Business process engineering. As mentioned earlier, BPE is an important early step within transformational outsourcing. It is usually applied as a "front end" to transformation projects and comprises a fundamental analysis of the core business process, thus eliminating or minimizing the possibility of outsourcing non-value-added activities. It analyzes existing business processes and defines radically new processes that offer the potential for dramatic improvement. BPE also defines the costs and savings of moving from the old process to the new in concrete quantitative terms.

In the past few years, the term "business process engineering" has become fashionable. Many approaches and methodologies have been developed in this area. There is clearly a convergence and similarity of approaches and techniques whether they are called BPR, BPE, business process design/redesign, cycle time reduction, or process simplification. The issue should not be one of terminology; it should be ultimately centered around the critical success factors and differentiators that ensure the positive results of process engineering.

SHL defines BPE to be "the radical application of scientific principles and analytical techniques to product or service delivery processes, systems of work, management systems, and organization structures and beliefs to achieve dramatic enterprise performance improvements."

Benefits of BPE. BPE results in improving customer satisfaction by speeding up the flow of value through an organization's value-creating process. This is achieved by eliminating non-value-added activities, simplifying the remaining activities, and applying information technology to the value-added activities. Benefits of BPE, over and above improved customer satisfaction, include increased asset availability, improved cash flow, higher employee morale, significantly lower costs, and improved quality. Sound like a panacea? It can be, but it requires a willingness to completely rethink the way organizations have structured themselves, in order to reflect customer-focused value-creating processes.

Radical thinking can be seen with the elimination of price-based selection of suppliers; the empowerment of customer-contact employees, who give customers what they want when they need it; and the use of technology that spans information across the value-creation process without starting and stopping in each functional pipe stack. The results one should expect include cycle time reductions of 40 to 90 percent, cost reductions of 20 to 40 percent, the elimination of paperwork discrepancies, and the reduction of process steps by at least 50 percent. Applied correctly, BPE can enhance the benefits of transformational outsourcing.

In summary, transformational services within a transformational outsourcing arrangement allows organizations to achieve a smoother transition to newer technologies. Transition risk is reduced because the supplier can provide the necessary skills, experience, and methodologies to ensure a successful and timely transformation.

8.3.7 Application systems management

Many organizations are addressing the challenge of transforming their application portfolio and support staff by outsourcing their application development and maintenance department, an approach known as application systems management (ASM). Under this arrangement, the application staff are employed by the vendor, who assumes total responsibility for the application development and maintenance function. Through skills transfer, resource management, service-level commitments, and strong management practices, the vendor can provide companies with cost savings, comprehensive support services, and improved delivery of software projects.

Why do companies outsource applications management?

Major cost item. Applications management has become a significant cost item for many organizations. Large investments have been made and a valuable asset created. This function, however, is coming under the same pressure as other functional areas. These include demands for accurate measurement of return on investment, achievement of efficiencies, and overall cost reduction. This presents a challenge to most organizations, as they are unable to measure return or productivity in this area.

Outsourcing enables an organization to measure return on investment and productivity more accurately. The vendor achieves this through skill transfer, efficient resource management, the introduction of productivity metrics, and a commitment to service levels. Return on investment is visibly enhanced, and overall cost reductions may be achieved.

Fixed cost. Applications management costs are primarily fixed. Most organizations achieve some level of variability by employing outside contractors; however, this is usually only a small percentage of total headcount. New projects can require significant spikes in resource demand over short periods of time, and the flexibility to vary costs as demand increases or decreases is seldom available.

ASM transforms applications management from a fixed cost to a demand-based level of service with predictable costs. The required resources are available on demand from the vendor, who has a large pool of IT professionals and has the flexibility to provide them when needed and easily reassign them during periods of low demand.

High attrition rates. It is becoming increasingly difficult for organizations to attract, develop, and retain IT staff. Attrition rates for in-house IT departments are usually very high. Many employees leave to further their career and acquire skills in newer technologies, and others leave because they are finding that their skills in older technologies command a premium in the marketplace.

Morale and attrition frequently become even more of an issue as companies shift to client-server systems and retraining and motivating those employees who are engaged in maintaining the older technology through the transition period becomes harder. The new work is being done by either external consultants or their own colleagues. Career progression and job security become the focus of attention, attrition often increases, and user service levels can be seriously jeopardized.

ASM relieves organizations of this problem and makes the required level of resources and skills available when needed. The vendor is able to deal with the problem more easily. Those employees who transfer to the employ of the vendor usually benefit from enhanced career opportunities, and employee morale and retention is usually high. The vendor has the advantage of being able to retrain and redeploy personnel more easily as the older systems are replaced.

Client-server skills. Accessing client-server design and implementation skills can be a difficult task for an internal IT department. Most organizations cannot afford the long lead times required to build these skills internally. People who already have these skills are scarce and in high demand. They also usually command a significant premium in the marketplace and can therefore be expensive to acquire.

Transformational outsourcing provides organizations with access to client-server skills and also provides an effective method of technology skill transfer.

User dissatisfaction. Organizations frequently experience user dissatisfaction with internal applications management services. One- to three-year application enhancement backlogs are commonplace. Even minor enhancements can seemingly take forever to implement. Cost and schedule overruns are often accepted as the norm.

ASM can resolve many of these issues. It requires users to rationalize enhancements and other changes on a cost/benefit basis. Accountability is enhanced through user chargeback mechanisms. Productivity is also enhanced, and performance metrics enable accurate management reporting. Under ASM, the application management function is seen as adding value to the organization, as opposed to being viewed as an overhead cost center.

What are the service elements of ASM?   The services in this area address all elements of the application life cycle, from the identification and analysis of a requirement, to post-implementation support and maintenance. Mainframe, minicomputer, PC/LAN, and client-server applications are supported. There are two primary categories of service: major projects and maintenance.

Major projects are usually managed through a formal life-cycle process. This entails formal project planning and approval, architecture, design, development, and implementation. The necessary levels of skills and resources are made available by the vendor through all project phases. Major projects are usually planned and identified in a one- to three-year plan which sets the mandate and scope for this service.

Maintenance consists of four primary service elements: enhancements, corrective maintenance, adaptive maintenance, and application support.

Enhancements.   This service involves the provision of resources to keep applications consistent with the business environment in which they operate (such as changes in business procedures) and to undertake reasonable minor amendments to maintain the usability and usefulness of the application. The service includes relevant advice, evaluation of change requests, and implementation of agreed-upon changes. Small projects and changes are provided through this service if they can be accommodated with the resources allocated. Otherwise they are treated as major projects and handled in the appropriate planning process. Urgent cases are handled on an exception basis.

Corrective maintenance.   This service involves the investigation and resolution of all operational failures of supported applications, and all instances where an application fails to perform to the agreed-upon specification. The work includes program/system testing, updating of program documentation, and liaison with users and the operations staff as necessary.

Adaptive maintenance. This service ensures that an appropriate technical environment for developing, implementing, operating, and supporting applications is maintained. It includes the enhancement of applications to reflect the acquisition and implementation of new releases of hardware and network and operations software.

Application support. This service involves training, advice, and support to users and operations staff. Examples include training and advice on the following: the effective use of applications and related query programs, third-party and supplier liaison, batch scheduling, the operational efficiency of live applications, data security and confidentiality, and disaster planning and recovery.

Management processes and reporting. A range of sophisticated management processes are implemented as part of the service. These include problem, change, backlog, and release management.

Enhancements to development and maintenance methodologies standards, tools, and supporting environments are also included as part of the service, which usually significantly improves overall productivity.

Performance and activity reporting is provided to show the volume and level of activity of the contracted services. Reports include a commentary on significant achievements and problems, and, in the case of the latter, an account of their resolution or proposals to bring them to a satisfactory conclusion. Actual performance against committed service levels is also provided.

In summary, ASM relieves an organization of the many operational and transformational challenges in this area. What was previously a fixed-cost infrastructure with questionable productivity and return is now a demand-based service with predictable cost and measurable productivity and returns.

8.3.8   Transformational outsourcing service pricing

The industry currently provides a variety of fee-for-service pricing options in the host and telecommunications environments. The shift to client-server computing will generate a demand for fee-for-service pricing in the distributed environment. This implies a fee per user which includes capital, maintenance, and ongoing support services. Technology refreshment will be included, and the fee will need to reflect the level of functions and service provided.

IT services in the networked systems environment can be provided on an all-inclusive cost-per-workstation basis. The price is structured to include all elements of networked systems computing, i.e., capital, technology acquisition, deployment, disposal and refreshment, maintenance and field services, training, application services, Super Help Desk, and systems management services.

This approach provides many benefits, including the availability of an all-inclusive and predictable cost per workstation and elimination of the need for future capital expenditures through the inclusion of technology refreshment in the cost per workstation.

In summary, transformational outsourcing can transform IT services from a fixed to a variable cost. It allows expenses to be more easily aligned with revenues, which is a significant benefit. Organizations can thus vary IT costs with usage and internally charge back IT costs to the actual user. This is similar to the manner in which company telephone charges are now internally allocated to operating units and telephone users.

8.4   Selecting a Transformational Outsourcing Supplier

Selecting a supplier is an important early step in any transformational outsourcing initiative. An industry view on this subject is presented below.

The Yankee Group* believes that the rapidity of change in IT and in business conditions will drive rapid changes in the outsourcing market and in the computing industry at large. The requirements that are emerging revolve around five themes (see Fig. 8.9):

- *Flexibility.*   Because of rapid change in both business and technology, arrangements must be modifiable.

- *Cooperation.*   To deal with uncertainty, customers and vendors must plan to work cooperatively over time.

- *Relationship.*   To weather inevitable difficult times, a good mutual relationship is invaluable.

- *Value.*   Financial arrangements are likely to change over a contract's duration.

- *Expertise.*   A constant value that has been seen is expertise, developed through experience. This will have to be expertise across a range of technologies and business knowledge, not just expertise in the data center or the network.

---

*"Outsourcing War Stories," The Yankee Group, Management Strategies Research Group, March 1993.

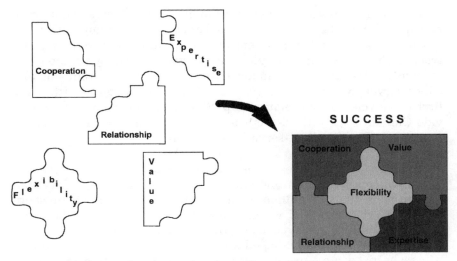

Figure 8.9 Fitting together outsourcing pieces. (*Source: The Yankee Group, 1993.*)

Suppliers' references are also an important indication of capability. These should be thoroughly researched.

8.5 Transformational Outsourcing Case Studies

This section examines four illustrative case studies of clients of SHL Systemhouse:

- Canada Post Corporation
- Amoco Canada*
- Central Guarantee Trust*
- Nova Scotia Government*

8.5.1 Canada Post Corporation

Canada Post's 10-year contract with SHL Systemhouse is the largest enterprisewide transformational outsourcing deal to date.

Under the agreement, SHL Systemhouse will assume responsibility for Canada Post's Computing and Communications Utility, which is a

---

*Excerpts from Oliver Pflug, "Business Audit of Outsourcing Contracts—North American Market," G2 Research multiclient study, November 1993.

nationwide communications network linking 12,000 devices and users to two mainframe data centers and a number of midrange computer sites.

What makes this deal different from a traditional outsourcing contract is the transformation plan, under which SHL Systemhouse is responsible for changing Canada Post's technology environment to a client-server system. That evolution should be complete within the first three years of the relationship. SHL Systemhouse will then provide Canada Post with its networked systems management services to manage the new client-server environment.

Introduction.   Canada Post collects, processes, and delivers close to 10 billion communication messages and parcels annually. This mail goes to more than 11 million points of delivery throughout the country—to rural homes and villages and to Canada's major urban centers. Mail is also received from and dispatched to the rest of the world. This volume is managed and processed through a network of 25 mechanized mail processing plants. The corporation employs a workforce of 57,000 full- and part-time employees, a fleet of some 5,300 vehicles, and thousands of contracted services from air and surface transportation companies. Canada Post markets its products and services through more than 17,200 points of sale nationwide, more than 70 percent of which are operated by private business.

In the face of a difficult business climate, the corporation has been able to maintain both its financial viability and the high level of its services through the introduction of new cost-effective technology, innovative products, and service enhancements. Outsourcing is an integral part of CPC's strategy. Many of its air and surface transportation functions are outsourced, and in 1992 CPC decided to outsource its IT operations.

Contract overview.   The transformational outsourcing contract was awarded to SHL Systemhouse in 1993. It is a 10-year contract with a value of $1 billion. The contract includes Super Help Desk, networked systems management, telecommunications, mainframe processing, and transformational services. Application systems management services are provided under a separate agreement.

Functions and responsibilities previously provided for CPC by its Computing and Communications Utility group (C&CU) will be provided by SHL Systemhouse under the outsourcing arrangement. These include the planning, specification, acquisition, installation, operation, and ongoing support and management of computing and communications technology in use by Canada Post. Management of CPC's production application environment and technical consulting to other departments is also included.

SHL Systemhouse acquired CPC's IT assets, which included a variety of mainframe and distributed computers: two IBM 3090s, an IBM 4381, 40 DEC VAXs, 2 IBM AS/400s, and several Tandems; CPC's network, which includes Postpac (X.25), Postcct (frame relay), and Posttel (voice); and various PC/LAN assets.

SHL Systemhouse extended employment offers to all full-time affected CPC staff. A high percentage accepted the offers and are now pursuing new careers with SHL Systemhouse.

The contract provides the flexibility to significantly reduce mainframe usage over time. Several mainframe systems will be downsized in the early stages of the agreement. This will allow CPC to realize significant savings in total operational costs. Future cost savings will offset the development and operational costs of the transformation projects and the required remote systems support infrastructure.

Approximately 12,000 devices will be connected over 250 (new) local area networks as part of the deal. A full suite of networked systems management services will be provided.

Benefits. From a financial perspective, the following benefits were accrued by CPC:

- Reduced IT costs
- Fee-for-service pricing of IT services
- Conversion of assets to cash
- Reduction of future capital expenditures

From a general business perspective, the following benefits were accrued by CPC:

- Ability to concentrate on core business
- Implementation of IT service-level agreements
- Downsizing of internal IT staff
- Continual technology refreshment
- Transformation of the technical environment from older mainframe technology to new client-server technology (utilizing the mainframe within the overall architecture)

CPC's comments included, "It was consistent with CPC's business and financial goals and objectives for improved efficiency and cost reduction"* and "SHL came to us with a unique strategy to achieve

---

*Hank Klassen, Vice President of Information Technology, Canada Post Corporation.

the transformation to client-server computing, which matched our future strategy for technology."*

8.5.2 Amoco Canada

Introduction. At Amoco Canada (AC), prior to the outsourcing decision, the responsibility for both IT decision making and application development had been decentralized to the business units, so that Corporate IT had retained only the data center and the network. This discussion covers the outsourcing contract for these last pieces of the IT infrastructure.

The oil industry for the most part (and Amoco in particular) uses the Ernst & Young benchmark of Barrel of Oil Competitive Equivalent Cost as a business measurement, and Amoco Canada conducted industry comparisons on the IT cost portion of this. This was the driver for looking at ways to simultaneously reduce costs, improve performance, and allow for future IT capacity growth.

Over the years, Amoco had had a history of cutting the DP budget by 25 percent per year. In effect, this had gradually put them in a position where they had virtually nowhere to go but to outsourcing to continue this kind of improvement. Unusually, the U.S. parent company was a bidder for the outsourcing contract (through its own IT department), so this was very much a showcase test of the viability of outsourcing for Amoco as a global corporation. The company is now in a position to clearly measure the results by comparing old and new headcount and the DP budget from past years against the costs being charged today.

Contract information. The outsourcing contract was awarded to SHL Systemhouse on October 1, 1992. It is a five-year contract with a value of $70 million. The contract included the data center IT assets, the network, all system software licenses, and a floor space sublease (which is now the Western Data Centre for SHL, with room for expansion).

It does not include responsibility for future application software development, nor does it include ownership of the Amoco Canada application code for existing applications or maintenance of same. The network is currently operated on a cost-plus basis, but will become a fixed-price contract in the near future.

Major business goals that drove outsourcing. Amoco Canada primarily wanted to achieve a focus on its core competencies through outsourc-

---

*Hank Klassen, Vice President of Information Technology, Canada Post Corporation.

ing, but also saw it as a way to complete the decentralization of IT. Outsourcing also represented

- A technique for accomplishing downsizing and providing a cost-controlled transition from a data center to a client-server environment
- A means to achieve IT cost and staff headcount reductions gracefully
- A way of providing improved career opportunities for the IT staff
- A means of providing competitive flexibility
- A means of accelerating the downsizing process

Not targeted by the outsourcing agreement were

- Productivity improvements
- Quality improvements
- Customer service issues
- Technology management issues

Although IT assets were sold, liberating the cash from these was not a major factor in the decision. Consultants were not used in either the decision to outsource or the vendor selection process, only a parent company review.

Vendor selection criteria. In selecting vendors, technology platform skills, project methodology, price, supplier size, and geographic coverage were considered; financial strength and knowledge of the oil business were not. With assistance from the parent company, technology risk, cost of nonperformance, business risk, and vendor assumption of risk and residuals were considered. SHL, ISM, and Amoco Corporation were short-listed.

SHL Systemhouse was ultimately selected based on

- Its focus on client-server solutions (and the skills associated with that process)
- The best plan for transition from a centralized data center and network control to the client-server environment
- The best plan for handling the Amoco Canada IT personnel

Results. In the customer's opinion, this outsourcing contract was a very clear success in all respects. Specifically, all cost and staff reductions were achieved, with excellent "people chemistry" between the two organizations. For example, the original IT staff of 130 has been reduced to 23 people. It is noteworthy that within the corporation, the Canadian division is now viewed as the model for the future DP organization.

Amoco Canada has retained responsibility for desktop acquisition decisions, but has delegated selection and negotiation for all other areas to SHL.

Lessons learned. Outsourcing has been a very positive experience for Amoco Canada, but AC says that this is a critical business decision that must be backed up by a fair and objective business case in the beginning. A maximum amount of work should be done prior to the RFP and negotiation stages, particularly in looking at the user's 5- and 10-year requirements for platforms and architecture to ensure that they are dealt with effectively in the contracting process.

8.5.3   Central Guarantee Trust

Introduction. Central Guarantee Trust (CGT) is a Halifax-based Canadian trust company that has recently completed the sale of all its assets. This also involved an outsourcing decision.

In 1991, financial concerns in other divisions caused CGT to consider selling trust assets (branch networks) in Atlantic Canada as a first step. Federal regulatory authorities then required CGT to sell the Ontario branch network also, so that creditors would be treated correctly.

In this situation, one of the largest IT installations in the province of Nova Scotia faced a very significant downsizing and relocation (to central Ontario). Therefore, while the cost savings inherent in outsourcing were the major objective, the critical success factor was preserving the skilled people and application development software base to allow a successful transition to the new owner.

Contract information and scope. Central Guarantee provided all data processing services to every functional department and all affiliated companies (such as mortgage companies, real estate, etc.). No formal methodology was employed to assess the value of outsourcing, but an external consultant was used in the decision-making and vendor selection processes.

SHL Systemhouse was the successful bidder, and in July 1992 a five-year contract was awarded; this subsequently became a one-year contract for $7 million as a result of the regulatory change referred to above.

Major business goals that drove outsourcing. After several years of organizational downsizing, morale was very low, and there was a substantial risk that key development personnel would leave en masse during the transition/move.

The number one goal was the divestiture of assets mentioned above. The associated staff reductions, productivity improvements, and focus on core competencies were significant; however, the defensive factors predominated.

Vendor selection criteria. In choosing a vendor, the cost of outsourcing was important only insofar as it had to be in a reasonable range. Knowledge of the business was not a requirement, and project work-plan, methodology, and technical skills were assumed rather than vetted. A Halifax-based data center location and an ability to mitigate the employment issues were the key criteria.

SHL Systemhouse, ISM, and EDS were short-listed, with SHL Systemhouse winning because of geographic preference. The critically important transition stage was completed with outstanding results in substantially improving development productivity and morale in a difficult situation.

These circumstances resulted in some very unusual contracting conditions: a fixed-price agreement with

- Cancellation rights for change of control
- Liquidation given preference over termination rights
- Very short notification periods

Results. A staff reduction from 126 to 25 was accomplished with stability, control, and development productivity enhancement.

The "benefits" under this contract were allowing liquidation and meeting a difficult liquidation schedule.

Liquidation of the company, while clearly unfortunate, required performance by the involved vendors in a true partner spirit, over and above the terms of the contract.

Lessons learned. While this is an unusual example of outsourcing, it focuses attention on the time dimensions of an outsourcing contract. For example, completion time, uptime, response time, and people response time all require greater focus on time dimensions and quality, with less attention to other, more traditional parts of contracting.

It also suggests fully exploring the degree to which short-listed companies will commit to dealing with alternative scenarios and will have the flexibility to resolve issues outside the contract in a true partnership fashion.

In summary, outsourcing in this case was a positive experience and could almost be viewed as a formal management technique for transition.

8.5.4 Nova Scotia government

Introduction. The Information Technology Department of the Nova Scotia government is responsible for providing all computing and networking requirements to the various government departments within the Province of Nova Scotia. In late 1991 and early 1992, the provincial government faced economic challenges and was reviewing a number of potential government organizations as candidates for privatization. In this period, an unsolicited proposal was received from SHL Systemhouse that met economic objectives in a cost sense and also provided an IS technology infrastructure plan for the province. The proposal was positively received and acted upon in parallel with a related proposal for infrastructure integration with Maritime Telephone.

Contract information and scope. The contract was awarded to SHL Systemhouse and has a seven-year duration and a value of $51 million. It involves the outsourcing of the data center operation and its assets, as well as systems programming support. The data center has become the Eastern Canada Data Center for SHL Systemhouse, which uses it as a tenant on a rental basis with the government as landlord.

Major business goals that drove outsourcing. The Nova Scotia government, as part of Atlantic Canada, was facing pressures from high unemployment and a shrinking tax base. These factors, in turn, had led to significant pressure to reduce costs and consider privatization of some government activities. Atlantic Canada also faced many challenges in enticing high-technology companies to locate and grow in Nova Scotia. As a result, an industrial benefits approach that offered a full-blown technology infrastructure plan for the province and resulted in new employment commitments was highly attractive to all levels of government.

Vendor selection criteria. This contract was not competitively tendered, and no consulting firm was used in the selection or contracting process. The major selection criterion was timing in meeting the government's goals as stated above.

Contractual conditions. This is a fixed-price contract with a base charge and a set of volume-related escalators or reductions. The only termination right is for cause. SHL Systemhouse has assumed vendor selection and negotiation responsibilities for the data center. Desktop decision making has been retained by the Nova Scotia government.

Results.   Results have been very effective, with a headcount saving of 33 on a base of 58 planned and fully achieved (57 percent). In addition, the industrial benefits are on target with the proposal. However, it is too early in the contract to determine whether the agreement will be extended or will have to be submitted to an RFP process prior to renewal.

Lessons learned.   Outsourcing, according to the user, has been a very beneficial experience that merits full consideration as a business strategy. However, the personnel implications for affected departments are highly significant. A strong recommendation would be for very effective and open communication with employees as early in the process as possible.

8.6   Conclusion

As corporations worldwide continue downsizing and reengineering their business processes to remain competitive, information technology will continue to play a critical role in their transformation. The decision to move away from legacy systems, to the more cost-effective and flexible client-server architecture, aligns with goals focused on improved efficiency, reduced costs, and core business excellence. Transformational outsourcing both accelerates and finances a company's downsizing, while it allows the company to take advantage of new and evolving technologies. Given the speed of today's global market changes, staying current with technology is not just good business sense, it's paramount to success.

Index

ABOUT THE AUTHOR

Daniel Minoli is an expert in the data communications and telecommunications fields. In his capacity as strategic communications planner and principal consultant at DVI Communications, Inc., he has recently turned his attention to multimedia, imaging, and outsourcing issues. He is the author or coauthor of a number of books, including *ATM and Cell Relay Service for Corporate Environments, Imaging in Corporate Environments: Technology and Communication*, and *1st, 2nd, and Next Generation LANs*, all published by McGraw-Hill, as well as 200 technical and trade articles. Mr. Minoli is also an Adjunct Associate Professor at New York University's Information Technology Institute, and a frequent speaker at industry conferences.